FAMILY SYSTEMS AND CULTURAL CHANGE

The International Union for the Scientific Study of Population Problems was set up in 1928, with Dr Raymond Pearl as President. At that time the Union's main purpose was to promote international scientific co-operation to study the various aspects of population problems, through national committees and through its members themselves. In 1947 the International Union for the Scientific Study of Population (IUSSP) was reconstituted into its present form. It expanded its activities to:

- stimulate research on population
- develop interest in demographic matters among governments, national and international organizations, scientific bodies, and the general public
- foster relations between people involved in population studies
- disseminate scientific knowledge on population.

The principal ways through which the IUSSP currently achieves its aims are:

- organization of worldwide or regional conferences and operations of Scientific Committees under the responsibility of the Council
- organization of training courses
- publication of conference proceedings and committee reports.

Demography can be defined by its field of study and its analytical methods. Accordingly, it can be regarded as the scientific study of human populations primarily with respect to their size, their structure, and their development. For reasons which are related to the history of the discipline, the demographic method is essentially inductive: progress in the knowledge results from the improvement of observation, the sophistication of measurement methods, the search for regularities and stable factors leading to the formulation of explanatory models. In conclusion, the three objectives of demographic analysis are to describe, measure, and analyse.

International Studies in Demography is the outcome of an agreement concluded by the IUSSP and the Oxford University Press. This joint series is expected to reflect the broad range of the Union's activities and, in the first instance, will be based on the seminars organized by the Union. The Editorial Board of the series is comprised of:

Family Systems and Cultural Change

EDITORS:

ELZA BERQUÓ
PETER XENOS

Clarendon Press · Oxford
1992

Oxford University Press, Walton Street, Oxford OX2 6DP
Oxford New York Toronto
Delhi Bombay Calcutta Madras Karachi
Kuala Lumpur Singapore Hong Kong Tokyo
Nairobi Dar es Salaam Cape Town
Melbourne Auckland Madrid
and associated companies in
Berlin Ibadan

Oxford is a trade mark of Oxford University Press

Published in the United States by
Oxford University Press Inc., New York

© IUSSP 1992

British Library Cataloguing in Publication Data
Data available

Library of Congress Cataloging in Publication Data
Family systems and cultural change / editors, Elza Berquó,
Peter Xenos.
p. cm.—(International studies in demography)
Includes bibliographical references and indexes.
1. Family demography. 2. Family—Cross-cultural studies.
I. Berquó, Elza. II. Xenos, Peter, 1943- . III. Series.
HQ759.98.F37 1992 306.85—dc20 92-12428
ISBN 0-19-828384-9

Typeset by Joshua Associates Limited, Oxford
Printed in Great Britain
on acid-free paper by
Bookcraft (Bath) Ltd
Midsomer Norton, Avon

Preface

The conference that gave rise to these papers brought people together from seventeen countries on five continents. Since then they seem to have dispersed in two or three directions each. The editors are in Brazil and Honolulu, the publisher is in England, the authors are in numerous other places, and everyone is always travelling. Or, at least, so it seemed as we sought to complete our task as editors.

Throughout the long gestation of this 'child', to pick up on Charlotte Hohn's metaphor in Chapter 1, there has been a remarkable amount of help—administrative, logistical, clerical—from the East–West Population Institute in Honolulu and its Director, Dr Lee-Jay Cho. The names of those who typed, photocopied, and otherwise laboured are too numerous to list here, but a special expression of thanks must go to Sandra Ward who, as Senior Editor at the East–West Population Institute, gave the redrafted papers a very thorough going over. We have received considerable help as well from the International Union for the Scientific Study of Population (IUSSP), particularly from Marc Lebrun. Our thanks also go to the authors of these chapters who, mostly, have been patient throughout.

EB
PSX

Contents

List of Figures   ix
List of Tables   x
List of Contributors   xii

Part I: Introduction

1. The IUSSP Programme in Family Demography   Charlotte
   Höhn   3
2. Editors' Introduction   Elza Berquó and Peter Xenos   8

Part II: Regional and Global Comparisons

3. Convergence or Compromise in Historical Family Change?
   Peter McDonald   15
4. Family Systems and Cultural Change: Perspectives from Past
   and Present   Chris Wilson and Tim Dyson   31
5. Family Systems: Their Viability and Vulnerability   John C.
   Caldwell and Pat Caldwell   46

Part III: Processes and Institutions

6. Traditional Family Systems in Rural Settings in Africa
   Christine Oppong   69
7. The Role of the Family in the Process of Entry to Marriage in
   Asia   Lita J. Domingo and Elizabeth M. King   87
8. Celibacy, Solitude, and Personal Autonomy: Individual Choice
   and Social Constraints   Elizabeth Jelin   109
9. The Slavery Period and its Influence on Household Structure
   and the Family in Jamaica, Cuba, and Brazil   Verena Stolcke   125
10. The Slavery Period and its Influence on Family Change in the
    United States   Richard Steckel   144

Part IV: Directions

11. The Centrality of Time in the Study of the Family   Norman B.
    Ryder   161

12. Analysing Household Histories   Mei Ling Young   176
13. Family Change and Family Process: Implications for Research
    in Developing Countries   Maria Coleta F. A. de Oliveira   201

Name Index   215
Subject Index   219

List of Figures

7.1 Aggregate Hypotheses for Nuptiality Transition   91

12.1 Hypothetical Structure of the Life-Course Diagram   185

12.2 Superimposition of Summary Statistical Index of Critical Move on Life-Course Diagram   189

12.3 Life-Course Diagram of Household History: Case Study 1   190

12.4 Life-Course Diagram of Household History: Case Study 2   191

List of Tables

4.1 Age Gap at Marriage between Males and Females in Northern and Southern India   32

6.1 Marriage Transactions and Kin Groups in Africa   73

7.1 Mean Age at Marriage and Percentage Distribution of Selected Indicators of Mate Selection and Courtship, by Country, Demographic Characteristics, and Socio-economic Status   97

7.2 Percentage Distribution of AMS Respondents' Siblings (15 Years Old and Older) and Mothers, by Socio-economic Status, Country, and Type of Occupation   99

7.3 Participation of Daughters in the Choice of Husbands, by Country, and Daughters' Occupations before Marriage   100

7.4 AMS Respondents' Opinions of the Amount of Education Required for Boys Relative to Girls   102

7.5 Percentage Distribution of Ever-Married Women by Whether or Not They Gave Support to Parents before Marriage and by Timing of Marriage: Philippines   103

7.6 AMS Respondents Who Would Not Choose Their Daughters' Spouses, by Residence and Socio-economic Indicators   105

8.1 Nuptuality and Celibacy in Latin America   119

8.2 Marital Status, by Sex: Brazil, 1960 and 1980   119

8.3 Age at Marriage and Percentage Celibate, by Sex: Brazil, 1960 and 1980   120

10.1 Percentage of Marriages in which the Husband and Wife had Different Owners, Classified by Median Plantation Size in the County of Residence in 1860   148

10.2 Age Distribution of Slaves Destined for Gulf Coast Ports, by State of Origin   149

10.3 Estimated Slave Heights Compared with Modern Standards   151

10.4 Mortality Rates per Thousand for Slaves and the Entire Population of the United States, 1830–60   152

10.5 Daily Cotton-picking Rates before and after Giving Birth 153

10.6 Numbers of Mothers and Fathers, the Ratio of Fathers to Mothers, and the Expected Ratio of Fathers for Various Pairs of Births 155

List of Contributors

ELZA BERQUÓ

JOHN C. CALDWELL

PAT CALDWELL
LITA J. DOMINGO

TIM DYSON

CHARLOTTE HÖHN

ELIZABETH JELIN

ELIZABETH M. KING

PETER MCDONALD

MARIA COLETA F. A. DE OLIVEIRA

CHRISTINE OPPONG

NORMAN B. RYDER

RICHARD H. STECKEL

Centro Brasileiro de Analise e Planejamento (CEBRAP), São Paulo, Brazil.

Director, Health Transition Centre, National Centre for Epidemiology and Population Health, The Australian National University, Canberra, Australia.

Weetangera, Australia.

Population Institute, University of the Philippines, Quezon City, Philippines.

Department of Population Studies, London School of Economics and Political Science, London, UK.

Bundesinstitut für Bevölkerungsforschung, Wiesbaden, Germany.

Centro de Estudios de Estado y Sociedad (CEDES), Buenos Aires, Argentina.

Education and Employment Division, Population and Human Resources Department, The World Bank, Washington, DC, USA

Deputy Director for Research, Australian Institute of Family Studies, Melbourne, Australia.

Nucleo de Estudos de Populacao, Universidade Estadual de Campinas (UNICAMP), Campinas, Brazil.

Employment Planning and Population Branch, International Labour Office, Geneva, Switzerland.

Office of Population Research, Princeton University, Princeton, NJ, USA.

Department of Economics, Ohio State University, Columbus, Ohio, USA.

Verena Stolcke

Universitat Autònoma de Barcelona, Departament d'Història de les Societats Pre-capitalistes, Barcelona, Spain.

Chris Wilson

Department of Population Studies, London School of Economics and Political Science, London, UK.

Peter Xenos

East–West Population Institute, Honolulu, Hawaii, USA.

Mei Ling Young

Malaysian Institute of Economic Research, Kuala Lumpur, Malaysia.

Part I

Introduction

1   The IUSSP Programme in Family Demography

CHARLOTTE HÖHN

Scientific committees of the International Union for the Scientific Study of Population (IUSSP), like families and individuals, have a life course or life cycle. They are formed by decision of the IUSSP Council, they expand their activities, their 'offspring' are seminars, and they publish the seminar proceedings. This launching phase of mature children, however, often occurs well after the dissolution of the committee. Such disorder of phases is not provided for in the concept of the family life cycle. To reconcile theory and reality is one of the major mandates of scientific committees of the IUSSP.

Family demography is a relatively new aspect of population studies. Hervé Le Bras (1979: 52) wrote in a study of household and family statistics undertaken for the Organisation for Economic Co-operation and Development (OECD): 'Married life punctuated by marriage and divorce, procreative life marked by birth, and life itself ending in death, are three chapters of demography, whereas all these events are experienced in families.' Le Bras's implied criticism is based upon the observation that few textbooks on population contain a chapter devoted to the demography of the family. Where such a chapter does exist, it is generally shorter and more superficial than those that deal with fertility, mortality, nuptiality, and migration, or with the dynamics of age structure.

There are good reasons for this neglect of family demography. The traditional demographic analysis of such events as births, marriages, divorces, deaths, and migration has the advantage that numbers of these events can be related to individuals in the same age group and can, therefore, be measured more easily and included in models. The inclusion of other family members in such analyses causes difficulties because they will generally differ in age and sex, and complications are also introduced because they do not generally live together continuously. Family and household size varies with time: a family is founded, grows, contracts, and is dissolved within the lifetime of each member. To cope with these difficulties, much more complex analytic methods and data-collection techniques are required. Some problems can be overcome by using micro-simulation or the multi-state life-table approach. Since many of the transition probabilities required are lacking, there is a continuing reluctance to include family variables in demographic studies, and they tend to be disregarded as potential explanations of demographic developments. But, as Le Bras remarks, almost all demographic events occur within a family context, and it seems reasonable to assume that the occurrence and frequency of such events will depend, at least in part, on the structure of the family.

It would be a gross exaggeration to state that there have been no studies of family demography. The last ten years or so have seen a plethora of formal methodological, as well as substantive-descriptive, studies of the family. The activities of the IUSSP Committee on Family Demography and the Life Cycle give vivid evidence of important progress. And before the committee was founded, two valuable studies, by Burch (1979) and Bongaarts (1983), reviewed the state of the art and stressed that the subject formed one of the less developed aspects of demography.

To advance research on family demography, the IUSSP Council in 1982 convened a Scientific Committee that was given the task of elaborating the essential aspects of family demography within a period of two years. John Bongaarts was chairman and Thomas Burch, Kenneth Wachter, Gustav Feichtinger, Hervé Le Bras, and Elza Berquó were members. The committee's terms of reference were not confined to family demography but included, as its name indicates, the family life cycle. In establishing the committee, the IUSSP Council may have been under the impression that the study of the life cycle would be among the less difficult of the committee's tasks. Though the family life-cycle concept has a history of at least 40 years, this view proved to be mistaken (Höhn, 1982; 1987).

The committee began its work by asking a number of experts to draft chapters for a textbook on concepts and applications of family demography. The drafts were discussed at a workshop held in New York in December 1983, and the revised papers were published in 1987 (Bongaarts, Burch, and Wachter, 1987). As a follow-up to this work, to the birth of its first 'offspring', the committee intended to organize two seminars devoted respectively to the early and the later phases of the family life cycle. For reasons that are no longer relevant, its fertility intentions were reduced. The last 'child' was a seminar on the later phases of the family life cycle, which took place in Berlin in September 1984. The second 'child' reached the launching phase, and the proceedings (edited by Höhn, Grebenik, and Mackensen) were published in 1989. The mandate of the committee, however, expired at the end of 1984. This short first life cycle was followed by a longer, four-year cycle—the time frame of a second committee of the same name.

There have been some links and transitions between the two cycles. The principal objective of the first committee was formal, whereas the second, present, committee has been asked to devote its activities to the substantial aspects of family demography. In this respect the Berlin seminar on the later phases of the family life cycle, combining methodological and substantial aspects, can be considered as a valuable bridge to the second committee's work. There have also been two personal transitions from the first to the second committee: Elza Berquó and, in a special sense, myself. I was actively involved in both events of the prior committee. Early in 1985 I agreed to chair the new committee and to outline the work programme. The committee's first meeting, with Elza Berquó, Louis Roussel, Peter Xenos, and Jan Trost as committee members, took place in Florence, Italy, in 1985 upon the occasion of the IUSSP General Conference. I was elected IUSSP Council member at that conference and, in accordance with the rule that council members should not be committee members at the same time, resigned from the committee. Elza Berquó became its chair.

The committee consequently has developed an interesting life course. It has a chairman who was a member of the prior 'family', then re-entered the second 'family' and eventually became 'head of family'. At the same time the nucleus of the 'family' contracted in size. Charlotte Höhn was launched from the family of orientation but remained a not too distant relative, a kind of godmother considered as a permanent guest. The simple core family is smaller now, but the household has been made more complex by a co-residing unrelated household member.

That the present committee was asked to focus on the substantial aspects of family demography does not mean that its work will be purely speculative. Undoubtedly, theoretical considerations, concepts, and hypotheses are indispensable to an understanding of cultural, social, economic, and psychological determinants and consequences of family forms and changing family structures. But demography is a quantitative discipline, with application to important problems, and it cannot neglect data. This committee intends that every effort should be made to integrate knowledge about the family as a social and cultural institution as such knowledge is provided by anthropologists, sociologists, and historians. To evaluate existing work from adjacent disciplines and from demographic surveys was the objective of the Seminar on Family Structures and Life Courses in Less Developed Countries and of the committee's work programme.

In addition, the seminar was organized to overcome one major criticism of the prior committee's work, the neglect of less developed countries. It is widely believed that family demography should not be restricted to formal and Western-centred studies, as was the case with the former committee. It must be acknowledged, however, that formal family demography and in particular the family life-cycle concept do apply best to families of the nuclear, Western type. In addition, formal family demography is represented almost entirely by experts from the more developed countries. There are two reasons for this state of affairs. Firstly, formal demography must be tested with empirical data. Because most of the data are gathered in countries with a long tradition of collecting statistical data, and these are the more developed countries, methods and results have been restricted to them. Secondly, the Western type of family has been, at least until recently, less complex and more uniform than other family types, and for this reason easier to analyse.

The committee decided to start its activities with the Seminar on Family Structures and Life Course in Less Developed Countries. It is delighted that the seminar was co-sponsored by the East–West Center and convened in Honolulu. It provided an opportunity for participants to discuss demographic and ethno-graphical data from a variety of countries and surveys designed to measure household and family structures and changes within them. Our objective was to understand marriage and kinship systems, family life cycles, household development cycles, and life courses in Asia, Latin America, and Africa. Cultural differentiations were to be described, measured, and explained. Together we tried to define cultural areas of family systems, to determine different morphologies and ways of change. Is such change induced culturally or historically, by internal or external influence (or both), by political intervention or socio-economic development? These are important and difficult issues.

The seminar was the first 'baby' of the new committee. The second event in our expansion phase was a Seminar on New Forms of Family Life in More Developed Countries, which took place 6–9 October 1987 in Vaucresson, France, and has been published (Prioux, 1990). It focused on the diversification of living arrangements; the nuclear family; the monoparental family; the re-constituted family; the young, the middle-aged, and old persons living in one-person households; and the various types of informal union, such as cohabitation, 'living together apart', communes, and informal networks. Specific problems for children in complete and incomplete families and as step-children were included. Studies on differential incidence were brought together to develop explanations for the diversification of familial arrangements.

The committee also organized a session for the IUSSP's African Conference in Dakar, Senegal, in 1988. Its purpose was to study important aspects of family systems in Africa.

A third seminar was on 'Theories of Family Change' (Tokyo, 29 November–2 December 1988), while a final activity, a session at the IUSSP General Con-ference 1989 in New Delhi, was devoted to a synthesis of the committee's work. The nuclearization hypothesis is that family systems change in the course of modernization, of demographic transition, from a prevalence of extended families in rural societies to a dominance of the conjugal family in industrialized societies. The debate is already quite old, but still controversial. The very influ-ential work by William Goode and by the Cambridge Group for the History of Population and Social Structure has shown many facets that cast doubt on this hypothesis. Like the concept of demographic transition, it is much too simple and smooth to explain a complex and diverse reality.

Discussions at the Honolulu seminar bore in mind this hypothesis of modernization and nuclearization. What is the experience in major cultural areas in Asia, Latin America, and Africa? We must be careful about definitions and statistical collecting procedures. What does the word 'family' mean in different cultural contexts? How important is co-residence? How strong are the links and influences between generations? What are the roles of kinship systems, of social networks? How do religion and tradition affect family systems? Are there cultural constants that resist external influences? Are there 'only' particular, culturally specific systems and unique, uncomparable types of change, or are there some common trends and features that should allow us to formulate a general theory of family systems and change within them?

References

Bongaarts, J. (1983), 'The Formal Demography of Families and Households: An Overview', *IUSSP Newsletter*, 17: 399–416.

—— Burch, T. K., and Wachter, K. W. (eds.) (1987), *Family Demography: Methods and their Application*, Oxford University Press, Oxford.

Burch, T. K. (1979), 'Household and Family Demography: A Bibliographic Essay', *Population Index*, 45 (2), 173–95.

Höhn, C. (1982), *Der Familienzyklus: Zur Notwendigkeit einer Konzepterweiterung*, Schriftenreihe des Bundesinstituts für Bevölkerungsforschung, xii, Boldt, Boppard.

—— (1987), 'The Family Life Cycle—Needed Extensions of the Concept', in J. Bongaarts, T. K. Burch, and K. W. Wachter (eds.), *Family Demography: Methods and their Application*, Oxford University Press, Oxford.

—— Mackensen, R., and Grebenik, E. (eds.) (1989), *Demography of the Later Phases of the Family Life Cycle*, Oxford University Press, Oxford.

Le Bras, H. (1979), *Child and Family: Demographic Developments in the OECD Countries*, Organisation for Economic Co-operation and Development, Paris.

Prioux, France (ed.) (1990), *La Famille dans les pays développés: Permanences et changements*, Institut National d'Études Démographiques, Paris.

2 Editors' Introduction

ELZA BERQUÓ AND PETER XENOS

Family demography is a recent and relatively underdeveloped branch of population studies, in large part owing to the complex problems of data collection and analysis that are encountered. As a step towards amending this situation the International Union for the Scientific Study of Population (IUSSP) in 1982 established a Scientific Committee on Family Demography and the Life Cycle. That committee convened a group of experts at the Population Council in New York, and ultimately produced a volume of concepts and applications in the field (Bongaarts, Burch, and Wachter, 1987). Another seminar was conducted in Berlin on the later phases of the family life cycle, the proceedings of which resulted in a second volume (Grebenik, Höhn, and Mackensen, 1989).

When the committee's term expired in 1984 it was superseded by a new committee, the objective of which was to advance the substantive demography of the family and the life cycle. The new committee planned three seminars: the one recounted here, on Changing Family Structures and Life Courses in Less Developed Countries (Honolulu, Hawaii, 5–7 January 1987); another on New Forms of Family Life in More Developed Countries (Vaucresson, France, 6–9 October 1987); and the third on Theories of Family Change (Tokyo, 29 November to 2 December 1988).

The first committee had focused almost exclusively on developed countries and on the nuclear family model most readily applicable there. That focus of course reflected the geographic concentration of both appropriate data and relevant experts. Nevertheless, it was felt even then that strenuous efforts should be made to rectify this situation. The subsequent efforts of the new committee focused on developing countries. Its mandate was to reveal the need, and the possibilities, for models of family demography and family change more attuned to the world's socio-cultural diversity.

The Honolulu seminar was co-sponsored by the East–West Population Institute and took place at the East–West Center. Over a three-day period there were nineteen formal presentations of papers by a total of twenty-three experts. The seminar comprised an overview session on 'Themes and Concepts' and five main substantive sessions dealing with 'Life Cycle and Household Histories', 'Marriage Systems', 'External Pressures on Family Systems', 'Rural Family Systems', and 'Family Systems and Cultural Change'. Thirteen contributions by seventeen authors are included in this volume.

The call to the Honolulu seminar affirmed an interest in 'marriage systems'—how such systems have evolved and how they function in specific socio-cultural settings and economic conditions. Only by examining the wide range of actual marriage systems over time and space, it was felt, could ethnocentrism be avoided. At the same time scholars were encouraged to seek out the common threads, 'the anthropological basis of the family' underlying the various marriage systems world-wide. A related goal was to document the paths to change under modern conditions. Central here was critical examination of the nuclearization/convergence idea, as well as investigation of more specific forces operating on the family, for example the historical institutions of slavery and of colonialism.

There has been a return recently to comparative and historical analysis of family systems world-wide. For a long time comparative family theory had been largely evolutionary and heavily Western in orientation and in that sense ethnocentric. In the absence of empirical investigation, theory was often deductive and grounded in evolutionary or functionalist principles more than in systematic observation. Generalization across all times and places was the overarching goal. The central idea that emerged posited a process of convergence of family forms on the nuclear family roughly as found in the West of the early to mid-twentieth century. In this view, contemporary developing societies differ because their traditional social organization has not yet, or not fully, been transformed by industrialization and modernization.

However, the last several decades have seen much new historical research on the Western family as well as thorough documentation of the rather divergent recent trends in Western family systems; these have, in Oliveira's phrase 'destroyed a whole set of mistaken images' about Western families and seriously undermined the simple convergence view. At the same time the developing countries have seen, in different degrees, unmistakable change in their family systems.

The way has been opened to new research on family systems throughout the world, now much more firmly grounded in both anthropological field studies and large-scale household surveys in a variety of cultural settings covering much of the developing world. This volume of new essays and research documents, synthesizes, and contributes to the new family research. It illustrates the ongoing revision in our views of the family systems of developing regions.

Also reflected well in this volume are some of the emerging styles and methodological directions of family research on developing countries. Modern data collection in the developing world is rich and varied. Standardized methods of large-scale data collection (especially traditional interviews with ever-married women) are well developed, and there has been movement recently toward forms of in-depth data collection such as life-history reconstruction, focus-group interviews, micro-level community studies, and richly textured functional studies of households. The preferred investigations, judging from many of the contributions in this volume, are fine-grained in their detail, and multi-levelled in the way that they link conditions and processes from the local through the national to the global society. Still, reservations are expressed throughout the volume, about both multi-purpose surveys and detailed life-history data collection. Proponents of those approaches are challenged to make clear the advantages of the additional effort that is inevitably involved, and in particular to demonstrate the value of the data already collected. A middle ground is recommended by some, between simplistic life-cycle and highly complex life-course information.

A demographic paradigm pervades this volume, with its stress on the systematics of space and time (residence and age) as essential components of family organization. N. Ryder begins with the force underlying all demographic process, time's passage, and examines the problems this raises for individuals (aging, survival) and populations (replacement). He identifies the family as the institution meant to solve these problems at both levels, as the 'prototypical formulation of family demography'. Practical observations stem from Ryder's comments, among them: the need to treat events individually; the need to stress the variances around mean ages at occurrence, particularly in developing countries where often these variances are great 'in every dimension'; the need to explore viewpoints other than that of the respondent generation (the child's viewpoint for example); the need to examine male as well as female outlooks (e.g. gender differences in generation length); and the importance of the marriage market in studying issues of population growth.

The overarching if not always explicit theme of the collection is diversity among family systems, even prior to the recent period of rapid change. The J. and P. Caldwell notion of a universal 'traditional family' notwithstanding, evidence of that pre-transitional diversity is abundant. The collection is rich with expositions of historical and contemporary variety, from the experience of families under slavery (V. Stolke; R. Steckel), to that of Malay households under the pressure of urbanization (M. Young), to the changes taking place in the process of entry to marriage in the Philippines (L. Domingo and E. King), and the evolving institutions of consensual union and celibacy in Latin America (E. Jelin). V. Stolcke, drawing on the revisionist work that has appeared over the last decade, examines and compares Jamaica, Cuba, and Brazil. The resulting analysis casts light on family systems under extreme tension. This is an important aspect in the contemporary world situation, characterized as it is by massive refugee populations and other kinds of movements. Similarly, R. Steckel examines the ante-bellum slave family in the United States, as to forces weakening and forces strengthening. Both Stolcke's and Steckel's analyses are important as well for their insights into families of intermarriage, in settings where this is not accepted because important social boundaries, often racial or religious, are being challenged—another notable feature of family change in the modern world. M. L. Young considers the lives and family relationships of young, working Malay women in Malaysia, with their divided loyalties, yet continued sharing of earnings with families left in the villages. L. Domingo and E. King seek to understand the shift to later marriage that is occurring across Asia. The explanation they develop centres firmly on the family and especially on intergenerational issues of control, resource transfer, and family continuity. E. Jelin relates female celibacy in Latin America to broader institutional changes.

There is little support in these chapters for the one-time consensus view of family convergence under conditions of industrialization. A wide range of evidence is cited by P. McDonald as exceptions to the convergence idea. Many of the contributions (that by C. Wilson and T. Dyson, for example) further emphasize that variety exists not only in family form and function, but also in the nature of the family's links to the rest of the local community and even to the entire society and to the world as a whole. For example, Wilson and Dyson question the stress often placed on the generational principal in family analysis, and particularly its utility when studying family systems in social and cultural contexts, such as South India, where marriages may take place among close kin. They suggest instead considering all relevant interrelations within the family.

The paucity of theory regarding family change is noted by many of the authors. This is attributed to the great variability of family forms and functions globally. An implicit question underlies many of the contributions: Is it really possible to have theories about the family that are plausible cross-culturally for the whole of the transformation from pre-industrial to industrial society? The collection reflects the long-standing tension between understanding specific phenomena holistically versus the scientific goal of generalization. The Caldwells' contribution offers such a generalization, though it should be noted that they are 'generalizing' to families that are 'patrilineal, patriarchal, virilocal, exogamous, peasant, and with a closed agricultural frontier and recognized, inheritable land tenure'. The more prevalent contrary view is illustrated by C. Oppong's assertion that Western concepts are largely ineffectual in understanding African reality: 'The simple addition of polygyny or "extended household/family" to the repertoire of (Western) concepts is in no way adequate.' She examines the diversity of African family and household systems and implicitly their differences with systems elsewhere in the world. This is demonstrated by C. Oppong in regard to kinship, rules of residence, rules of sexual access, and other important features.

There are numerous suggestions regarding the future of family and household studies in developing countries. Conceptual and analytic problems are identified as blocks to progress. For example, N. Ryder's discussion emphasizes the all too frequent use of a female reference-point for data collection and the construction of indicators. He also derides the pursuit of modelling for its own sake rather than for the purpose of answering research questions. It is noted that considerable ambiguity remains regarding certain fundamental dimensions of household. Thus, N. Ryder argues that residence and descent are critical dimensions whereas E. Jelin suggests 'everyday maintenance' and 'descent' as more appropriate. C. Wilson and T. Dyson stress demographic maleability and the importance of lateral relationships, thus their questioning of the adequacy of generational concepts. Another example of conceptual ambiguity is the notion of celibacy: as E. Jelin points out, it remains to disentangle such dimensions as 'alone-ness', virginity, and childlessness. She calls for a view of celibacy giving equal place to the positive elements of solitude and autonomy, and to the underlying forces of individuation and female emancipation. Oliveira emphasizes the value of the historical research that has been carried out on Latin American societies. She urges further work of this kind, drawing on a wide range of qualitative and quantitative sources. However, a significant difficulty in trying to reconstruct the processes of family change in developing societies is the fact that many historical studies rely mainly on family systems prevailing in the dominant élites or castes.

Another point of agreement concerns the necessity of linking family and marriage systems with other important features of society, for example with issues of gender stratification, the societal process of individuation (namely, E. Jelin's view of marriage and celibacy decisions in the context of women's roles and the individuation process), the changing value of daughters (namely, L. Domingo and E. King on Asia, remarking that daughters are more and more fulfilling family obligation by providing income and, in certain cases, prestige and in turn enjoying more autonomy in decision-making).

One factor—the technology of data collection and data processing—has been of undeniable importance in the last decades and will be a dominant influence in the future. The hand of technological change is clearly reflected in the recent paths of family studies, and the present volume is a microcosm of this. Underlying many of these studies is a vast quantity of highly detailed data which has been subject to interactive manipulation in ways unimagined only two decades ago, and imagined perhaps but certainly unavailable only a few years ago. One senses that the future trajectory of the field will likewise be impelled by the possibilities that technologies of information processing will bring within reach. This applies equally to studies of the past and of the present.

A final comment on the scope of these chapters. It should not be necessary to point out that not all viewpoints and methodologies are represented here. This is a collection of papers either centred on or in some way responsive to the categories and topics of demography.

References

Bongaarts, J., Burch, T. K., and Wachter, K. W. (eds.) (1987), *Family Demography: Methods and their Application*, Oxford University Press, Oxford.

Grebenik, E., Höhn, C., and Mackensen, R. (eds.) (1989), *Later Phases of the Family Cycle: Demographic Aspects*, Oxford University Press, Oxford.

Part II

Regional and Global Comparisons

3 Convergence or Compromise in Historical Family Change?

PETER McDONALD

The Convergence Theory of Family Structure

The development of theories of social change has a distinctly Vedic character. The players are portrayed in the roles of creator, preserver, or destroyer. The creator is the great god who appears on the scene from time to time and sets down a grand theory. Subsequently the preservers get to work; they refine, they embellish, they teach, they pay homage. Last on the scene are the destroyers. Their weapons are hindsight and the exception, and their methodology consists of categorizing and labelling the theorists. The labels used range from the socio-logical, such as 'reductionist', 'functionalist', and 'structural determinist', to the impolite, such as 'culture-bound', 'self-serving', and 'naïve'. Theories that survive this process and continue into the next round of debate are identified by the prefix of 'neo'.

The creator of the convergence theory of family structure is William Goode. Goode predicted the inevitable convergence of family systems around the globe to the Western, conjugal type in his important book *World Revolution and Family Patterns* (1963: 368–70): 'It is clear that at the present time a somewhat similar set of influences is affecting all world cultures. All of them are moving towards industrialization. . . . Their family systems are also approaching some variant of the conjugal system.' He asserted that there was a 'theoretical harmony' between the conjugal family system and the modern world and that the time perspective for change was the next ten to twenty years, a period that has now elapsed.

In asserting harmony between the conjugal family and the modern world, Goode was merely following an earlier creator, Parsons. Using the structural–functionalist approach, Parsons postulated that the process of differentiation in modernizing societies is the main explanatory principle for the rise of the nuclear family (Parsons and Bales, 1955). The modern nuclear family is charac-terized, according to Parsons and Bales, by its structural isolation, the intensive nature of family life, and a rigid role segregation of husband and wife. These characteristics better equip the nuclear family to operate in the modern world, which revolves around individual achievement and social and geographic mobility. In turn, both Goode and Parsons owe much to the earlier great gods,

Marx and Weber, who saw society and its structures moving through evolution-ary phases, with the final stage being the advanced capitalist or socialist mode of production characterized by urbanization, industrialization, individualism, and predominance of the nuclear family (Macfarlane, 1978). All four great gods owe much to misinformation about the history of the family in Western Europe (Laslett, 1965).

With the aid of hindsight and an accumulation of exceptions, I must throw in my lot with Siva, the destroyer. One of the principal tactics of the destroyer is to complicate the argument excessively, and it is to that end that I devote much of this chapter.

Definitions and other Complications

'Define your terms' is the sociological equivalent of 'choose your weapons'. A judicious choice of definition is easily half the battle or, in this instance, half the chapter. Already I have used two terms, the 'conjugal family' and the 'nuclear family', as coterminous. The term 'nuclear' was used by Parsons but is unaccept-able because of its implication that the unit of husband, wife, and their children constitutes the smallest possible family or kin grouping. Goode's use of 'con-jugal family' is therefore to be preferred as long as the meaning of 'conjugal' is extended to include *de facto* relationships. Goode, however, does not define his convergence theory simply in terms of the conjugal family; he explicitly refers to the Western conjugal family. In doing so, he excludes polygamous conjugal families but also extends convergence theory beyond the structural dimension to the functional and ideological dimensions: 'Everywhere the ideology of the conjugal family is spreading. It appeals to the disadvantaged, to the young, to women, and to the educated. It promises freedom and new alternatives as against the rigidities and controls of traditional systems' (Goode, 1963: 369).

In their time context, Goode and Parsons were referring to the Western conjugal family of the 1950s. To repeat, this family was seen as structurally isolated (independent of other families), intensive, and having a rigid role segre-gation of husband and wife. Thus, the proof of convergence theory is dependent upon the emergence of this family form 'everywhere'. Recall also that Goode set a time frame of 10–20 years for convergence to be realized. Hindsight and a bag full of exceptions, many of which I shall refer to in subsequent discussion, prove that Goode was wrong at least in his time frame.

To salvage convergence theory, we must, therefore, complicate it. The theory depends on the notion that family systems change as an inevitable consequence of inevitable structural and ideological changes. The inevitable structural changes are industrialization, urbanization, proletarianization, and centraliza-tion of power. The inevitable ideological change is the acceptance of Western family values of the 1950s. To abstract further, the theory is based upon a model that sees micro-level social organization as inevitably changing in response to changes in macro-level social organization. Political, technological, or ideo-logical change at the macro-level is seen as inconsistent or incoherent with micro-level social organization, which must inevitably adjust to the macro-changes.

The theory postulates that, because the macro-changes are Western, the micro-changes must of necessity also be Western. This framework allows us to disaggregate (complicate) the argument regarding convergence theory. Granted that convergence has not yet occurred, is this because (1) the model is correct but the process of change is much slower than originally envisaged, (2) macro-changes are not conforming to the process of evolution envisaged by the pro-ponents of the theory, (3) social change is not unidirectional from macro-systems to micro-systems, or (4) macro- and micro-systems are not so rigidly linked as the proponents of the theory insist? If proposition (1) applies, then convergence theory remains intact. If proposition (2) applies, then convergence theorists can perhaps be forgiven. If proposition (3) or (4) applies, convergence theory is invalid.

Questions of Measurement

The debate over convergence theory has often diverged into two important questions of measurement; flying the measurement protest flag is another conventional tactic of the destroyer. The two measurement protests are: (1) evidence in favour of convergence theory is often based on a co-residence criterion of measurement as distinct from a co-operation criterion, and (2) the incidence of conjugal family households should be interpreted in the context of the development cycle of domestic groups. Further complication of the argu-ment necessitates that we give these protests a full judicial hearing.

The Falsity of the Co-Residence Criterion

Data on family structure are often collected on a household basis. Particularly in censuses, the household is defined in an internationally consistent and Western way. By this means it is possible to measure a high incidence of conjugal families in settings where there may actually be a substantial amount of co-operation between related households. In measurement, therefore, we must allow for the possibility of multi-household families. This objection greatly complicates the discussion because it implies that a functional definition of the family be applied in the measurement process, a task that any dictionary of sociology will reveal is difficult. The difficulty is overcome if convergence theory proponents are prepared to accept Parson's emphasis on the isolated nuclear family—that is, a family household that owes no allegiance to other related households, has no obligations to or co-operation with other related households, and, perhaps unfairly, has no affective relations with other related households. If this emphasis is not accepted, convergence theorists at the very least would need to apply equivalent definitions in Western and non-Western contexts of the form and intensity of any co-operation between related households that they regarded as being consistent with the dominance of the conjugal family. I would contend that the application of either of these definitions is easily refutable.

Recent research on family support networks in Western countries reveals an enormous amount and variety of co-operation between related households. The Western conjugal family household is not, and never has been, isolated. Inheritances pass to related households, grandparents provide child-care assistance, parents provide financial assistance to new couples, families care for their aged, relatives often form business partnerships, adult children may return to their parents' home when their marriages break down, related families provide domestic and household assistance particularly in times of crisis, and family members are often turned to for emotional support. (An extensive bibliography of studies documenting family support networks in Western settings is contained in d'Abbs, 1982, and, for the Australian context, in Whithear, 1984, 1985, and 1986.) Further, it is difficult to argue that this range of co-operation between related households in the West is exactly replicated in form and intensity in non-Western contexts.

The evidence of co-operation between related households in non-Western societies is voluminous. Oppong (1982: 134–6) using evidence from Ghana, has criticized the new household economics framework for its focus upon bounded conjugal family units. She points out that child care is often provided by persons outside the conjugal household. Arnould (1984) reports considerable variation in the degree of co-operation among agnatically related family clusters in the performance of household tasks among the Hausa, but that the ideology of the traditional multiple family *gida* is maintained. In the context of the Thai village, Foster (1984) has described the division of labour in the performance of household tasks by related households. Campbell and Brody (1985), citing the strong obligation upon Japanese children to support their aged parents, warn that we should not limit our attention to co-residential families. Similar statements are made by Eickelman (1984: 41) about the *hayyan* family cluster in Oman, by Smock (1977*a*) in reference to Ghana, by Plakans (1984: 165) in respect of the Russian Baltic provinces in the nineteenth century, and by Netting, Wilk, and Arnould (1984: xxiv) in respect of all of South-east Asia. Digard (1986: 45) goes so far as to state that the differences between extended families and conjugal families have been overdone, and that they differ only according to integrating or defining characteristics, which may be residence, authority, support, affection, and so on.

The argument here is not that households are not a meaningful unit of analysis but simply that we cannot assume that households are isolated from other related households. Convergence theory cannot therefore be based upon the incidence of conjugal family households; it must instead be based upon changes in the structural and functional linkages between related households.

The Development Cycle in Domestic Groups

The second protest flag used against convergence theory relates to errors that can arise when family structure is measured at various times rather than over the life course of the domestic group. This flag was raised as early as 1958 in Fortes's introduction to the book, *The Developmental Cycle in Domestic Groups* (Goody, 1958). The argument is a simple demographic argument which fell into the hands of Cambridge social anthropologists.

It states that even if a society aims to its fullest extent towards a joint family system, there will always be a proportion of simpler families because of the events of life and death, the timing of events such as marriage and prescribed departures from the joint family household, and varying age and sex structures of sibling sets. Of course, the incidence of cyclically determined simpler families in any particular society will depend upon the size or complexity of the joint family ideal. If the joint family is very large and complex, its structure will be relatively resilient to demographic events. If, however, the ideal is a three-generation stem family with no lateral extension, then its structure will be highly dependent upon demographic events. Attempts have been made to construct simulation models of kinship systems (Wachter, Hammel, and Laslett, 1978); but as Caldwell, Reddy, and Caldwell (1984: 217) have pointed out, the difficulty—often greater than admitted—lies in specifying the model.

Besides the original proponents of the development cycle, many writers have pointed to its significance in determining cross-sectional household structure. These include Foster (1984) and Kundstadter (1984: 306), both writing about Thailand; Caldwell, Reddy, and Caldwell (1984: 227) on India; Wolf (1986) on China; Smith (1985: 276) on Japan; Janssens (1986: 38) on Holland; Duben (1985) on Turkey; and Gould (1968) on India. Kundstadter lists 12 ways in which mortality and four ways in which fertility influences family structure in Thailand. Smith claims that demographically induced changes were so significant in nineteenth-century Japan that cross-sectional measurement of family structure displayed little regularity of pattern despite an underlying ideal. Finally, in their study of south India Caldwell, Reddy, and Caldwell (1984: 227) conclude: 'the evidence is clear and supports the development cycle argument. There is no evidence of change in the pattern of family structure during the past several generations and no real evidence that the present situation has not persisted almost indefinitely.' The relevance of the development-cycle protest flag is thus well established. Its raising greatly complicates statistical proof of convergence theory.

Initial Family Systems

The preceding complications deal with definition and measurement of the final family system, the conjugal family. We can also ask the question, What particular initial social unit will converge to the conjugal family? In many cultures the family system can be conceived as being hierarchical. The archetypal system would consist of a vast tribe or clan made up of a number of lineages, which in turn subdivide into extended family households or clusters of conjugal family households. Is the entire system to converge to the conjugal family, or only a part of it?

Following the theoretical framework already outlined, which postulates that convergence theory deals with micro-level family systems, we could conclude that the theory treats the tribe or clan, the macro-level, as exogenous. Its attention, therefore, is focused on the survival of the lineage and the extended family. The decline of the tribe or clan in the face of powerful centralized authority (the kingdom or state) is, of course, literally the story of civilization, a story that has been millennia in its making. Nevertheless, survival of the tribe or clan, through the weakness of the centralized authority or through integration with the centralized authority, remains an important reason for the continuation of extended family systems, particularly in parts of Africa and central Asia. Furthermore, even after the military power of the tribe or clan has been brought under control, the tribe may still constitute an important resource network for its members.

Evidence in Favour of Convergence Theory

While the bagful of exceptions is sufficient to disprove convergence theory because universality is one of its tenets, a less rigidly defined theory of the impact of changing macro-level systems upon micro-level family systems is supported by evidence from many societies. The extended family system that existed until relatively recently in Eastern Europe (east of the Leningrad–Trieste line) has all but faded away. The decline of the *zadruga*, the patrilineage that dominated the region of modern Yugoslavia, has been reviewed by Tisay (1985: ch. 3). Following Hammel (1969), she attributes this decline to landlessness, monetarization of the economy, urbanization, and acceptance of modern ideologies. Peristiany (1976: 2) also accepts the view that 'socio-economic environmental uniformities are undermining the extended households' in the Mediterranean region and that the 'conjugal family is gradually but surely replacing the large groups'.

In like manner, Palmer (1984: 240–4) reports that as late as the 1820s, work in the rural areas of the north-eastern states of the United States was arranged along familial lines, cash was not a universal equivalent, authority was vested in legal control over land, and a large family was a sign of prosperity. This system managed to stave off its ultimate reckoning through migration to the west, but it eventually capitulated to the rise of commercialized agriculture, capitalism, land policy, speculation, technical innovation, and regulation. This trend towards proletarianization was accompanied by the emergence of evangelical religions that satisfied the ideological needs of those at the lower end of the newly differentiated social order.

The notion that proletarianization, in either its capitalist or its socialist form, is the essential element in the replacement of extended families by conjugal families is a very powerful one and is well developed in the contributions to the book *Proletarianization and Family History* (Levine, 1984*b*). The excellent contribution by Palmer has already been described, but Levine also documents a similar process in England between 1500 and 1850. He refers (1984*a*: 99) to the crucial role played by the state in the proletarianization process: 'The law— with its bewigged judges, elaborate rituals, and powers over life itself—took the place of religion and magic as the social glue cementing the lower classes to their stations.' In the same collection Tilly (1984) addresses demographic aspects of the rise of the European proletariat, and Lis and Soly (1984) confirm the crucial role played by centralized authority structures.

The book thus revolves around the theme that familial production normally requires a family unit larger than that of the conjugal family but that the rise of a centralized economic system, either capitalist or socialist, transforms the majority into membership in the wage-earning proletariat. This process is abetted by technological innovation in the hands of the central powers and rigid regulation and policing by central authorities. Urbanization, industrialization, and ideological change are likely to accompany the process, but they are not the motor. Scarcity of resources, particularly of land, will hasten the process. Familial production is an unequal competitor to these forces, and so the extended family is stripped back to its conjugal base. This, to my mind, is the most convincing formulation of theory related to the emergence of the conjugal family, but the cogency of the argument undoubtedly owes much to the fact that the papers in the book relate only to Northern and Western Europe and to the United States. What, then, is the evidence in non-European settings?

It would be fair to say that currently, in non-European settings, the exceptions appear to outweigh the favourable examples. Exceptions will be considered in the succeeding sections, but there are many studies that support, at least in part, elements of convergence theory. Oke (1986: 191) reports that in Nigeria socially upwardly mobile people attempt to avoid their kinship responsibilities, and Caldwell (1968) has made similar observations about urban élites in Ghana. Epstein (1982: 161) asserts that the nuclear family predominates among landless labourers and marginal farmers in India. The intervention by the state in family systems is claimed for the Philippines and Mexico (Hackenberg, Murphy, and Selby, 1984) and for China (Wolf, 1986; Johnson, 1983: 217). Wolf emphasizes the significance of state intervention in counter-argument to Whyte and Parish (1984), who argue, in line with convergence theory, that industrialization and urbanization are responsible for changes in the Chinese family system. State intervention, however, must also be considered to be part of the macro-system and therefore consistent with Goode's formulation. The predominance of nuclear families is also reported among settlers in Egypt's newly reclaimed lands (Sukkary-Stolba, 1985: 185).

Examples Counter to Convergence Theory

In contrast to the research just reviewed, many studies report resilience of extended family systems even when considerable change has occurred in macro-social systems. The south Indian study by Caldwell, Reddy, and Caldwell (1984) has already been quoted. Persistence of the extended family in Ghana is reported by Oppong (1982), Fortes (1978), and Smock (1977a). Oke (1986: 186–7) reports that in Nigeria the interests of the extended family transcend those of the individual and that the larger the circle of one's kin, the greater one's social and political importance. In Senegal (Mogey and Bachmann, 1986: 234) the caste system is familial and the council of heads of noble families retains political authority. In this case, as evident throughout much of Northern Africa and the Middle East, endogamous marriages tend to perpetuate the familial-based social strata and hence the extended family (Patai, 1971: 429–36). This same view is put forth by Atran (1985: 661), who states that in the Arab world endogamous marriage 'has proven to be a historically robust form of what, at least at first glance, appears to be essentially a tribal means of alliance and descent, and is even today a powerful factor in the area's politics and economics.' Endogamous marriage solidifies a lineage against fission and reunifies competing segments (see also Smock, 1977b: 400; Smock and Youssef, 1977b: 43; Eickelman, 1984: 41).

Continuation of the importance of the extended family is also reported for Latin America. Elmendorf (1977: 140) claims that in Mexico, despite pressures towards the nuclear family, many traditional forms of the extended family are maintained and constitute the basis of the political and financial power of privileged social groups. Deere (1985) notes that in 13 Latin American countries agrarian reform, in designating households as the beneficiary, was designed not to challenge existing family structure. Mallon (1986: 149), referring to central Peru, concludes that patriarchal relations will not change in a specific, predictable, and automatic way with a change in the mode of production.

More remote communities, such as those of the West African Sahel (Bovin, 1983) and the Pakhtu of Afghanistan (Boesen, 1983) are reported to be almost unchanged, still steeped in the extended family kinship system. At the other extreme, persistence of the importance of extended families in Japan is documented by Hodge and Ogawa (1986), by Kobayashi and Tanaka (1984), and by Morgan and Hiroshima (1983). Convergence to the Western conjugal family is also belied by the flourishing of husband–wife relationships in Africa that diverge greatly from the Western type, such as polygyny (Ware, 1979) and separateness of residence and resources (Abu, 1983: 156–8).

Much of the evidence in favour of convergence theory in non-European contexts is related to urban areas and to migrant groups. In an interesting study of rural China, Johnson (1983, 215–24) claims that government policies restricting mobility and emphasizing village self-sufficiency have buttressed patrilineal extended family practices. Thus, although the state has been instrumental in the destruction of the traditional clan loyalties that threatened it (the macro-level), its strategies have supported family practices at the micro-level. The collective and the cadre system, according to Johnson, have simply been superimposed on pre-existing village organization.

A final study of interest because of its experimental methodology is that of Kundstadter (1984) of the Karen, Lua', and Hmong groups in north-western Thailand. He shows that different ethnic groups that shared precisely the same environmental circumstances had divergent family systems, an argument against the notion that family systems are environmentally determined. He also observed the same groups in 1968 and 1981, between which years considerable economic development occurred. His observations related to three environmental settings: highland subsistence with communally held land, lowland cash-crop agriculture with individual ownership, and a suburban area of wage workers. Development substantially affected all three areas, but there was little observed change in kinship structure even in the suburban area. Kundstadter concludes that economic structure is less important to family systems than are cultural patterns or ideals. This point of view clearly contrasts sharply with the European proletarianization argument outlined above, perhaps pointing to the importance of examining the ideological underpinnings of proletarianization. The theme of reconstitution of family systems arising through compromise between ideology and economic structure is the new direction in the theory of social change and the family, and it is to that theme that I now turn.

Social Change and Family Reconstitution

Boudon (1983) regards convergence theory as structural determinism. He rejects the notion that particular structural features are essential to the detection and explanation of the main trends of social change. He suggests that observed features of social structure may not be logically linked and harmonious but instead may be conflicting and under strain. He rejects social order theories including convergence theory and suggests that the effect of industrialization upon family structure is highly dependent on the context and that the causal direction is sometimes reversed. Development, states Boudon, occurs as people try to reconstruct their society through individual or joint action.

Farber, Mogey, and Smith (1986), drawing upon Boudon, postulate that 'essential structural relationships are transformed to maintain social continuity' and that integration of the new with the old is a normative rather than a natural process. Thus, social constraints such as religious values may be highly significant in defining the options for change. The Summer 1986 special issue of the *Journal of Comparative Family Studies* contains several papers that serve as examples of this reformulation of theories of family change. Ramu (1986: 179), for example, describes how Indian tax laws favour extended family corporations and that the extended family remains an important element in the credit structure. Ekong (1986) describes how each of three groups in Nigeria experienced development in a manner consistent with its own social and cultural history and structure. Mogey and Bachmann (1986: 234–6) describe how social change in villages in Senegal depended upon the effectiveness of the local council; while the council controlled the local status system, traditional family practices were maintained.

This theoretical construct is supported by studies that have shown increases in the incidence of extended family households in particular settings (Laslett, 1965; Laslett and Wall, 1972; Netting, 1965; Anderson, 1971; Linares, 1984; Janssens, 1986). Economic necessity is producing this result in advanced societies in respect of care of the aged (Morgan and Hirosima, 1983) and post-separation co-residence of adult children and their offspring with parents (McDonald, 1986).

Other writers refer to the emergence of dual family systems, with some functions being more importantly functions of the conjugal family and others functions of the extended family. This viewpoint is put forth by Backer (1983: 62) in respect of the Albanian minority in Yugoslavia, by Halpern and Anderson (1970) in respect of Yugoslavia, and by Smock (1977a) and Okali (1983) in respect of Ghana. Their work perhaps is little different from earlier anthropological studies showing that differing familial and social units functioned in different situations (Fortes, 1949; Goody, 1958; Geertz, 1967). It is also a common strategy of immigrant groups in the United States (Mindel and Habenstein, 1981) and Australia (Storer, 1985). James (1985: 161) also reports how people involved in resettlement in Southern Africa experienced a lapse of some kinship bonds while other bonds intensified. Households in the resettlement area were likely to be extended collaterally, not in a traditional form but in a new form that emphasized the need to share.

The notion that development produces a compromise of the maintenance of social continuity while essential structural relationships are transformed is strongly espoused by scholars of the Muslim world. They assert that Islamic family values are maintained while modernization proceeds. This is the resounding theme of papers from a conference in Tunis. Behnam (1985) claims the persistence of Islamic family values from Morocco to Iran despite considerable variation in economic and social change. The Iranian extended family, the *tayefeh*, is said to persist in Iranian villages, extensive socio-economic relations are maintained within the kin group, and the evolution of the extended family has followed an Iranian rather than a Western path (Nassehi-Behman, 1985: 560–2). In respect of Turkey, Vergin (1985: 574) writes:

in spite of secularization policies, socio-economic development and change in attitude towards political and economic life, the Turkish family, far from disintegrating, is surviving as a unit which is particularly resistant to external pressures. An examination of research results has shown that the percentage of extended families in Anatolia has scarcely changed since the Tanzimat reforms and that the current changes in rural infrastructure have not affected the family. Moreover, the rural exodus and urbanization have not resulted in the dissolution of kinship relationships. These data should allow us to develop, contrary to the evolutionist theories which predict unilinear changes in the family, a model of differential change that accounts for the variety of concrete situations.

A similar argument is made by Sow (1985: 563–70) for Black African Muslim societies, by Rugh (1984) for contemporary Egypt, and by Rezig (1983) for Algeria. In making the same argument for Arab societies, Minces (1982: 24, 112) makes the additional point that persistence of Islamic values involves direct rejection of Western values. The West is perceived as 'a dominating force to be shut out lest it destroy the character and personality of the region', and there is 'a fear that any tampering with the socio-cultural edifice based on Islam will lead to disintegration of civilization itself'.

The final example of compromise is an urban example, Hong Kong, but the process described could hold equally well in a rural setting. Salaff (1981), following Farber (1975), postulates that, when faced with developmental changes, some societies take on a factional form in which extended families stratify the community as power bases to manipulate other institutions. Primary loyalty of members of the kin group is demanded in order to mobilize labour and political power in the competition with other kin groups for scarce resources.

Conclusion

The remaining weapon available to the destroyer is labelling. As we have seen, the sociological labels, such as the dreaded 'structural determinism', have already been applied by others to proponents of convergence theory. It remains for me to provide some impolite labels.

With the aid of hindsight, convergence theory can be regarded as a product of its time, the era of familism and Western chauvinism that pervaded the 1950s and 1960s. It was an era in which leading psychologists declared persons who divorced or did not marry as immature or deviant (Ehrenreich, 1983), the era in which Rostow (1962) gave us the universal path to economic growth applicable to all countries, the era in which the 'modern man' was re-invented and blatantly defined in our own image (Lerner, 1958; Inkeles and Smith, 1974). Inkeles (1983) indicates that the era, for some, extends beyond the 1960s. The assumption of cultural superiority underlying the era's ideology approximated that of the social evolutionists of the late nineteenth century. Convergence theory not only failed to predict the path of changes in family systems in the non-Western context, it also failed to predict the movement away from the idealized version of the conjugal family that has occurred in the West itself in the past twenty years.

References

Abu, K. (1983), 'The Separateness of Spouses: Conjugal Resources in an Ashanti Town', in C. Oppong (ed.), *Female and Male in West Africa*, Allen & Unwin, London.

Anderson, M. (1971), *Family Structure in Nineteenth Century Lancashire*, Cambridge University Press, Cambridge.

Arnould, E. J. (1984), 'Marketing and Social Reproduction in Zinder, Niger Republic', in R. M. Netting, R. R. Wilk, and E. J. Arnould (eds.), *Households: Comparative and Historical Studies of the Domestic Group*. University of California Press, Berkeley, Calif.

Atran, S. (1985), 'Managing Arab Kinship and Marriage', *Social Science Information*, 24 (4), 659–96.

Backer, B. (1983), 'Mother, Sister, Daughter, Wife: The Pillars of the Traditional Albanian Patriarchal Society', in B. Utas (ed.), *Women in Islamic Societies: Social Attitudes and Historical Perspectives*, Curzon Press, London.

Behnam, D. (1985), 'The Tunis Conference: The Muslim Family and the Modern World', *Current Anthropology*, 26 (5), 555–6.

Boesen, I. W. (1983), 'Conflicts of Solidarity in Pakhtun Women's Lives', in B. Utas (ed.), *Women in Islamic Societies: Social Attitudes and Historical Perspectives*, Curzon Press, London.

Boudon, R. (1983), 'Why Theories of Social Change Fail: Some Methodological Thoughts', *Public Opinion Quarterly*, 47(2), 143–60.

Bovin, M. (1983), 'Muslim Women in the Periphery: The West African Sahel', in B. Utas (ed.), *Women in Islamic Societies: Social Attitudes and Historical Perspectives*, Curzon Press, London.

Caldwell, J. C. (1968), *Population Growth and Family Change in Africa: The New Urban Elite in Ghana*, Australian National University Press, Canberra.

—— Reddy, P. H., and Caldwell, P. (1984), 'The Determinants of Family Structure in Rural South India', *Journal of Marriage and the Family*, 46 (1), 215–29.

Campbell, R. and Brody, E. M. (1985), 'Women's Changing Roles and Help to the Elderly: Attitudes of Women in the United States and Japan', *Gerontologist*, 25 (6): 586–92.

d'Abbs, P. (1982), *Social Support Networks: A Critical Review of Models and Findings*, Australian Institute of Family Studies, Melbourne.

Deere, C. D. (1985), 'Rural Women and State Policy: The Latin American Agrarian Reform Experience', *World Development*, 13 (9), 1037–53.

Digard, J. (1986), 'On the Family and Change in the Middle East', *Current Anthropology* 27 (1), 45.

Duben, A. (1985), 'Turkish Families and Households in Historical Perspective', *Journal of Family History*, 10 (1), 75–97.

Ehrenreich, B. (1983), *The Hearts of Men: American Dreams and the Flight from Commitment*, Anchor Press, Garden City, NY.

Eickelman, C. (1984), *Women and Community in Oman*, New York University Press, New York.

Ekong, S. C. (1986), 'Industrialization and Kinship: A Comparative Study Of Some Nigerian Ethnic Groups', *Journal of Comparative Family Studies*, 17 (2), 197–206.

Elmendorf, M. (1977), 'Mexico: The Many Worlds of Women', in J. Z. Giele and A. C.

Smock (eds.), *Women: Roles and Status in Eight Countries*, John Wiley and Sons, New York.

Epstein, T. S. (1982), 'A Social Anthropological Approach to Women's Roles and Status in Developing Countries: The Domestic Cycle', in R. Anker, M. Buvinic, and N. H. Youssef (eds.), *Women's Roles and Population Trends in the Third World*, Croom Helm, London.

Farber, B. (1975), 'Bilateral Kinship: Centripetal and Centrifugal Types of Organization', *Journal of Marriage and the Family*, 37 (4), 871–88.

—— Mogey, J., and Smith, K. S. (1986), 'Introduction: Kinship and Development', *Journal of Comparative Family Studies*, 17 (2), 151–60.

Fortes, M. (1949), *The Web of Kinship Among the Tallensi: The Second Part of an Analysis of the Social Structure of a Trans-Volta Tribe*, Oxford University Press, London.

—— (1978), 'Family, Marriage and Fertility in West Africa', in C. Oppong, G. Adaba, M. Bekombo-Priso, and J. Mogey (eds.), *Marriage, Fertility and Parenthood in West Africa*, Australian National University Press, Canberra.

Foster, B. L. (1984), 'Family Structure and the Generation of Thai Social Exchange Networks', in R. M. Netting, R. R. Wilk, and E. J. Arnould (eds.), *Households: Comparative and Historical Studies of the Domestic Group*, University of California Press, Berkeley, Calif.

Geertz, C. (1967), 'Tihingan: A Balinese Village', in R. M. Koentjaraningrat (ed.), *Villages in Indonesia*, Cornell University Press, Ithaca, NY.

Goode, W. J. (1963), *World Revolution and Family Patterns*, Free Press of Glencoe, New York.

Goody, J. (1958), *The Developmental Cycle in Domestic Groups*, Cambridge University Press, Cambridge.

Gould, H. A. (1968), 'Time Dimension and Structural Change in an Indian Kinship System', in M. B. Singer and B. S. Cohn (eds.), *Structure and Change in Indian Society*, Aldine, Chicago.

Hackenberg, R., Murphy, A. D., and Selby, H. A. (1984), 'The Urban Household in Dependent Development', in R. M. Netting, R. R. Wilk, and E. J. Arnould (eds.), *Households: Comparative and Historical Studies of the Domestic Group*, University of California Press, Berkeley, Calif.

Halpern, Joel and Anderson, David (1970), 'The Zadruga: A Century of Change', *Anthropologica*, 12, 83–97.

Hammel, E. A. (1969), 'Economic Change, Social Mobility and Kinship in Serbia', *South-Western Journal of Anthropology*, 25.

Hodge, R. W., and Ogawa, N. (1986), *Arranged Marriages, Assortative Mating and Achievement in Japan*, NUPRI Research Paper Series, No. 27, Population Research Institute, Nihon University, Tokyo.

Inkeles, A. (1983), *Exploring Individual Modernity*, Columbia University Press, New York.

—— and Smith, D. H. (1974), *Becoming Modern: Individual Change in Six Developing Countries*, Harvard University Press, Cambridge, Mass.

James, D. (1985), 'Family and Household in a Lebowa Village', *African Studies*, 44 (2), 159–87.

Janssens, A. (1986), 'Industrialization Without Family Change? The Extended Family and the Life Cycle in a Dutch Industrial Town, 1880–1920', *Journal of Family History*, 11 (1), 25–42.

Johnson, K. A. (1983), *Women, the Family and Peasant Revolution in China*, University of Chicago Press, Chicago.

Kobayashi, K., and Tanaka, K. (1984), 'Population of Japan: Families, Households and Housing', NUPRI Reprint Series, No. 12, Population Research Institute, Nihon University, Tokyo.

Kundstadter, P. (1984), 'Cultural Ideals, Socioeconomic Change, and Household Composition: Karen, Lua', Hmong and Thai in Northwestern Thailand', in R. M. Netting, R. R. Wilk, and E. J. Arnould (eds.), *Households: Comparative and Historical Studies of the Domestic Group*, University of California Press, Berkeley, Calif.

Laslett, P. (1965), *The World We Have Lost*, Scribner, New York.

—— and Wall, R. (1972), *Household and Family in Past Time*, Cambridge University Press, Cambridge.

Lerner, D. (1958), *The Passing of Traditional Society: Modernizing the Middle East*, Free Press, New York.

Levine, D. (1984*a*), 'Production, Reproduction, and the Proletarian Family in England, 1500–1851', in D. Levine (ed.), *Proletarianization and Family History*, Academic Press, New York.

—— (1984*b*), *Proletarianization and Family History*, Academic Press, New York.

Linares, O. F. (1984), 'Households among the Diola of Senegal: Should Norms Enter by the Front or the Back Door?' in R. M. Netting, R. R. Wilk, and E. J. Arnould (eds.), *Households: Comparative and Historical Studies of the Domestic Group*, University of California Press, Berkeley, Calif.

Lis, C., and Soly, H. (1984), 'Policing the Early Modern Proletariat, 1450–1850', in D. Levine (ed.), *Proletarianization and Family History*, Academic Press, London.

McDonald, P. (1986), *Settling up: Property and Income Distribution in Divorce in Australia*, Prentice-Hall of Australia, Sydney.

Macfarlane, A. (1978), *The Origins of English Individualism: The Family, Property, and Social Transition*, Blackwell, Oxford.

Mallon, F. E. (1986), 'Gender and Class in the Transition to Capitalism: Household and Mode of Production in Central Peru', *Latin American Perspectives*, 13 (1), 147–74.

Minces, J. (1982), *The House of Obedience: Women in Arab Society*, Zed Press, London.

Mindel, C. B., and Habenstein, R. W. (1981), *Ethnic Families in America: Patterns and Variations*, 2nd edn., Elsevier North Holland, New York.

Mogey, J., and Bachmann, H. (1986), 'Kinship under Two Strategies of Development', *Journal of Comparative Family Studies*, 17 (2), 233–44.

Morgan, S. P., and Hirosima, K. (1983), 'The Persistence of Extended Family Residence in Japan: Anachronism or Alternative Strategy', *American Sociological Review*, 48 (2), 269–81.

Nassehi-Behman, V. (1985), 'Change and the Iranian Family', *Current Anthropology*, 26 (5), 557–62.

Netting, R. M. (1965), 'Household Organization and Intensive Agriculture: The Kofyar Case', *Africa*, 35 (4), 424–9.

—— Wilk, R. R., and Arnould, E. J. (1984), 'Introduction', in *Households: Comparative and Historical Studies of the Domestic Group*, University of California Press, Berkeley, Calif.

Okali, C. (1983), 'Kinship and Cocoa Farming in Ghana', in C. Oppong (ed.), *Female and Male in West Africa*, Allen & Unwin, London.

Oke, E. A. (1986), 'Kinship Interaction in Nigeria in Relation to Societal Modernization: A Pragmatic Approach', *Journal of Comparative Family Studies*, 17 (2), 185–96.

Oppong, C. (1982), 'Family Structure and Women's Reproductive and Productive Roles: Some Conceptual and Methodological Issues', in R. Anker, M. Buvinic, and N. H. Youssef (eds.), *Women's Roles and Population Trends in the Third World*, Croom Helm, London.

Palmer, B. D. (1984), 'Social Formation and Class Formation in North America, 1800–1900', in D. Levine (ed.), *Proletarianization and Family History*, Academic Press, New York.

Parsons, T., and Bales, R. (1955), *The Family: Socialization and Interaction Process*, Free Press of Glencoe, New York.

Patai, R. (1971), *Society, Culture and Change in the Middle East*, University of Pennsylvania Press, Philadelphia.

Peristiany, J. G. (1976), *Mediterranean Family Structures*, Cambridge University Press, Cambridge.

Plakans, A. (1984), 'Serf Emancipation and the Changing Structure of Rural Domestic Groups in the Russian Baltic Provinces: Linden Estate, 1797–1858', in R. M. Netting, R. R. Wilk, and E. J. Arnould (eds.), *Households: Comparative and Historical Studies of the Domestic Group*, University of California Press, Berkeley, Calif.

Ramu, G. N. (1986), 'Kinship Structure and Entrepreneurship: An Indian Case', *Journal of Comparative Family Studies*, 17 (2), 173–84.

Rezig, I. (1983), 'Women's Roles in Contemporary Algeria: Tradition and Modernism', in B. Utas, *Women in Islamic Societies: Social Attitudes and Historical Perspectives*, Curzon Press, London.

Rostow, W. W. (1962), *The Stages of Economic Growth: A Non-Communist Manifesto*, Cambridge University Press, Cambridge.

Rugh, A. B. (1984), *Family in Contemporary Egypt*, Syracuse University Press, Syracuse, NY.

Salaff J. W. (1981), *Working Daughters of Hong Kong: Filial Piety or Power in the Family?* Cambridge University Press, Cambridge.

Smith, R. J. (1985), 'Transformations of Commoner Households in Tennojimura, 1757–1858', in S. B. Hanley and A. P. Wolf (eds.), *Family and Population in East Asian History*, Stanford University Press, Stanford, Calif.

Smock, A. C. (1977*a*), 'Ghana: From Autonomy to Subordination', in J. Z. Giele and A. C. Smock (eds.), *Women: Roles and Status in Eight Countries*, John Wiley and Sons, New York.

—— (1977*b*), 'Conclusion: Determinants of Women's Roles and Status' in J. Z. Giele and A. C. Smock (eds.), *Women: Roles and Status in Eight Countries*, John Wiley and Sons, New York.

Smock, A. and Youssef, N. (1977), 'Egypt: From Seclusion to Limited Participation', in J. Z. Giele and A. C. Smock (eds.), *Women: Roles and Status in Eight Countries*, John Wiley and Sons, New York.

Sow, F. (1985), 'Muslim Families in Contemporary Black Africa', *Current Anthropology*, 26 (5), 563–70.

Storer, D. (1985), 'Introduction', in D. Storer (ed.), *Ethnic Family Values in Australia*, Prentice-Hall of Australia, Sydney.

Sukkary-Stolba, S. (1985), 'Changing Roles of Women in Egypt's Newly Reclaimed Lands', *Anthropological Quarterly*, 58 (4), 182–9.

Tilly, C. (1984), 'Demographic Origins of the European Proletariat', in D. Levine (ed.), *Proletarianization and Family History*, Academic Press, London.

Tisay, L. (1985), 'Yugoslav Families', in D. Storer (ed.), *Ethnic Family Values in Australia*, Prentice-Hall of Australia, Sydney.

Vergin, N. (1985), 'Social Change and the Family in Turkey', *Current Anthropology*, 26 (5), 571–4.

Wachter, K., Hammel, E. A., and Laslett, P. (1978), *Statistical Studies of Historical Social Structure: Advances in Historical Demography*, Academic Press, New York.

Ware, H. (1979), 'Polygyny: Women's Views in a Transitional Society, Nigeria 1975, *Journal of Marriage and the Family*, 41 (1), 185–95.

Whithear, D. (ed.) (1984, 1985, 1986), *Australian Family Studies Database*, vols. i–iii, Australian Institute of Family Studies, Melbourne.

Whyte, M. and Parish, W. (1984), *Urban Life in Contemporary China*, University of Chicago Press, Chicago.

Wolf, A. P. (1986), 'The Preeminent Role of Government Intervention in China's Family Revolution', *Population and Development Review*, 12 (1).

4 Family Systems and Cultural Change: Perspectives from Past and Present

CHRIS WILSON AND TIM DYSON

Our purposes in this chapter are straightforward: we aim to examine family structures in India and Europe and in doing so to consider the utility of various theoretical approaches to this subject. Although the focus of the volume is on the contemporary family in the developing world, we try wherever possible to adopt a historical perspective. We do this in the belief that a full picture of present trends can be gained only through an awareness of their origins. This is especially important when considering the family, about which, in the absence of detailed information, there is a great temptation merely to assume that we know the nature of past structures. The history of the academic study of the family is full of such cases. The grandfather of family demography, Le Play himself, is a celebrated but far from sole example. In this frame of mind we undertake our exploration of the family in India and Europe, starting with the Indian Subcontinent.

India

We preface our discussion of India with a few general observations. Though their views vary in detail, almost all commentators suggest that there is an underlying basic similarity of family structure in much of India, despite wide variation by region, caste, etc. As in many agricultural societies, kinship, family, and marriage relationships dominate most people's lives; even inter-village relations may be conceptualized in kinship terms (Lewis, 1986: 154). Indian scholars sometimes seem reluctant to admit the extent to which traditional Hindu family forms, especially those found among high castes, may be changing (e.g., Kapadia, 1966: 332–3). However, this may partly reflect ambiguities concerning the direction of change. There is also a serious shortage of hard data on Indian family demography.

A controversy exists as to the nature and extent of regional variation in traditional kinship structures (Karve, 1953; Dumont and Pocock, 1957). It has revolved around north–south contrasts; less is known about variation in eastern India's kinship and family forms. In general, southern Indians marry people who are closer in both kinship and spatial terms. Among some southern groups it is common for a man to marry his mother's brother's daughter. This matrilateral, cross-cousin marriage form is compatible with the key Indian marriage principle of hypergamy. Another 'preferred' marriage partner for a southern man is his elder sister's daughter. The existence of a fairly high proportion of analogous close-kin unions across the generations is a key factor accounting for the systematically larger age gap at marriage found throughout the southern states (shown in Table 4.1). In contrast, in northern India spouses must be unrelated in kinship terms, and marriages take place over much greater distances. Prior to the marriage season northern fathers may spend months in which they 'scour the countryside' far and wide for potential husbands for their daughters (Lewis, 1986: 163).

This basic contrast between north and south may have been overstated, however. The coexistence of both northern and southern marriage forms in geographically intermediate areas has long been acknowledged. In Mahar-

TABLE 4.1. Age Gap at Marriage between Males and Females in Northern and Southern India (Computed from 1971 Census Data)

Region	Age gap at marriage (in years, male–female)
South	
Kerala	5.73
Tamil Nadu	6.34
Andhra Pradesh	6.49
Karnataka	7.23
Maharashtra	6.03
North	
Gujarat	3.78
Rajasthan	4.45
Uttar Pradesh	3.85
Madhya Pradesh	4.73
Punjab	3.14
Haryana	3.88

(i) The figures represent differences between male and female singulate mean ages at marriage (SMAMs) calculated with 1971 census data. Similar statistics from previous censuses indicate that this regional pattern is of very long standing.
(ii) The North/South categorization of states is that devised by Dyson and Moore (1983) when exploring regional variation in Indian kinship and demography.
(iii) The pattern of regional variation shown in the table is an important yet rarely noted feature of India's kinship and demography.

Source: India, Registrar General and Census Commissioner, 1983.

ashtra, for example, many groups exhibit a preference for matrilateral cross-cousin marriage (Karve, 1953). Dumont and Pocock (1957) go further in criticizing Karve's classic depiction of north–south variation. For example, cross-cousin marriage forms are found in some low-caste groups in Rajasthan, and in south India a significant proportion of marriages has probably always been between unrelated persons (i.e., they were not the preferred marriage forms). Perhaps the most important point to note from the work of Dumont and Pocock, aside from the much more prevalent existence of cross-cousin marriage in the south, is that both northern and southern systems were governed by the same basic principles (e.g. hypergamy, patrilineality, patrilocality). Hence the north–south contrast may be best viewed as quantitative (i.e. one of mix) rather than qualitative (one of kind) (Dumont and Pocock, 1957).

These common kinship principles between north and south take on particular importance with reference to another shared feature of both regions in the past—the Hindu joint family. The ideal of this family form stressed filial and fraternal solidarity (Mandelbaum, 1970). It should be clear from the foregoing summary of north–south variation that the joint family was probably in some respects more readily identifiable in the north than in the south, for, in the former region, patrilineality and patrilocality were in no way compromised by preferred marriage forms to close kin. In the south there was not always sharp distinction between agnates and affines. Relatedly, in the south preferred marriage forms 'across the generation' blur the distinction between inter- and intragenerational marriages. Of course, joint families could exist within the southern kinship system, but their boundaries would not have been so precisely defined. Let us now briefly summarize the ideal of the traditional Hindu joint family before examining how it may have changed.

In this family brothers stayed in their parents' house after marriage, worked together, and supported and revered their parents. Thus, the prime kin links were both vertical and lateral, and in the male line. The joint family was the main unit of production, consumption, and security for its members. It existed semi-autonomously within the village. Family property was jointly owned and worked. Sons would eventually inherit on an equal (though not necessarily individual) basis. Daughters received no share, though the women of the family (both daughters and in-marriers) had rights to basic maintenance. Proper relations between brothers, and between father and son, were deemed extremely important. An outward symbol of family unity was joint worship and dining among the family's adult males (Mandelbaum, 1970; 1972; Kapadia, 1966).

Given the above precepts, the joint family functioned to assimilate in-marrying women (who might be regarded as a potential threat to family solidarity) and to minimize the conjugal bond. The presence of the husband's parents also hindered the growth of husband–wife communication. The joint family also functioned as a reproductive unit; its continuance rested with the production of male heirs, for which there was intense social pressure upon the in-marrying women. The joint family also may have facilitated early marriage for both sexes. Beyond the production of male heirs for the family, a woman's status depended upon her husband's position within the family hierarchy. In general this family form promoted sharp separation of male and female activities, especially in the north. Should a woman be widowed, her husband's family would maintain her; she would probably not remarry, although among some northern groups levirate remarriage was (and is) widespread. In sum, the traditional joint family structure was hierarchical and heavily male-oriented. It embodied firm parental authority, respect for elders, and fraternal accord.

Clearly, this family form had many facets. Some of its aspects have changed more radically than others. It is important to stress, however, that much of the ideal, as depicted above, is misleading as a representation of most Indian families in the past.

Firstly, it is clear that the joint family would have followed a cyclical pattern of development and decay. At some stage (e.g., at the death of the senior male) fission became inevitable. If brothers had duties to co-reside, these did not extend in force to the next generation (i.e., to their sons). In most cases there would be no shortage of tensions to act as the excuse for division at the moment of fission. For example, the joint family often involved rivalry between the wives of brothers and the suppression of those wives by the family matriarch. Thus, to quote Goode (1968: viii) 'we can be sure that the very large household was probably not ever common at any time in India, simply because the forces of fission were great . . .'.

Secondly, arguably the most important unifying feature of the traditional joint family was its coparcenary holding of family land. What we have described above is really the ideal form of the high-caste landholding family. Indeed, it was so hierarchical in structure precisely because of the key issue of control over land. But it is probable that family structure among many lower-caste groups with less land tended to differ substantially from such an ideal, possibly involving less hierarchy and greater independence for women. Interestingly, surveys of contemporary India show that, to the extent that joint families remain, they are found among large landholders, and are rare among small landholding castes (Mandelbaum, 1970: 50).

What, then, of family and household structure among landless groups in the past? In this connection research is increasingly suggesting that the image of Indian villages consisting historically of a number of joint families, semi-autonomous, each with its own land, living fairly harmoniously together, is largely a high-caste myth (Kumar, 1965). Great differentiation among the agricultural population existed long before the colonial era; a fairly significant proportion of India's population has probably been landless for centuries (Breman, 1974). This is significant because it casts further doubt upon the frequency of joint families (as described above) in the past. Equally important, it directs us to extra-familial aspects of the traditional village social structure which, for most of the poor, served some of the functions achieved for some high castes by the joint family. Let us briefly consider the context of these extra-familial relations.

Historically, many regions of India experienced a significant level of heredi-tary servitude, institutionalized in labour bondage. The relationship came into being when an agricultural labourer approached a high-caste landowner for a loan, in many cases connected with marriage expenses. Given interest pay-ments, the debt could well increase over time, and the wife and children of the agricultural labourer would work to pay off the initial debt, probably inherit the debt, and incur further debts (Breman, 1974). The result was a semi-permanent tied relationship between landlord and agricultural labourer families. Although exploited, these subservient households were due a measure of social security from the patron. This potential support extended to all members of the subservient family unit. Some relationships between patron and client families could be fairly amicable. Members of both types of family might work together in the fields. Labourer families would receive loans of cash and grain in difficult times. Security for such families, then, came from outside the confines of their own households. Thus, there is little point in analysing family structures of client groups without reference to stratification and patron–client relations within the traditional village.

Multi-couple families may have occurred among landless castes, but they were certainly much rarer than among landed groups and their situation was very different. To reiterate, hierarchical patron–client relationships provided the main source of economic and social security to the majority of the population—not the joint family. Other village-level mechanisms, such as the giving of alms, also existed to serve broadly similar ends (Karve, 1953: 301). In general, kinship and family structures among low-caste groups with little or no land deviated very significantly from the high-caste forms, which have often been taken as the traditional norm. Further, even among high castes, the joint family was very much a cyclical institution—a fact that must be remembered when considering basic changes in the Indian family (Mandelbaum, 1972; Shah, 1964).

The foregoing provides a backcloth against which to examine briefly the changes in kinship and family patterns of the past few decades. In these developments such factors as new external cultural models, population growth, and the increasing intrusion of market forces have played major and, on balance, disruptive roles. They have affected both family forms and patron–client relationships, especially for low castes.

One cannot neglect changes in the latter when considering changes in the former. Some aspects of traditional family forms have proved remarkably resilient, and old ideals are certainly still acknowledged and sometimes operationalized. But in general the trend has been towards separating out (and making more vulnerable) individual families and households—that is, towards smaller and simpler forms.

The possibility of selling agricultural produce in the market has increasingly led to the commercialization of the relationship between landlord and client families formerly in labour bondage. The relationship is now much less personal and hinges on income maximization for landlords. Monetization now means that individual members of low-caste families are increasingly paid wages for specific amounts of work. The previous generalized obligation of landlords to aid and protect subordinate families as complete entities is on the wane, and it has not been assumed by other agencies. This process of 'depatronization' (Breman, 1974) has also been fuelled by rapid population growth, since patrons have been faced with absorbing larger numbers of clients. This disintegration of traditional forms of security has wide implications. It is almost certainly one of the main forces behind fertility decline. Depatronization has highlighted, and increased, the direct costs of children to parents in low-caste rural groups. In some areas—for example, Tamil Nadu and Orissa—poor, rural, low-caste women are certainly over-represented among sterilization acceptors, though this phenomenon may also reflect the provision of financial incentives (IIPS, 1985). In our view the frequency of multi-couple households among lower castes has probably declined as relationships between high and low castes have generally become more fluid. For example, families of low-caste brothers are now less likely to work for the same landowner or to co-reside.

Other factors have altered the traditional joint family of high-caste land-owners and affected low-caste family structures too. External changes have exacerbated internal tensions. Legal rulings, sometimes following changes in practice, have helped to undermine traditional family patterns (Kapadia, 1966). Thus, in Kerala the imposition of a maximum ceiling on landownership contributed to the collapse of Namboodiri joint family organization (as did the Madras Namboodiri Act of 1933, pertaining to marriage). Elsewhere in India the courts have generally ruled against joint family coparcenary in favour of individual interest. Legislation (e.g., the Hindu Marriage Act of 1955) has also encouraged the already rising age at marriage.

Migration has also affected the joint family. It can be argued that this family form facilitates village out-migration because some family members will be able to remain in the rural area and cultivate ancestral lands. An urban brother and his family often provide rural relatives with cash, advice, information, and other benefits in exchange for food. In some ways, therefore, the extended family may continue to function as a total entity. Nevertheless, proximity counts for much in maintaining intrafamilial ties. Further, some urban migrants resent the financial demands of joint family members back on the land. In general, monetization highlights the unequal contribution made by individual family members to the overall joint family, thus worsening existent internal tensions. Moreover, it is possible that technological developments such as improved grains and fertil-izers and increased irrigation have made the subdivision of family lands more feasible, thus contributing to the decline of larger family forms (Kapadia, 1966; Mandelbaum, 1970).

Demographic developments are also weakening larger traditional family structures. The rise in marriage age means that, *ceteris paribus*, a couple can become more resource-independent at an earlier stage of the family life cycle. An older in-marrier is more difficult for a mother-in-law to condition, especially if the newcomer is educated. The increased incidence of widow remarriage in India (Bhat and Kanbargi, 1984) reflects the changing position of women; in general, they are less subservient to joint family pressures than in the past. Increasing independence of women is both facilitated by and reflected in fertility decline. Rural mothers looking after smaller numbers of children are not only able to care for them better, they can also ward off the mother-in-law's interference as to how the children should be reared.

Perhaps the most telling demographic change, in so far as the traditional joint family is concerned, relates to increased survivorship. Mortality decline has stretched both vertical (father–son) and lateral (brother–brother) links within larger family structures, and it is the former that have emerged less scathed. The greater viability of vertical links partly reflects the fact that there was potential for acrimony between co-residing brothers and their wives. Moreover, older generations have had to reduce the degree of authority and discipline they exerted over the young. But as Gore (1968: 235) notes, it may also indicate that in the past 'the fraternal or collateral joint family was never the most common form'. Thus, study of change can throw light on the relative strength of intrafamilial links in the past. The above developments have all occurred alongside a trend towards a stronger conjugal bond (Mandelbaum, 1972: 643) and less separation of male and female activities.

No one should underestimate the power of new, external (primarily Western) models of behaviour in influencing the general decline of larger family units. More than 30 years ago Karve (1953: 296) pointed to the role of 'culture contact' in shaping the modern Indian family. External ideas have much influence on changes in contemporary Indian values relating to the conjugal bond, fertility limitation, care of one's own children, etc., especially in urban areas. Yet some of the related changes have certainly been adverse. While still very important, larger family structures today provide less security for poorer and more peripheral members than was probably the case in the past. If the dominant trend is towards smaller and simpler family forms, then, *ceteris paribus*, these also tend to be more vulnerable, especially in a context of collapsing village supports. Increased insecurity for many, and the Western-inspired 'revolution of rising expectations' are two of the main factors underlying the India-wide move towards more and bigger dowries. In this respect, among some groups, the position of in-marrying women is probably deteriorating (Karkal, 1985).

The current spread of dowry throughout South Asia emphasizes the complexity of the interaction between family forms and socio-economic change. Everywhere there are widening gaps between occupational and kinship structures. Yet evidence from some studies indicates that in the initial stages of modernization in urban India, people actually moved to strengthen and elaborate traditional family structures (Singer, 1968; Kapadia, 1966). For wealthier groups such as the Marawari it became a matter of status: they could afford to support an extended family. Paradoxically, at first, modernization may strengthen some traditional forms. This sort of movement seems to have confused some analysts as to the more important dimensions of contemporary Indian family change, i.e. towards smaller and simpler structures.

This brief foray into India's kinship and family system illustrates several points. First, the distinction between inter- and intragenerational relations is of limited utility. This is especially true in south India, where marriages among close kin can lead to problems in the adequate definition of generations. A better strategy is probably to map all relevant interrelations within the family. Secondly, the traditional Hindu joint family was dominant only in the sense that it was subscribed to by the higher castes. Thirdly, for most of the population in the past one has to consider family structure in the overall community context— especially the patron–client relationship. Finally, in response to a myriad of influences, kin and family structures in India are certainly changing towards simpler and smaller forms. However, assessment of the nature and degree of such change is hampered by lack of information on the kinship and family forms of lower castes in the past.

Europe

Given the way in which smaller, nuclear family households are becoming increasingly common throughout the developing world, there is much to be gained from a consideration of European family history. As is now widely recognized, the nuclear family has long been the predominant form of household organization in Western and Northern Europe (Laslett, 1983). Moreover, the quality of European historical data, both demographic and socio-economic, provides us with a highly detailed picture of the family and its surrounding environment stretching back several centuries. In particular, evidence from England is unusually rich in economic and social detail, and can be set against the full range of demographic statistics calculated by Wrigley and Schofield (1981).

The fundamental pattern of traditional household formation in North-western Europe has been well specified by Hajnal (1982). This system can be summed up by three formation rules: (1) marriage was late for both partners; (2) before marriage many young people circulated between households as servants; and (3) after marriage the couple formed a new household separate from both sets of parents.

While these broad features are now well recognized, their deeper implications have received less attention. In particular, the profound importance of the interaction between family structure and community organizations is only now coming to light. In the following paragraphs we draw upon recent research about these interactions to illustrate the importance of considering the family as one part of the wider social framework.

In all family systems the nature of the human life cycle can impose great strain on household resources at certain times. The joint or extended family, with its overlapping generations, seems well adjusted to the task of balancing the numbers of producers and consumers within the household and thus minimizes life-cycle crises. The nuclear family is less well adapted to this task. As one of the earliest social researchers (Rowntree, 1906) observed, the life cycle of the British labourer around 1900 implied periods of poverty in childhood, during the years of child-rearing, and in old age. It is easy to confirm Rowntree's observation for earlier periods either by referring directly to historical records or by developing theoretical models (Smith, 1986). The latter enable us to see the range of possible strategies available to families, whereas the former provide clear evidence of the existence of life-cycle poverty and the measures taken to mitigate it.

Although institutional arrangements to cope with the hardships inherent in the nuclear family household system can be found throughout North-western Europe, they have been most convincingly documented for England. In that country a succession of institutions, from medieval manors and guilds to charitable organizations, parishes, and Poor Law unions, and finally to the state itself, managed the process of welfare distribution. Moreover, they demonstrated a remarkable consistency in defining who was eligible for relief and drawing a distinction between the 'deserving' and the 'undeserving' poor (Ault, 1972; Slack, 1984; Newman Brown, 1984; Thompson, 1980). The elderly, the sick, the widowed, and, in some cases at least, couples with young children constituted the 'deserving' category.

Unquestionably there was a great diversity of local circumstances, and not all communities were generous with their assistance. Nevertheless, evidence is now accumulating that the managers of these welfare funds adapted their use to keep pace with changing patterns of deprivation and dependency. For example, at times of relatively rapid population growth, such as the late sixteenth and late eighteenth centuries, there were large numbers of children in the population. Thus, the funds disbursed by those in charge of welfare went especially to young married couples with dependent children (Slack, 1984; Smith, 1986). In contrast, the later seventeenth century was an era of negligible population growth and modest youthful dependency. In these circumstances, as research on villages in southern and eastern England has shown, most support went to elderly couples and widows, with little given to young couples and their children (Newman Brown, 1984; Wales, 1984). The scale of such payments deserves comment. As Smith (1984) has pointed out, the elderly in the period around 1700 could be observed receiving weekly pensions that compared favourably with labourers' wages, in spite of having children living in the village or even co-residing. In short, weekly pensions were an integral feature of life in pre-industrial England.

As a postscript to this discussion of the institutional supports for the nuclear family, it is interesting to note that writers who ignore them are in illustrious company. Malthus, however perceptive his general judgements on demography, failed utterly to appreciate the significance of those institutions operating under his nose. He portrayed the family as being in a permanent state of tension with the wider community, in which individual interests could be met only at the expense of communal ones (Malthus, 1798). His failure to investigate thoroughly the working of the Poor Law as it affected individuals in his own day was perhaps his greatest oversight and remarkable in a man who otherwise took such pains to acquire accurate information.

Another institution whose importance was long neglected but is now receiving appropriate attention is the phenomenon of life-cycle service. Once again, Hajnal (1982) provides an excellent overview. It is clear from his collation of data from many areas of North-western Europe that a large proportion, often a majority, of the population, both male and female, was engaged in either domestic or agricultural service at some point during adolescence or young adult life. The system was based predominantly on the transfer of young people from poor households to those of the more wealthy, and as such was clearly exploitative. Nevertheless, it unquestionably provided a mechanism whereby the labour of the young was utilized more effectively than was feasible within their households of origin.

Service also played a crucial role in the process of household formation. In so far as it was an integral part of a system of youthful geographical mobility, it ensured that many individuals would meet, marry, and reside with a partner in parishes other than those of their birth. The resulting pattern of neo-local residence was characteristic of traditional North-western Europe and belies the notion of an immobile peasantry rooted for life to a single village.

The economic role of service also deserves comment. It enabled women to remain economically active until the time of marriage and gave emphasis to the accumulation of private savings in anticipation of the creation of the new household at marriage. Such features made possible the delay of marriage for around 10 years after the attainment of sexual maturity. It also provided a nexus linking general economic conditions to marriage and hence to fertility. Wrigley and Schofield (1981) have suggested, with considerable plausibility, that marriage trends in England between 1550 and 1800 responded to trends in real wages (albeit with a lag of about one generation). Their arguments are persuasive, whatever doubts may remain over the evidence on real wages, and posit a central role for service in the process of balancing economic resources and population growth at the aggregate level.

The implications of life-cycle service for our understanding of family structure are equally profound. By removing young people from their homes just at the point at which they were likely to become net economic producers, service reduced the utility that parents received from their children. This result was encouraged by the need to save for marriage during service rather than return money to the parental home. There is very little evidence indeed of children in service providing support for their parents. Nor does there appear to have been any expectation that they would. In sum, the rate of return on children must have been low for parents, even if society more generally experienced a higher one.

We are aware in making these arguments that traditional North-western Europe was a region with some very particular institutions and that few other societies at similar stages of economic development have shown analogous features. This is especially true for England, which can be regarded as the classic example of the North-western European type. From an early date land- and labour-markets were well developed, a reasonably strong state provided security of tenure, and its communally organized welfare system was particularly thorough. But, whatever the specifics of the European example, we believe that a sensitivity to the institutional context of family structures remains essential to a proper understanding of any family system.

Equally, an awareness of the ecological constraints on families can be of prime importance. Consider, for example, recent studies of family structure in the Alps, one of the most evidently constrained ecosystems in the world. In many Alpine areas extended households were traditionally dominant as an adaptation to the management of widely scattered resources (valley fields, high meadows for pasture, etc.). Indeed, as Sahlins (1957) noted in his classic study of contrasting family structures in Fiji, working spatially separated resources appears to be something to which extended households are especially well suited. However, the extended family is not universal in the Alps, and areas with nuclear family structure solve the problem of dispersed activities with a communal institution. The grazing of animals on the high meadows is delegated to small teams of specialists who tend the herds and flocks of the whole village (Netting, 1981; Viazzo and Albera, 1986: 33–4).

Discussion of the familial and communal arrangements of pre-industrial Europe inevitably raises the questions of how such institutions arose and how they were sustained. It is best, perhaps, immediately to sound a note of caution. Although historical demographers have been successful in describing the often complex social arrangements of Europeans in earlier centuries, the ultimate causes of these patterns remain a matter of contention. Broadly speaking, there are two schools of thought. One, found in the work of such scholars as Wrigley (1983), sees homeostatic patterns in the European record and stresses the role of unconscious rationality in arriving at them. The second school, most succinctly presented by Lesthaeghe (1980), gives greater emphasis to conscious 'short-term goal setting' on the part of élite groups, who controlled the welfare funds and set the prevailing moral guidelines. According to this line of reasoning, the institutions we have been discussing here are best seen as instruments of social control.

Ultimately the choice between conscious and unconscious rationality is likely to remain a philosophical one. Those who prefer to see complex institutions as proceeding from 'a logic of individual transactions', to borrow a phrase from McNicoll (1983: 10), will probably find Lesthaeghe's formulation appealing. In contrast, the less specific approach of the advocates of homeostasis may find favour with those who wish to emphasize the limitations of the instrumental approach. Both schools of thought offer many insights into the workings of traditional European society, and both may also be widely applicable in other cultures. For present purposes, however, lack of space precludes further elaboration of their respective merits.

A consideration of the demise of the traditional North-western European system is also revealing. Life-cycle service remained a major social phenomenon well into the nineteenth century in many areas of Europe before being replaced by wage labour. This transformation occurred earliest in the most economically sophisticated regions, such as south-eastern England (Snell, 1985). In that area there were already few rural servants by 1800. And the depressed real wages of the following two decades further encouraged farmers to stop hiring servants (who were mainly paid in kind in the form of food and lodging) and instead to hire wage labourers whose money wages were of diminishing value. This change was repeated, with some modifications, all over North-western Europe. In addition, industrialization and urbanization both served to undermine service by providing alternative employment. By 1900 in most parts of Europe only domestic service remained as a noticeable phenomenon, and this too largely vanished after the First World War.

The disappearance of life-cycle service did not, however, immediately lead to a breakdown of the traditional marriage pattern. Couples in most countries continued to marry in their mid- to late 20s until well into the twentieth century. In fact, it was only after about 1930 that the mid-century marriage boom began. In a similar way, there appears to be no strong link between the breakdown of service and household structure. Except for the replacement of servants with more lodgers, family composition remained virtually unchanged throughout the nineteenth century, the nuclear family remaining predominant. The fertility decline, when it came, also had no clear link to the patterns of service or welfare distribution of the kind expected by many theories of the transition. Indeed, in England the 1870s and 1880s, the decades when fertility control became widespread, were also marked by an attempt on the part of the Poor Law authorities to force children to care for their elderly parents and thus reduce the need for communal assistance (Thompson, 1980; Smith, 1988). This move to increase parental dependence on children for support, nevertheless, clearly failed to increase parents' demand for offspring.

In sum, while the traditional patterns of family and household organization in North-western Europe lead to straightforward conclusions, especially concerning the centrality of extra-familial institutions, the picture of how these traditional forms came to be replaced is much more confused. Why some aspects of behaviour (e.g., late marriage) should have remained largely untouched by the upheavals of urban and industrial growth remains obscure.

Thus, in so far as we are able to draw lessons from the European past that are relevant for contemporary developing societies, it is best to focus our attention on the traditional rather than on the transitional situation.

Conclusion

Our comments in this chapter have, of necessity, been brief and introductory. Nevertheless, we believe that we have illustrated a number of important points. Firstly, both the Indian and the European evidence suggests that it is essential to examine family systems in their wider social context. Thus, focusing exclusively on intrafamilial relations is likely to obfuscate rather than clarify. This is self-evidently so for historical Europe, where the predominance of the nuclear family makes it all but impossible to discuss the family in any depth without reference to communal institutions. However, we think that the admittedly more fragmentary evidence from India points in a similar direction. Moreover, it is equally clear from the Indian example that separation of intra- and inter-generational links is often a false dichotomy. The implications of these observations for our thinking about both family structures and related topics, such as transition theory, may be considerable.

References

Ault, W. O. (1972), *Open-field Farming in Medieval England*, Allen & Unwin, London.

Bhat, M., and Kanbargi, R. (1984), 'Estimating the Incidence of Widow and Widower Re-marriages in India from Census Data', *Population Studies*, 38 (1), 89–103.

Breman, J. (1974), *Patronage and Exploitation: Changing Agrarian Relations in South Gujarat, India*, University of California Press, Berkeley, Calif.

Dumont, L., and Pocock, D. (1957), 'Kinship', *Contributions to Indian Sociology*, 1 (1), 43–64.

Dyson, T., and Moore, M. (1983), 'On Kinship Structure, Female Autonomy, and Demographic Behavior in India', *Population and Development Review*, 9 (1), 35–60.

Goode, W. J. (1968), 'Foreword', in M. S. Gore (ed.), *Urbanization and Family Change*, Popular Prakashan, Bombay.

Gore, M. S. (1968), *Urbanization and Family Change*, Popular Prakashan, Bombay.

Hajnal, J. (1982), 'Two Kinds of Preindustrial Household Formation System', *Population and Development Review*, 8 (3), 449–94.

India, Registrar General and Census Commissioner (1983), *Key Population Statistics Based on Five Per Cent Sample Data*, Census of India 1981, Series 1, Paper 2 of 1983, New Delhi.

International Institute for Population Sciences (IIPS) (1985), *Report on the Baseline Survey on Fertility, Mortality and Related Factors in Orissa*, Bombay.

Kapadia, K. M. (1966), *Marriage and Family in India*, Third edn., Oxford University Press, Bombay.

Karkal, M. (1985), 'Health of Mother and Child Survival', in K. Srinivasan and S. Mukerji (eds.), *Dynamics of Population and Family Welfare 1985*, Himalaya Publishing House, Bombay.

Karve, I. (1953), *Kinship Organisation in India*, Deccan College, Poona.

Kumar, D. (1965), *Land and Caste in South India: Agricultural Labour in the Madras Presidency during the Nineteenth Century*, Cambridge University Press, Cambridge.

Laslett, P. (1983), 'Family and Household as Work Group and Kin Group: Areas of Traditional Europe Compared', in R. Wall, J. Robin, and P. Laslett (eds.), *Family Forms in Historic Europe*, Cambridge University Press, Cambridge.

Lesthaeghe, R. (1980), 'On the Social Control of Human Reproduction', *Population and Development Review*, 6 (4), 527–48.

Lewis, O. (1986), 'Peasant Culture in India and Mexico—A Comparative Analysis', in M. Marriott (ed.), *Village India: Studies in the Little Community*, Midway Reprint edition, University of Chicago Press, Chicago.

McNicoll, G. (1983), 'The Nature of Institutional and Community Effects on Demographic Behavior: An Overview', Working Paper 101, Center for Policy Studies, Population Council, New York.

Malthus, T. R. (1798), *Essay on the Principle of Population*, ed. A. Flew, Penguin, Harmondsworth (reissued 1970).

Mandelbaum, D. G. (1970), *Society in India*, vol. i. University of California Press, Berkeley, Calif.

—— (1972), *Society in India*, vol. ii. University of California Press, Berkeley, Calif.

Netting, R. M. (1981), *Balancing on an Alp: Ecological Change and Continuity in a Swiss Mountain Community*, Cambridge University Press, Cambridge.

Newman Brown, W. (1984), 'The Receipt of Poor Relief and Family Situation: Aldenham 1630–1690', in R. M. Smith (ed.), *Land, Kinship and Life-cycle*, Cambridge University Press, Cambridge.

Rowntree, B. S. (1906), *Poverty: A Study of Town Life*, Macmillan, London.

Sahlins, M. D. (1957), 'Land Use and the Extended Family in Moala, Fiji', *American Anthropologist*, 59 (3), 449–62.

Shah, A. M. (1964), 'Basic Terms and Concepts in the Study of the Family in India, Indian Economic and Social History Review, 1 (3), 1–36.

Singer, M. (1968), 'The Indian Joint Family in Modern Industry', in M. Singer and B. S. Cohn (eds.), *Structure and Change in Indian Society*, Aldine, Chicago.

Slack, P. (1984), 'Poverty and Social Regulation in Elizabeth's England', in C. Haigh (ed.), *The Reign of Elizabeth I*, Macmillan, London.

Smith, R. M. (1984), 'Some Issues in the Family Cycle of the Propertyless or Property Deficient', in R. M. Smith (ed.), *Land, Kinship and Life-cycle*, Cambridge University Press, Cambridge.

—— (1986), 'Transfer Incomes, Risk and Security: The Role of the Family and the Collectivity in Recent Theories of Fertility Change', in D. Coleman and R. Schofield (eds.), *The State of Population Theory: Foreward from Malthus*, Blackwell, Oxford.

—— (1988), 'Welfare and the Management of Demographic Uncertainty', In M. Keynes, D. A. Coleman, and N. H. Dimsdale (eds.), *The Political Economy of Health and Welfare*, Macmillan, London.

Snell, K. D. M. (1985), *Annals of the Labouring Poor: Social Change and Agrarian England, 1600–1900*, Cambridge University Press, Cambridge.

Thompson, D. (1980), 'Provision for the Elderly in England, 1831–1908', Ph.D. thesis, University of Cambridge.

Viazzo, P. P., and Albera, D. (1986), 'Alpine Marriage Patterns in Perspective', Paper prepared for the Ninth International Economic History Conference, Berne, August.

Wales, T. C. (1984), 'Poverty, Poor-relief and the Life-Cycle: Some Evidence from Seventeenth Century Norfolk', in R. M. Smith (ed.), *Land, Kinship and Life-cycle*, Cambridge University Press, Cambridge.

Wrigley, E. A. (1983), 'Malthus's Model of a Pre-industrial Economy', in J. Dupaquier, A. Fauve-Chamoux, and E. Grebenik (eds.), *Malthus Past and Present*, Academic Press, London.

—— and Schofield, R. S. (1981), *The Population History of England 1541–1871: A Reconstruction*, Edward Arnold, London.

5 Family Systems: Their Viability and Vulnerability

JOHN C. CALDWELL AND PAT CALDWELL

This chapter focuses on the forces that stabilize family systems, and on the transactional and demographic characteristics of such systems. It identifies their potential for destabilization when sufficient socio-economic change occurs. While it accepts the view that individuals have a major concern with the reproduction of their families and society, it also assumes that they are interested in attaining and maintaining positions of relative advantage in intra-familial relations. Thus, we treat the family not as an emotional unit but as an institution with the potential for internal conflict, particularly as is evidenced by social mechanisms for constraining and minimizing such conflict. (See J. C. Caldwell, 1982, for a fuller discussion of this view.)

One feels a certain unease in employing such concepts as the 'traditional family' and the impact upon it of 'modernization'. Yet, from Weber to Durkheim and on to Parsons, these concepts have been the mainstream of sociology. The simple dichotomy between the traditional and modern families may be surprisingly close to the truth; one of the problems we concentrate upon is why premodern families had so much in common and why there was not a greater diversity of types. We draw upon Marx to employ the valuable concepts of modes of production, the accompanying relations of production, and the (cultural) superstructure that they generate.

Our departure from orthodoxy is to argue that there have been only two modes of production and that these determine the two very different types of society that exist. The first is familial production, most of which is for subsistence and in which the producers are given work, direction, and rewards by relatives. The second is labour-market production, in which work, direction, and rewards are provided by the society and the economy, which are external to the family. There may be social and political institutions superimposed upon these systems: feudal lords may expropriate part of the production of the peasantry; the same lords or capitalists may expropriate unpaid employees or slaves; and the employers operating in the labour-market may be private firms or socialist governments and their institutions. These variations make sur-

Research assistance has been provided by Wendy Cosford, Betty Kavunenko, and Elizabeth Baker, with typing by Deirdre Wood and Kae Mardus.

prisingly little difference to the mode or relations of production; and, perhaps more importantly from our focus, they do not have much effect on family relations or demographic behaviour. Familial production is characterized by high and relatively uncontrolled fertility and usually by high mortality (a point to which we will return), whereas in advanced labour-market production both fertility and mortality may be low. These two demographic situations are separated by a period of change that demographers have entitled the 'demographic transition'. Perhaps we should emphasize that the important development is the labour-market rather than the market that distributes goods and services. Familial production can produce a surplus to sell on the latter market and can buy goods from it for very long periods without much effect on family production or other relations or on its demographic behaviour.

The situation is more complex than this, however, for two reasons. The first is that there is no simple transition from familial to market employment. For a very long time both types of employment have coexisted in most societies: there has certainly been a labour-market since the first cities appeared five thousand years ago, and the most advanced market economies still retain much familial production within households. Yet the balance has changed over time, and industrialization usually changes the balance quite dramatically as more non-familial employment becomes available and local employers known to the family are replaced by larger and more anonymous firms, a phenomenon accelerated by urbanization.[1] The second reason relates to what Marx called the superstructure or the institutional and cultural manifestations of a particular mode of production. For instance, familial relations of production are supported and justified by a massive superstructure of family morality and religion as well as legal and political support. Such superstructures, although undoubtedly originating in the mode of production, are almost certainly not bound as closely to it as much Marxist writing maintains. Much of the history of modernization of the family has been that of dismantling the superstructure of familial production, with resistances provided not so much by the economic system as by deeply entrenched beliefs and attitudes. Furthermore, this dismantling does not proceed at a steady pace dictated by economic change but has been accelerated and decelerated in the West by the generation of new ideologies or new interpretations of older ideologies, often not specifically focused on engendering family change (as will be seen below). In the Third World, imported cultural elements can produce family change, and it is even possible that social and political ideologies can move familial and demographic change ahead of the economic transition.

---

[1] Goldstone (1986) identifies such a change beginning in England after 1750 as a substantial proletariat developed with long-term employment prospects, not only in industry, but also in capitalist farming.

The Family of Familial Production

Traditional families, even those that we identify as deviant in the final section of the chapter, have so many similar characteristics in very different parts of the world that it is rewarding to look for some kind of internal logic in them and to relate it to the mode of production.

Fundamentally, this family is a production unit, as well as a consumption unit and a distributive system among its members. As a production unit it has in its mechanisms and attitudes more in common with the business firm than one might anticipate from the very different kinds of society that the two productive systems generate. Firstly, most familial production is concerned with food and its processing and, to a lesser degree, with clothing and housing. Nearly everyone works, beginning at 4–6 years of age in much of sub-Saharan Africa and mainland South Asia. Indeed, if baby care of a fairly passive kind (but important because it frees both parents for cultivation) in Nigeria is taken into account, the lower age limit can be reduced to 3 years (Okore, 1978). Such work is possible because it is not dependent on separate training but is learned on the job by imitating older relatives in an apprenticeship fashion and is similar to work going on in the whole community. Nevertheless, such work needs direction and sanctions against laziness or disobedience. The work is often long and arduous (it is described by Chayanov (1966: 6), as 'drudgery') and, if not done well, can result in destitution and death or at least in the loss of social, and possibly political, position.

Constant undisputed effort is achieved in three ways: by a pyramidal work direction system; by the segmentation of work according to sex, age, and family status; and by a system of familial morality that justifies and extols these devices. This moral system has been the major element in all human morality and still deeply penetrates our way of thinking.

Direction is normally given by the older to the younger, usually by relatives and, most often, by members of the same sex. When we employed continuous observation in rural Bangladesh to examine the working of traditional familial production, we found that these three conditions applied on average to family members for 80 per cent of their waking hours (J. C. Caldwell, Jalaluddin, *et al.*, 1980; 1984). When we used similar methods in rural south India to listen in on conversation, we found that 90 per cent of all working conversation consisted of direction, threats, moralizing or scorn and scandal based on moral stances, and excuses and explanations set within the same moral framework (J. C. Caldwell, Reddy, and P. Caldwell, n.d.). Age plays a pervasive role in the traditional family, so that deference is given not merely to parents but also to elder siblings. Indeed, one never hears a boy speak of his 'brother' but always of his 'elder brother' or 'younger brother'.

The segmentation of work (and of leisure) reaches an extraordinary degree in traditional families. This point is often not fully appreciated in work-input studies because of the use of broad work categories, sometimes predetermined by researchers. When we wrote descriptions of what Bangladeshi rural people were doing throughout the day, we found that there were hundreds of activities and that most were usually specific to a single sex and a limited age range (J. C. Caldwell, Jalaluddin, *et al.*, 1980, 1984). This is also true with regard to family status. A family head has duties distinct from those of a man of the same age who is still living with his father in a joint family; an elder brother has responsibilities and often work patterns that contrast with those of another man who is the same age but is a younger brother; and the daughter-in-law in a household has a different work pattern (and, in the studied rural Bangladeshi families, works harder) than the unmarried daughter of the household even where their ages are comparable. The segmentation by age and sex is buttressed by biological differences. The basis of the segmentation by family status, especially that of daughters-in-law, seems less immutable. A common way of guarding against the danger of reducing the contrast between family segments is exogamy, the importing of daughters-in-law from places beyond the immediate locality so that each long remains a stranger who needs instruction in local ways and those of the family.

Most of traditional morality is focused on justifying this work structure. The underlying fear is that affection ('affective individualism' as Stone, 1977, terms it) arising from parentalism or conjugal relations will erode the work authority structure. A need is felt for emotional distance, an attitude common in many firms and other extra-familial institutions. Thus, an emphasis is placed on the gulfs created by age and sex. Morality is needed both to make the system work and to ensure that it works almost automatically without continual emotional confrontations or *ad hoc* decisions based on the real logic of each new situation. It is also needed so that each family does not have to fight its own battle but, rather, has a community consensus so that external social pressures can be applied to potential rebels. The society is caught up in its own morality. Adults hate doing 'children's jobs', and this aversion enhances the value of children. When, by chance, a family has no persons of a certain type, the members are distressed. Substitutions are possible, if undesirable: if a daughter-in-law moves away, for example, the family may quickly remove their daughter from school. (See J. C. Caldwell, Reddy, and P. Caldwell, 1985: 42, for a discussion of substitutions.) Nevertheless, one of the values of larger aggregations of relatives, even if they are not in the same residence, is that larger groups are more likely to contain persons of each age–sex segment.

The age gap is fundamental but does have its anomalies. If the ability to work hard and control others were the measure, then we might expect control and respect to be maximized among adult men before physical decline began, with deference being shown to them by both their children and their parents. This usually is not the case. The reason would seem to be the difficulty of reversing the direction of moral imperatives. Children are likely to respect their parents and toil unprotestingly at their direction only if there is a clear moral rule about deference towards those who are older and obedience to their commands. It is likely to work unchallenged in this way only if the middle-aged treat the old in the same way. There is an ancillary life-cycle reason. The middle-aged are rapidly aging: the overthrow of the old would soon lead to their own undoing.

In practice the affirmation of the authority of the old is not left to such logic (J. C. Caldwell, 1986*a*). The old are said to possess superior wisdom arising from their longer experience and often both from the shared secret knowledge of the ancients and from occult powers. In sub-Saharan Africa, which may be fairly representative of all societies prior to sedentary farming, the power of the oldest member of the lineage lies in the fact that he alone can contact the ancestors; and these ancestors, while still remembered, play an important role in the lives of those members of the lineage now on earth (J. C. Caldwell and P. Caldwell, 1985). Related to this power is the capacity of the old to curse their descendants for being insufficiently filial—an action that will bring disaster on the descendants for the rest of their lives. In many societies children justify filial devotion as the reward for the grant of life itself, a concept that goes beyond simple biological explanation.

Not all confirmation of the authority of the old is as other-worldly as this. Most traditional societies exaggerate the quality and quantity of the work done by the old (thus greatly damaging many labour-input studies). This happens partly because of an exaggeration of the value of their managerial direction, which, involves, more often than is admitted, nagging about jobs which are being adequately done, following patterns repeated countless times, and, in times of crisis, agreeing to suggestions cautiously put forward by children or wives. In fact, an important stabilizing element in the traditional family is the inability to compare the labour or rewards of different family members arising from the segmentation of tasks and the belief that persons are inherently suited for work of different kinds in accordance with their sex and age. An important function of the old, where there is agreement in the society that this is a role primarily for the old, is, as apex of the family pyramid, to serve as its head in negotiations with similar heads of other families. This position as the only real representative of the family confers other powers: the father can negotiate for his children relations or employment with other families, and conversely, the young man who breaks with his father may find that he has nowhere to go. He may also find that he cannot marry.

Nevertheless, the position of the patriarch in hunting and gathering societies has never been completely secure because failing physical strength in the hunt is so visibly a sign of declining powers. Even in the community based on shifting cultivation, the existence of uncultivated land, and often distant cultivable land beyond the effective suzerainty of any family, has given strength to rebellious sons and has the potential for weakening the power of the family head. The religious blessing on the leadership of the old was always necessary. This was not so with the development of a peasantry with some fund of inheritable tenure on identifiable areas of land. The ownership of land, and often of housing and farming equipment, provided adequate power for, if need be, completely secular control of the family by the old, especially when political and legal systems reinforced this power. In theory, a combination of rebellious sons might present a threat to their father; in practice 'divide and rule' almost always triumphed, and family segmentation, especially the emphasis on age differentials, made it much more likely that each son would seek his father's favour rather than his brothers'. Thus, the most 'traditional' families, those that contrasted most markedly with modern families, were not the most ancient but those of the more recently developed peasantry. Even among peasant societies the power of the patriarch tended to increase over the centuries as population growth led to the closing of the frontier and the disappearance of free land so that a son's hopes rested solely on his father's beneficence.

Segmentation by sex is more complex. There are probably two major reasons for its existence. The cruder is that it makes the simplest family pyramid with a monarchical head rather than a dyarchical one. The patriarch shares neither power nor rewards. In addition the weakness of the dyarchy is avoided, for children cannot play off their parents against each other. The segmentation between husband and wife is usually by both sex and age. As the age gap is frequently up to ten years, the simple model of intergenerational relations and transactions hardly holds. The wife occupies a kind of intermediate position between the generations, and part of the strength of the patriarchy (and, as we shall see, its weakness when change begins) lies in the triangular relations between the patriarch, his wife, and their children. The second reason for sex segmentation is more important. The patriarchy works successfully only if a son believes he should do more for his father than for his own wife and children. Indeed, the joint family gets maximum work and obedience from a daughter-in-law only if her husband does not take her part and does not intercede to lighten her load or to render ambiguous the unquestioning obedience she owes to her mother-in-law.

A still more fundamental aspect of sex segregation, however, is the strength of maternal devotion for infants in the traditional family. (Either Europe was very different from contemporary rural India and probably the rest of the Third World, or Shorter (1977), is wrong in his failure to find such overweening maternalism in older Europe.) This devotion is probably inherent and biological, a necessary mechanism for infant survival. It is probably also a recognition by the mother that it is the existence of the child (especially, usually, if it is a son) that gives her a claim to be anything but a stranger in the family and eventually to attain a good deal of matriarchal power. This maternalism can easily broaden to include older children and always presents the possibility that the young wife will assert, and her husband will agree, that the children are also his and deserve priority. She gives pride of place when young to her children, not only because of whatever her biology may dictate, but also because her in-laws are still essentially strangers to her as she is to them. This tension, usually simplified as that between mother-in-law and daughter-in-law, is ultimately, when change occurs, the fatal flaw in the traditional family.

The only way of overcoming this weakness in family structure is to keep the conjugal tie between the younger couple weak and to prevent an effective nuclear family from crystallizing out from the larger economic and emotional family. This is done partly by the usual segmentation of the family by sex— indeed, it is one of the main purposes of that segmentation—so that wife and husband do not work together and are rarely on their own (often even when sleeping). Nevertheless, the danger always exists that the sexual relation between the younger couple will form the basis for an emotional link that is stronger than that between the husband and his parents. The only safeguard against this danger is a downgrading of marital sexual relations. This, we suggest, is the major ground for the obsession, by most traditional societies, with female sexual purity. If females have not acquired favourable attitudes toward sexual relations by their practice before marriage, then other attitudes can be moulded after marriage. One study of a Greek mountain village came to conclusions that would be appropriate in mainland South Asia: 'maidens must be virgins, and even married women must remain virginal in thought and expression. . . . The sexual shame of women is no doubt related to the ambivalent attitude . . . towards sexual relations even in marriage' (Campbell, 1974: 270). Once female sexual purity is taken this seriously, then it is a resource that is of great value when brought in the form of virginity to marriage. After marriage, female adultery with a member of another family is such an important relational act that it has the potential for greatly weakening the family.

The distinction made between the daughter of the family and the daughter-in-law is partly the 'us-and-them' contrast that makes the patriarchal family homogeneous and weakens the position of the imported foreigner. It is also based on the fact that female productivity in the family will depend for years to come on the work habits of the daughter-in-law, whereas, in contrast, a growing tenderness, marked often by a reluctance to enforce strict obedience or to exact the last ounce of work, is exhibited toward the daughter who will soon be cast out to survive as best she can in an alien family.

The most important single point is that all these relationships, which follow the inherent logic of familial production, are enshrined in popular morality and its precepts, proverbs, and stories, and also in religion and ultimately in law and political practice. Their enshrinement is justified because they are following clear moral and religious rules. This superstructure acquires a life of its own in providing an additional logic for behaviour as productive relations change and can render some family structures economically rewarding to the decision-makers to an extent that would not be true in the absence of the moral and religious sanctions.

These sanctions are enforced by interested parties. The interests of the old are enforced by an aged hegemony so that horror will be the society's reaction to any family not giving most respect to the old. To judge at least from the public expression of criticism of female deviance, women seem to play an even more important role than men. A 'virtuous' wife can gain a good deal of moral ascendancy over a husband who is less certain of right and wrong. A patriarch who has a liberal attitude toward his relations with his wife and children may be regarded as weak and can be a source of considerable embarrassment to the family. He can also be rightly suspected by other families of offering daughters for marriage who may bridle at strict discipline or back-breaking work.

One weakness in the system that results from the large spousal age gap is that the patriarch's mental faculties, including his judgement, can begin to deteriorate while his wife is still a major force in the family. She can begin to assume considerable powers ostensibly in his name, or, perhaps more commonly, she and her eldest son can form an alliance, which will also help her position once her husband is dead. In India this practice is institutionalized with the explanation that the feeble old man has capped his successful life by entering its third or fourth phase, in which he devotes himself to religious and philosophic thought, withdrawing from this world and usually from work and sexual relations.

Transactional and Demographic Implications of Traditional Family Structure

Transactions must be considered in two ways, first as resources received as a result of intrafamilial distribution in the form of goods and services, and secondly as labour inputs made. There is probably a more significant differential in material receipts than in labour inputs, partly because the segmentation of work means that family members take a certain pride in doing what they believe only they are adequate to perform.

In most traditional societies, in accordance with some objective biological assessment of need, males usually receive more and better food, better clothing, and more conscientious care than females. This is probably also true of the old compared with the young (d'Souza and Chen, 1980; J. C. Caldwell, Jalaluddin, *et al.*, 1984). Such flows are in the direction of respect, and it is that which justifies them. The respect actually hides many of the mechanisms, as our rural south Indian work demonstrates (J. C. Caldwell, Reddy, and P. Caldwell, 1983*b*). Males may not know how much (or little) food is left for females when the latter eat last. When small children try to grasp for more food at meal times, a boy is more likely to be allowed to succeed than is a girl, because his action may show that he is growing up to be a suitably assertive male while her unfeminine forwardness may cause horror. When weak or sick, an old man may be given rest and care (partly because of terror that this keystone of the family arch may die and so cause the whole structure to crumble), whereas a sick child may be quite unmaliciously chased off to look after the animals. Unless he is the oldest boy, his fever will probably not be noticed. Probably the single greatest lack in child care in many traditional societies is the failure to arrange for rest during sickness. The most cherished rewards that age can bring are the extra comforts that the family can provide, mostly in the form of additional effort. Help and the pleasure of direction also come to a woman when she becomes a mother-in-law. In a society where extra-familial honours are available to few, the ability to exercise the power of the patriarch and to receive services from the whole family is success indeed and is maintained by intrafamilial transactions.

The measurement of labour inputs is difficult. It is done mostly by analysing retrospective statements by family members. In an effort to diminish bias and recall failure, we undertook measurement by direct observation in Bangladesh even though this meant employing a large observational group and a limited number of families for observation (J. C. Caldwell, Jalaluddin, *et al.*, 1980; 1984). Although all Bangladeshi observers had Masters' degrees in the social sciences and had been thoroughly trained, the measure of work intensity was demonstrably useless because both male and female interviewers classified most male work as more intensive than female work and older male work as surprisingly intensive even though we were certain that the relative assessments were very different from that which would be shown by an ergometer or any other objective system. This result is evidence of the grip of traditional familial morality. So too is the division that many modern social scientists make between 'productive' and 'household' work, a distinction that is usually meaningless and so distorts our understanding of family activity that it is usually very misleading as to the balance of intrafamilial transactions and their demographic implications. For that reason we defined 'wealth flows' (or transactions) as 'all the money, goods, services, and guarantees that one person provides to another' (J. C. Caldwell, Jalaluddin, *et al.*, 1980; 1984). When we measured services or labour inputs in rural Bangladesh, the average weekly inputs were for adult women (i.e. females 15+ years of age) 76.5 hours (index = 100); adult men, 65.3 hours (85); male children, 35.2 hours (46); and female children, 33.9 hours (44) (J. C. Caldwell, Jalaluddin, *et al.*, 1980: 6). When the time spent on education, travel connected with work or other necessary tasks, and business or trading negotiation and ancillary talk was added, these measures became for adult women 77.8 hours (100); adult men, 74.7 hours (96); male children, 48.7 hours (63); and female children, 46.8 hours (60) (J. C. Caldwell, Jalaluddin, *et al.*, 1980: 6–7). In terms of work inputs there was little transactional advantage. The study did show that girls were working adult hours by 11–12 years of age and boys by 13–14 years, and that each had reached half adult hours by 8–9 years (J. C. Caldwell, Jalaluddin, *et al.*, 1980: 12). We undertook a supplementary study which confirmed that transactional advantage lay mostly in the receipt of additional food, clothing, and services, and that children lived sufficiently austerely for the balance of cost over work to be of little significance beyond 8–9 years of age and none soon afterward (J. C. Caldwell, Jalaluddin, *et al.*, 1984).

In terms of demographic significance the situation during normal years may be misleading. In south India, where drought-induced famine strikes rural communities every few years, we studied the impact of the 1980–3 drought (J. C. Caldwell, Reddy, and P. Caldwell, 1986). By 1983 the proportion of the families describing their nutritional and health condition as still being 'fair' or safe had declined with increases in the size of households, and the proportion identified as suffering from hunger had increased along with the number of children under 12 years of age (one of Chayanov's (1966) dictums, which he related to stages in the life cycle). We found little agreement among families as to which of their members bore the brunt of the famine, but it is noteworthy that 60 per cent of families reporting illness arising from the drought listed as those afflicted only women, children, and old people. Other demographic effects of the drought were a dramatic decline in marriage, largely because of the inability to meet dowry and wedding expenses, and a resulting diminution in births. The same phenomenon was reported in famines in the West African Sahel (J. C. Caldwell, 1975), China (J. C. Caldwell and Srinivasan, 1984), and Bangladesh (Cain, 1981). It may be noted that the measurement of the mortality impact of extreme famine conditions in Bengal in 1943–4, when it was known that both individual and family survival was at stake, demonstrated preference being given to the survival of middle-aged active male household heads, whereas the highest mortality was experienced by the old and the young (Greenough, 1982).

The study of the implications for mortality of relative advantage of the sexes within the traditional family has begun in South Asia, where most areas are still characterized by higher female than male mortality (Visaria, 1961; Miller, 1981; d'Souza and Chen, 1980; Dyson and Moore, 1983). Similar studies on relative advantage by age have been rare, partly because of the difficulty of determining what is an advantage-free mortality structure. Certainly with a change from traditional to modern society an extraordinary reversal occurs in the balance of deaths: the Princeton 'West' model life tables, based on historical experience, show for stationary populations with life expectancies of 40 years one-third of all deaths taking place before 15 years of age, compared with only one-fiftieth when life expectancy reaches 75 years (Coale and Demeny, 1966).[2] Most of this difference arises from the fact that much of the reduction in mortality depends upon the near elimination of transmittable diseases, which particularly attack young children. Yet this reduction of childhood diseases has often been given as the only reason for the change in the balance of deaths, thus obscuring the fact that one component has inevitably been a redirection of the internal flow of care within the family to the young. Relative differences in care can yield very substantial differences in mortality. In our 1973 study of all married fecund women 40–59 years of age in Ibadan City, Nigeria, who had deliberately and successfully restricted their family sizes, we found that those with 1–5 live births had experienced less than half the child loss found in the total community, and those with 1–4 children less than one-fifth (equivalent to

[2] These figures represent the individual risk or that found in stationary populations. In a population with a life expectancy of 40 years and growing at 2.5 per cent per annum (i.e. CDR = 24, CBR = 49, TFR = 6.8), three-fifths of all deaths would take place among persons under 15 years of age.

differences in life expectancy of 15 and 23 years, respectively). Controlling for socio-economic factors did little to reduce those differentials (J. C. Caldwell and P. Caldwell, 1978). In recent work in Mali it has been shown that neighbouring cultural groups with similar levels of adult mortality lose very different proportions of their children by 5 years of age—ranging from 30 to 50 per cent, differences that almost certainly reflect different allocations of family resources and time (Hill, 1985: 48, 51).

The fertility implications of the traditional family are more easily studied. In spite of much anthropological writing on fertility or population control in pre-modern societies, most of the evidence for any significant level of control is suspect (J. C. Caldwell, P. Caldwell, and B. Caldwell, 1987). The demographic evidence is clearly against significant levels of marital fertility control in traditional societies (Knodel, 1977). The only exceptions in large populations have probably been found in China and Japan, where densely settled peasant areas had reduced landholdings to a size where extra family growth produced little more usable family labour while putting a critical strain on the supply of food that could be produced.

There are both positive and negative reasons for identifying the traditional family with uncontrolled marital fertility. On the positive side, high fertility is of value in that children nearly pay their own way in production from an early age and eventually become the major work-force of the family and the guarantors of comfort for their parents' old age. By their numbers, they discourage the development of too much maternalism and paternalism and encourage sibling rivalry, which consolidates the patriarchy. Those situated at the apexes of traditional families receive the loyalty and benefit from the transactional flows of a unit that combines production, consumption, and defence. Their situation is very much that of the directors of firms who receive both material benefits and adulation as the company grows. Both can influence decisions about the rate of growth. In the traditional society the headship of a large family is, for most, the only way of gaining the esteem derived from institutional leadership. The negative reasons are those associated with conjugal sexual relations and female purity. Women who were supposed not to dwell too much on sexual relations or to have too intimate relations with their husbands were only too easily thought to be polluted if they discussed fertility control or were involved in its practice. This was the antithesis of the wife–mother image, and husband–wife discussion of the matter was easily thought to be indecent and even unnatural. Furthermore, continued childbearing kept women engaged in demonstrably female activities and reinforced family segmentation. It may have made them less sexually attractive to other men. The delay in fertility decline in Victorian England (which, relative to levels of urbanization and the proportion of the labour-force working outside agriculture, was probably the most delayed transition) probably owed something to images of female purity and problems of husband–wife communication about fertility control. The major pre-modern controls on marital fertility, lengthy breast-feeding, and the practice of post-partum and terminal female sexual abstinence, had other primary goals than depressing fertility and were, not coincidentally, behaviour that reinforced rather than eroded female sexual purity.

Fertility is also affected by nuptiality patterns. Most traditional societies favour a substantial age gap between husband and wife for a range of reasons. It weakens the conjugal emotional bond. Rural Indians, for example, believe that a wife who is close to her husband in age will effectively influence him against his parents and brothers and the larger family interests (J. C. Caldwell, Reddy, and P. Caldwell, 1983*a*). It allows a male to marry at a mature age while still bringing a very young wife into the family household—one still young enough not to have become set in her ways and to be able to take instruction from her mother-in-law, and also still young enough (preferably pubescent) to be likely to be a virgin. It ultimately allows the husband to receive net transactional gains or wealth flows from his wife as well as from his children. The heart of this nuptiality system is the arranged marriage and the marriage payment. It is still clear in rural India that most parents regard a marriage primarily as a means of adding a new member to the family and only secondarily as providing a spouse for their son (J. C. Caldwell, Reddy, and P. Caldwell, 1983*a*: 348); thus, they are prime actors, not merely because often only they can provide or organize the raising of the resources, but also because only they can appropriately make the payments. The demographic impact of a substantial age gap between spouses is considerable (J. C. Caldwell, 1966: 9). In growing populations it means that wives come from different birth cohorts (almost different generations) from their husbands'. With an age gap of ten years and an annual growth rate of 3 per cent, there will be about 35 per cent more potential wives than husbands. This imbalance may encourage polygamy or spinsterdom and discourage the remarriage of widows. It thus reinforces the inferior position of women and, except possibly in some polygamous societies, tends to depress fertility (Muhsam, 1956; Page, 1975: 50–1; Bean and Mineau, 1986). This depressive tendency is reinforced by two other factors. The earlier part of the marriage may occur during the period of female adolescent subfecundity, whereas during the latter part of the wife's reproductive span the husband may be old and coitus may be reduced or nonexistent. Furthermore, not only is widow remarriage discouraged, but also women, being much younger than their husbands, are widowed earlier in their potentially reproductive period. Some evidence suggests that once mortality falls, with consequent increase in the rate of population growth, the resultant imbalance in the marriage market and the mechanisms devised to overcome it (such as large dowries accompanying older brides close in age to their husbands) can begin to reduce the spousal age gap. Thus, the cause is demographic change rather than fundamental social change, although considerable social change can result, even of the type feared by the traditional family.

The Impact of Social and Economic Change

Much of the discussion so far has centred on a traditional family that is patri-lineal, patriarchal, virilocal, exogamous, peasant, and with a closed agricultural frontier and recognized, inheritable land tenure. The majority of pre-modern populations, at least over the last millennium, have been of this type. Until recent times it mattered little whether societies were characterized by this tight, arche-typal family structure. Even more ambiguous structures secured net trans-actional flows from the young to the old and from female to male. Older males also received maximum care, although in high-mortality conditions this did not greatly increase their chances of survival. Fertility was not maximized because social ends often outweighed such maximization: sometimes marriage at puberty was not particularly favoured, often widow remarriage was felt to violate the rules of female purity and devotion to one patriarch (as well as presenting com-plicated inheritance problems), resumption of sexual relations too soon after birth could endanger a child's survival and also evidence a dangerously strong sexual attraction between spouses, and sexual relations after a woman had become a grandmother or a mother-in-law could lead to a conflict between grandmaternal or mother-in-law's roles and maternal roles. Nevertheless, maternal fertility was not controlled in order to limit ultimate family size except to an extent that can no longer be determined in some of the densely settled older Asian peasant societies. We have also frequently implied joint-stem residential families. Such families probably have rarely been the most common form of residence; but close residence, shared or inheritable landed resources, and the successive living of the newly married in a stem family all produce rather similar family situations wherein the patriarch receives obeisance and the mother-in-law has considerable directive power over the daughters-in-law. This pattern of joint-stem family residence is somewhat weakened in India when a couple moves to a new residence, but land may still be held or farmed jointly and many mutual activities persist indefinitely.

Ultimately, these family systems are being dissolved as an increasing pro-portion of all work is contacted through the labour-market—a process by no means yet completed, and with ultimate family structures and relationships beyond our comprehension. Meanwhile, modifications successively appear that ultimately have both transactional and demographic implications.

The form of family morality that most completely protects the traditional family system is that which is associated with some type of ancestor worship. The major religions, those of the Great Tradition, reveal truths beyond the family and have a potential for emphasizing matters other than the rights of the old and cutting across those rights by appealing directly to younger members of the family. It is perhaps no accident that their rise was associated with the establishment of the great peasant societies, which had consolidated the power of the old by land control and legal and political measures. Most of the world religions drew on familial morality to stress respect for the old and female purity.

The position of Western Christendom, however, appears to have long been anomalous, particularly in the sense that its main thrust was not the sacredness of the traditional family. This may have been because its genesis was in the Roman Empire, with its urban populations, or it may have been because the large extra-familial institution then established in the form of the Church found itself thereafter locked into battle with the traditional family for the adherence of individual members, especially, as Goody (1983: 83–102) argues, with respect to inheritance. Hence, the Christian Church did not give priority to the rights of the family, either by teaching the unquestioned wisdom of the old or by giving primacy to keeping family possessions within the family. To a considerable extent it thus struck at intrafamilial transactions. By the eleventh century it was intervening in marriage to the point of forbidding arranged marriages (Davis, 1977), and this fact may well be of fundamental importance in explaining the preponderance of neo-local and nuclear family residence in the West. The Christian Church did stress female purity, but not to the point of contesting delayed marriage nor of tolerating death for female pre-marital sexual activities. The lack of stress on early marriage or, indeed, on marriage at all allowed the development of a mechanism for regulating population growth in accordance with economic growth, although the relationship was probably not one linked through concepts of avoiding Malthusian limits but of the sufficiency needed to establish a household (Wrigley and Schofield, 1981; Goldstone, 1986). This link was possible because of neo-local and nuclear residence. The newly married couple had, to a large extent, to support themselves, and in return their labour did not go primarily to their parents. If they could marry, they would benefit from the labour of their own children, but only until the latter married. Demographically, the situation was potentially unstable.

The familial morality that developed, with the strong conjugal tie that was possible with neo-local residence, became part of Western culture. It is possible that this non-traditional family morality made changes from familial production to labour-market production easier. Several points should be noted. There was still a strong familial morality which taught that there could be greater trust between family members than between non-relatives. Although this morality has been condemned in our own time for blocking economic and social progress (Banfield, 1958), it allowed urban bourgeois families with unrestricted fertility to flourish, for instance, in the Renaissance because wages could not buy employees as loyal as adult children, especially in managerial positions or in negotiations where trust was essential. It was also a specialized form of this morality that, beginning in the nineteenth century, as industrialization enlarged the labour-market but could not provide employment for all adults, allowed the perfection of a two-tiered productive system whereby the husband as breadwinner worked for money outside the house while a familial production system within, employing the wife and, to successively lesser extents, daughters and sons, competed successfully in the production of household services and finished goods with labour-market production (J. C. Caldwell, 1978). This Western family morality was to be of more than local importance, for Western economic growth invaded the whole world by means of its strength, its colonization, and its education. It was essentially the secular morality that caused change; Christianity alone did not even alter the arranged marriage system (for example, in India). Most other world religions at least sanctioned the traditional family. Islam gave strong support to most of its separate elements to a point where social change was challenged on religious grounds when it tended to erode divisions by age or sex. This is almost certainly the reason that most Muslim countries, certainly in the religion's heartland from Mauritania to Pakistan, have higher fertility and child mortality than their per capita incomes would imply (J. C. Caldwell, 1986b).

In the West itself the two-generation family morality, together with the two-tiered productive system, provided an intrafamilial transactional system that meant that unrestricted marital fertility did not endanger parental living standards until the late nineteenth century. Ultimately, the process was hastened by the development of ideologies that emphasized child-centredness, the reduction of child work at least outside the home, and, most importantly, the erection of universal education systems. More recently the ideology of the women's movement, essentially aimed at further liquidating the morality of family production and replacing it by one more in keeping with the individualism of a developed labour-market economy, has hastened the decline of the two-tiered productive system. As both pregnancy and children can impair a woman's position in the labour-market, fertility has again declined.

Transactional and demographic change in the Third World owes much to the development of the labour-market. Fathers cannot expect so much from their sons nor mothers-in-law from their daughters-in-law when the sons can secure employment off the family farm or when the couple can depart for the distant town (J. C. Caldwell , et al., 1984). The situation during early industrialization or in the times of a colonial export economy is for a period far more complex than this. The existence of a familial economy allows urban, plantation, or mine wages to be lower than those that would support a whole family, and the young man's wife and children must stay with his parents, to whom much of his earnings must also go. In some ways this arrangement strengthens family morality, and, indeed, substantial remittances to the old may continue even when the whole younger family has moved away.

It would be impossible to understand the speed of transactional and demographic change in the Third World if the study were to be restricted only to labour-market changes. What has often allowed a cultural superstructure to change almost as fast has been the export of institutions, morality, and ideology from the West: missionaries, educators, administrators, schools, books and films, models of conjugal relationships, child welfare legislation, and concepts of greater equality within the family. Sometimes these ideologies are embedded in the programmes of successful revolutionary governments that, as in China, accelerate the movement towards equality within the family and towards women working outside the home. As in China, the transactional changes may be speeded by commune organization, and the demographic changes may even run ahead of what one might anticipate from productive changes because of the import of specific political ideologies with regard to child survival or fertility regulation.

Several important points should be noted about the interaction of imported and locally generated social change. Almost all the imported social influences stress—as a moral imperative—the need for the younger couple to strengthen their conjugal emotional link and for the young mother's maternalism towards her infant to spread to all children and to be paralleled by growing paternalism. It seems to be impossible for the relations between children and father and between wife and husband to move completely independently: improvement in the situation of one improves the other. Many external influences, especially those of the media, stress sexuality, and, although at first the influence of traditional family morality may lead husbands to interpret this as encouraging extramarital relations, it ultimately is likely to affect marital relations as well. New religions, growing secularism, and especially the message of education undermine the belief in the superior knowledge of the old. More objective measurements of work efficiency by cost-accounting employers lead to the retirement of the old from work and a preference for employing the young, a change that has a profound psychological impact on society. Such changes generate new catalysing indigenous ideologies blending new experience with older traditions and imported traditions.

Neither the rate of change of the mode of production nor the potential for importing new ideologies entirely determines the timing of demographic change. It is becoming clearer that long-existing elements of the cultural superstructure probably play an important role. The key elements appear to be the family structure and the family morality. There have long been societies at odds with our mainline model.

Before we deal with them, we should note that even the peasant society has elements for which our description does not hold good. In most peasant societies, historically, most families who wanted access to land could obtain access. With growing population densities, this is no longer true. In India there have always been artisan castes whose family structure worked like that of the peasantry because the old owned the tools, often had more skilled knowledge, and even could control entrance to the craft. However, there have also been landless labourers, chiefly the harijans. The patriarch seems to have controlled these families because he was the client in relation to the patron, the landlord, and through him the whole family was employed and received food. Nevertheless, our recent work in Bangladesh shows that the head of a landless family does have less control than the head of a landed family over both his children and his wife. This seems not to have produced a different articulated moral code or pattern of demographic behaviour.

Matrilineality is found among the Ashanti in Africa, the Nayars and Ezhivars of Kerala, and various groups in South-east Asia, the Pacific, and the Americas. Uxorilocality (i.e., matrilocality) and avunculocality (on the wife's side) have been common in South-east Asia. Polyandry has existed to some extent in Kerala and even in Sri Lanka. In every one of these areas the emphasis on female purity and subservience has been less than in the monolithic patriarchal model we explored. Female status has not always been high, but women's autonomy has often been marked. It is also possible that more equality has existed in intrafamilial transactional receipts, at least among children and younger adults. The study of social change in both Kerala and Sri Lanka suggests that it is this degree of female autonomy that has allowed mothers to exercise a good deal of control over their children's health and also to share equally in education, and these two factors have led to very marked declines in mortality (J. C. Caldwell, 1986*b*). Inevitably, at least among young married adults, matrilocality must lead to greater equality in transactional receipts—the description of the situation of the new husband in Thai matrilocal households certainly suggests that (R. B. Davis, 1973). Among the Javanese and Malaysia's Malays, women keep close contact with their households of origin; marital instability and high levels of divorce see to that. Similarly, in Jamaica and other parts of the West Indies female responsibility for running the household and bringing up the children— the latter often done by mothers and grandmothers—provides a substantial, if enforced, measure of female autonomy. In every one of these areas fertility decline has been marked and is ahead of that which might have been predicted by economic indicators alone (estimated by comparing rankings of fertility levels and fertility decline with rankings of per capita income as listed in World Bank 1984).

The unilineal descent group or lineage of sub-Saharan Africa, while providing great respect for older males, also weakens the conjugal link (to the point traditionally among the Ashanti and Ga of Ghana of not co-habiting). This weak link is further attenuated by the high level of polygamy, which nearly every woman feels to be potentially universal and so creates a psychological, social, and economic unit consisting of herself and her children—indeed, spouses often trade with each other as distinct families would (Abu, 1983; Vercruijsse, 1983). Fertility, however, has shown less evidence of decline there than in any other major society (J. C. Caldwell and P. Caldwell, 1985), for several reasons. One economic one is that the subdivision of the family means that a woman is far more likely to be dependent on her children than on her husband. Another is that the availability of free land has meant no closed frontier. The social one is the still widespread interpretation of bride wealth as implying that a woman's reproductive power is controlled by her husband's lineage. The ancestor cult means both a belief that more children are needed for the continuation of the lineage, and a fear of ancestral anger against not only barrenness but also deliberate fertility control.

Hunting and gathering societies are sufficiently different from the present model that the old may not always live well. Indeed, among some, of which certain Eskimo groups are best recorded, both senilicide and infanticide have been relatively common patterns. These practices appear to have been less a measure of population control than a measure to protect the group's mobility in search of food during particularly perilous times.

Conclusion

The term 'traditional society' has been employed here in a very specific sense, namely the society characterized by familial production and by the culture that flows from it and reinforces it. If one seeks a counterpart for some of the assumptions of traditional family production, one must look in the modern world not to the family, but to the business firm. In traditional society most transactions were within the family and were characterized by inequality, a characteristic that was held to be necessary to maintain production and that was justified by the whole culture. Characteristic demographic results were early marriage, uncontrolled marital fertility, and even higher infant and child mortality than might otherwise have been the case.

We are far from attaining or even guessing at the nature of the family and society that will characterize the fully developed extra-familial labour-market. The society will certainly have low mortality right across the age structure, although this may be slightly modified by a greater concentration of familial care on the very young than on the very old. It is becoming clearer that neither stable marriage nor perhaps formal marriage need characterize such a society. Nor will children be a transactional necessity. One might surmise that because of the lack of positive economic dictates on family behaviour, such societies will be subject to waves of ideology having as their content views on the nature of conjugal relationships, parenthood, and intergenerational relations. Such ideologies may well bring politics into the situation in order to create economic pressure towards the desired models.

Clearly, Northern Europe and English-speaking countries of overseas European settlement are already closer to this situation. Nevertheless, in most of Asia, conjugal links are strengthening relative to parent–son relations, and in both Asia and Latin America fertility is falling while child mortality is improving very much faster than adult mortality. There are great variations which could be treated only by undertaking separate studies to apply the model outlined to various societies with radically different traditions. The patriarchy of the Islamic Middle East and North Africa will tend to resist change, although wealth, and the education it eventually brings even for women, will provide an erosive force. The weak conjugal link was characterized in Indonesia and Malaysia, as well as in all Muslim countries, by high rates of divorce. Everywhere these rates are declining, almost certainly because of a weakening of extended family bonds relative to nuclear ones (even in South-east Asia, to the extent of grandparents not so readily taking in their grandchildren after a divorce as was the case earlier). Similarly, it is likely that the weak conjugal bond in sub-Saharan Africa will strengthen, possibly at the expense of some female economic autonomy. Finally, what of Latin America, with its heterogeneity, imported southern European traditions, and subsequent family adaptations to a *conquistador* society? In the Caribbean area, where slavery led to weak conjugal links and matrifocal societies, there may be a simple transition from pre-industrial to post-industrial female (and male) autonomy, although with a continuing reduction in fertility. In those Latin American societies characterized by *machismo*, social change, influenced by rising levels of female education and the global spread of the ideas of the women's movement, is already diminishing the phenomenon, with the consequence of an emotionally closer nuclear family and greater control over fertility. The direction of change, driven by the creation of a global economy and society, will be as outlined in this chapter, although different historical traditions will ensure diversity, even if diminishing, for generations.

References

Abu, K. (1983), 'The Separateness of Spouses: Conjugal Responses in an Ashanti Town', in C. Oppong (ed.), *Female and Male in West Africa*, Allen & Unwin, London and Boston.

Banfield, E. C. (1958), *The Moral Basis of a Backward Society*, Free Press, Glencoe, Ill.

Bean, L. L., and Mineau, G. P. (1986), 'The Polygyny—Fertility Hypothesis: A Re-evaluation', *Population Studies*, 40 (1), 67–81.

Cain, M. (1981), 'Risk and Insurance: Perspectives on Fertility and Agrarian Change in India and Bangladesh', *Population and Development Review*, 7 (3), 435–74.

Caldwell, J. C. (1966), 'The Erosion of the Family: A Study of the Fate of the Family in Ghana', *Population Studies*, 20 (1), 5–26.

—— (1975), *The Sahelian Drought and its Demographic Implications*, Occasional Paper, No. 8, Overseas Liaison Committee, Washington, DC.

—— (1978), 'A Theory of Fertility: From High Plateau to Destabilization', *Population and Development Review*, 4 (4), 553–77.

—— (1982), *Theory of Fertility Decline*, Academic Press, London and New York.

—— (1983), 'Direct Economic Costs and Benefits of Children', in R. A. Bulatao and R. D. Lee (eds.), *Determinants of Fertility in Developing Countries*, Academic Press, New York.

—— (1986a), 'Family Change and Demographic Change: The Reversal of the Veneration Flow', Plenary Session Address to American Sociological Conference, August–September, New York.

—— (1986b), 'Routes to Low Mortality in Poor Countries', *Population and Development Review*, 12 (2), 171–220.

—— and Caldwell, P. (1978), 'The Achieved Small Family: Early Fertility Transition in an African City', *Studies in Family Planning*, 9 (1), 1–18.

—— —— (1985), 'Cultural Forces Tending to Sustain High Fertility in Tropical Africa',

PHN Technical Note 85–16, Population Health and Nutrition Department, World Bank, Washington, DC.

—— —— and Caldwell, B. (1987), 'Anthropology and Demography: The Mutual Reinforcement of Speculation and Research', *Current Anthropology*, 28 (1), 25–43.

—— and Srinivasan, K. (1984), 'New Data on Nuptiality and Fertility in China', *Population and Development Review*, 10 (1), 71–9.

—— Jalaluddin, A. K. M., Caldwell, P., and Cosford, W. (1980), 'The Control of Activity in Bangladesh', Working Papers in Demography, No. 12, Australian National University, Canberra.

—— —— —— —— (1984), 'The Changing Nature of Family Labour in Rural and Urban Bangladesh: Implications for Fertility Transition', *Canadian Studies in Population*, 2 (2), 165–98.

—— Reddy, P. H., and Caldwell, P. (1983*a*), 'The Causes of Marriage Change in South India', *Population Studies*, 37 (3), 343–61.

—— —— —— (1983*b*), 'The Social Component of Mortality Decline: An Investigation in South India Employing Alternative Methodologies', *Population Studies*, 37 (2), 185–205.

—— —— —— (1984), 'The Determinants of Fertility Decline in Rural South India', in T. Dyson and N. Crook (eds.), *India's Demography: Essays on the Contemporary Population*, South Asian Publishers, New Delhi.

—— —— —— (1985), 'Educational Transition in Rural South India', *Population and Development Review*, 11 (1), 29–51.

—— —— —— (1986), 'Periodic High Risk as a Cause of Fertility Decline in a Changing Rural Environment: Survival Strategies in the 1980–83 South Indian Drought', *Economic Development and Cultural Change*, 34 (4), 677–701.

—— —— —— (n.d.), 'Measurement of Rural Conversation', data file in Department of Demography, Australian National University, Canberra.

Campbell, J. K. (1974), *Honour, Family, and Patronage: A Study of Institutions and Moral Values in a Greek Mountain Community*, Oxford University Press, Oxford and New York (first published 1964).

Chayanov, A. V. (1966), *The Theory of Peasant Economy*, ed. D. Thorner, B. Kerblay, and R. E. F. Smith, Richard Irwin, Homewood, Ill.

Coale, A. J., and Demeny, P. (1966), *Regional Model Life Tables and Stable Populations*, Princeton University Press, Princeton, NJ.

Davis, N. Z. (1977), 'Ghosts, Kin, and Progeny: Some Features of Family Life in Early Modern France', *Daedalus*, 106 (2), 87–114.

Davis, R. B. (1973), 'Muang Matrilocality', *Journal of the Siam Society*, 61 (2), 53–63.

d'Souza, S., and Chen, L. C. (1980), 'Sex Differentials in Mortality in Rural Bangladesh', *Population and Development Review*, 6 (2), 257–70.

Dyson, T., and Moore, M. (1983), 'On Kinship Structure, Female Autonomy, and Demographic Behavior in India', *Population and Development Review*, 9 (1), 35–60.

Goldstone, J. A. (1986), 'The Demographic Revolution in England: A Re-examination', *Population Studies*, 40 (1), 5–33.

Goody, J. (1983), *The Development of the Family and Marriage in Europe*, Cambridge University Press, Cambridge and New York.

Greenough, P. R. (1982), *Prosperity and Misery in Modern Bengal*, Oxford University Press, New York.

Hill, A. G. (1985), 'The Recent Demographic Surveys in Mali and Their Main Findings', in A. G. Hill (ed.), *Population, Health and Nutrition in the Sahel: Issues in the Welfare of Selected West African Communities*, Kegan Paul International, London.

Knodel, J. (1977), 'Family Limitation and the Fertility Transition: Evidence from the Age Patterns of Fertility in Europe and Asia', *Population Studies*, 31 (2), 219–49.

Miller, B. D. (1981), *The Endangered Sex: Neglect of Female Children in Rural North India*, Cornell University Press, Ithaca, NY.

Muhsam, H. V. (1956), 'The Fertility of Polygamous Marriages', *Population Studies*, 10 (1), 3–16.

Okore, A. O. (1978), 'The Value of Children among Ibo Households in Nigeria', Ph.D. thesis, Australian National University, Canberra.

Page, H. (1975), 'Fertility Levels: Patterns and Trends', in J. C. Caldwell (ed.), *Population Growth and Socio-economic Change in West Africa*, Columbia University Press, New York.

Shorter, E. (1977), *The Making of the Modern Family*, Fontana/Collins, Glasgow.

Stone, L. (1977), *The Family, Sex and Marriage in England, 1500–1800*, Weidenfeld and Nicolson, London.

Vercruijsse, E. (1983), 'Fishmongers, Big Dealers and Fishermen: Co-operation between the Sexes in Ghanaian Canoe Fishing', in C. Oppong (ed.), *Female and Male in West Africa*, Allen & Unwin, London and Boston.

Visaria, P. M. (1961), *The Sex Ratio of the Population of India: 1961 Census of India*, vol. i, Monograph 10, Office of the Registrar-General, New Delhi.

World Bank (1984), *World Development Report 1984*, Oxford University Press, New York.

Wrigley, E. A., and Schofield, R. S. (1981), *The Population History of England 1541–1871: A Reconstruction*, Harvard University Press, Cambridge, Mass.

Part III

Processes and Institutions

6 Traditional Family Systems in Rural Settings in Africa

CHRISTINE OPPONG

In this chapter I first define the traditional state of society and then examine aspects of African systems of domestic organization, kinship, and marriage. This is undertaken with a view to shedding light on the typical characteristics of traditional African family systems. These are systems that ensure the availability of the resources required for material existence in natural environments that are often harsh and demanding; the reproduction and survival of the human population in conditions of vulnerability to disease and consequent low life expectancy, and the transmission from one generation to the next of both material and cultural heritages, thus maintaining the viability and continuity of effective socio-economic groups from decade to decade, based upon descent and affinity.

The Traditional State of Society

The traditional state of society is not confined to any specific historical period or set of cultures, but rather consists of an interlinked array of features that persist to a greater or lesser degree at any given time and in any particular community. These features include beliefs; political, economic, demographic, and social systems; and associated personality types. In the realm of beliefs and perceptions there is reliance upon fate and destiny, witchcraft, magic and sorcery, and activities of spiritual beings, including ancestral spirits, rather than upon development and use of scientific knowledge, improved technology, and techniques (Hagen, 1962). Given the low levels of control over natural events such as births and deaths, levels of mortality and fertility are high. Women spend most of their reproductive years pregnant and nursing. People have little control over their natural environment and basic resources of food and water, which are subject to rapid and disastrous fluctuations due to climatic changes. These fluctuations are greater in some settings than in others and may lead to annual periods of hunger or drought before the major harvests or rainy seasons. Given the simplicity of tools for production and the primitive production techniques, divisions of labour are rudimentary and based mainly on sex and age, with the majority of individuals from an early age engaged in food production.

Adults in societies with such a poor economic and scientific knowledge and resource base are made continually aware of their vulnerability to natural calamities—drought, disease, crop failure, floods, and storms. Death is an omnipresent feature, especially the death of infants and of mothers in childbirth and death due to warring activities and vengeance.[1] Disasters and death are understood only in a mystical sense, attempts to explain and control them being made on the spiritual plane, hence the prevalence of belief in witchcraft, magic, and sorcery (Carroll, 1981). The structure of authority is hierarchical; respect is associated with age and individual social positions are ascribed by birth, rather than being individually achieved. Traditional behaviour patterns change little from one generation to the next, being governed by custom (ibid.). The state of nature and existing social organization are accepted as immutable givens, and the anxiety that individuals feel in new situations is assuaged by reliance upon custom or traditional authorities. Thus, elders often reach decisions by discussion and consensus. The authoritarian personality prevails, satisfaction being gained from both yielding to superiors in a hierarchy based on descent, age, sex, and by dominating those in inferior social positions (Hagen, ibid.).

In view of the uncontrollable fluctuations in numbers of people and availability of material resources, effective systems are required for distributing the burdens of dependency of young and old (e.g. elderly widows, orphans, and the sick) among the fit and able; for replacing deceased mothers, fathers, and offspring; for allocating fluctuating resources; and for economic co-operation, since considerable inputs of labour may be needed periodically for farming, especially where a village or tribe is threatened by aggressors. Thus, the individual adult or couple with small children is not usually capable of survival alone but is dependent upon mutual help, joint responsibility, and co-operation. This co-operation is gained through a network of mutual obligation and the exchange of resources between kin. Investments are made in people, in relations of kinship and affinity, which can be called upon in time of need, ideally providing a permanent source of sustenance and security.

Such traditional features of belief systems, economies, polities, and personality are still found to a greater or lesser extent in contemporary sub-Saharan rural societies, as in many other societies around the world, both contemporary and historical. The basis of the discussion that follows is social–anthropological studies carried out through prolonged periods of ethnographic work, mainly during the 1960s. The societies considered here are not assumed to be static nor to have been unaffected by colonial regimes. However, there is ample evidence in the literature of the continued prevalence of traditional social organization. For the sake of simplicity the anthroplogical present tense is mainly used.[2]

---

[1] Given the prevalence of parental bereavement in contemporary Africa, parents' preference for their children's survival has been observed to be not necessarily attached to specific living children. This phenomenon presumably helps protect parents from the ravages of child loss (Frank and Dakuyo, 1985).

[2] Present-tense exposition has been normal practice in many ethnographic accounts. For some classic ethnographies of the past half century see Bohannan (1965), Evans-Pritchard (1951), Fortes

Characteristics of African Family Systems

What are the characteristics of traditional family systems, given that the prevailing economic, demographic, political, and religious spheres are congruent and associated roles are overlapping? One is that the head of the kin group combines religious, political, and legal authority. The co-operative working group—which clears land or hoes together, is frequently the core of the local religious congregation, and sacrifices to the same ancestors—is the political group for dealing with external aggressors and the local court for settling internal disputes.

A second prominent characteristic of traditional family systems is the openness or lack of boundaries of the nuclear family system.[3] Associated with this is the lack of personal individuation. These characteristics are further discussed below; but stated briefly, they are related to the prevalence of sibling group solidarity, the sharing of conjugal rights and duties, and the frequent substitution of persons in parent–child relationships.

These three features make the conjugal family open and the roles of the individuals easily subject to substitution in time of death or crisis, thus maintaining the continuity of the fragile nuclear family. In addition to the lack of structural differentiation of institutions and the lack of functional individuation of the nuclear family, a third pervasive characteristic of African traditional family systems is the prevalence of descent as an organizing principle and the extent to which descent groups of one kind or another are important building blocks of society, in the community, the economy, and the religious and political organizations. In addition, at the individual level, political, economic, legal, and religious roles are frequently ascribed on the basis of descent.

Domestic Organization

Domestic organization does not necessarily focus upon one multi-functional, co-resident unit that emerges in all domestic situations. (Witness the problems of field research encountered in Ghana by, for example, Vercruijsse, 1974, when one uses inappropriate concepts of domestic organization.) Various groups of individuals emerge in different situations, including reproduction, production, consumption, and socialization; and the individuals who constitute these groups do not necessarily reside in the same dwelling.

In addition to the fact that dwelling groups are composed of people who are related to each other in various ways, kin tend to live in neighbouring houses,

(1938, 1970*a*, 1970*b*, 1970*c*), J. R. Goody (1962*a*, 1962*b*, 1973*a*, 1973*b*, 1976), E. N. Goody (1973, 1978), Gray and Gulliver (1964), Levine (1964, 1982), Radcliffe-Brown and Forde (1950).

[3] For a full discussion of openness versus closure of the nuclear family system and methods of indexing and comparing these dimensions in various areas of nuclear family functioning, see Oppong (1982).

either within village communities or in more dispersed patterns. Domestic organization includes the activities and relations involved in the systems of sexual congress, procreation, production, consumption, and socialization, as well as the ownership, management, and use of property. For studies of varied developmental cycles of domestic groups see J. R. Goody (1962*b*) and Sanjek (1983). Each of these sets of activities may be carried out by different configurations of individuals in separate locations. There is no basis for assuming that a single set of people referred to as a 'family' co-resides, has a single fund of resources, eats from the same pot, or socializes all the children begotten by or born to the adult members of the group.

The observed reality is that activities associated with one of the domestic processes enumerated may be typically divided between two or more spatially separate residential units. For example, children and youths under systems of fostering and apprenticeship may stay for training in different houses from the ones in which they were born. (Cf. Aries, 1962, on European patterns of child-rearing.) The use of certain types of property may be controlled by dispersed kin-group members or by kin living in neighbouring dwelling groups. Adults and children from several nearby dwelling groups may co-operate in production for subsistence. At the same time members of the same residential group may split into separate cooking and eating units, and sexual partners (spouses) may live in separate residences.

Food processing and cooking traditionally are mainly women's work, but the way in which these activities are organized among women in the compound varies greatly from ethnic group to group. In some cases each wife maintains her own hearth and stores of grain and tubers. In others, wives take turns cooking for the household. In yet others, cooking for the husband rotates among wives, but each cooks for herself and her own children. (For an indication of the potential complexity of cooking arrangements in Malian households, see Wéry, 1987.) The elderly, the young, or those without children may not have hearths and therefore join with other women. Two features are typical of food consumption: husbands and wives generally eat separately, and mothers with their small children.

Fostering of children by non-parental kin is prevalent. In addition, even when continuing to live in the same household, children are normally cared for by a variety of caretakers other than the father who begot them and the mother who bore them (Weisner and Gallimore, 1977). Hence, on all accounts the openness of the nuclear and conjugal family prevails.

Land and Labour in Family Production

Mutual self-help and reciprocity are vital for carrying out many subsistence tasks, and frequently exploitation of natural resources occurs through co-operation by relatives. The necessary labour is organized and provided by spouses and kin, and the necessary skills are learned in the domestic context

Table 6.1. Marriage Transactions and Kin Groups in Africa

	Type of kin group			
	Patrilineal	Matrilineal	Double	Bilateral
Marriage transactions				
Bride-wealth	154	22	12	7
Bride-service	10	8	0	1
Dowry	0	0	0	0
Gift-exchange	1	0	0	0
Sister-exchange	8	0	0	2
Token or absent	3	7	0	3
Total	176	37	12	13

Source: Goody, 1973: 50 (Table 6).

(Gray and Gulliver, 1964). Produce is distributed through family relationships to family members, some of whom may be residing in other domestic groups. Individual members of the family are allocated rights and obligations with respect to the ownership, control, exploitation, and consumption of resources, according to their status, ascribed on the basis of kinship and marriage. As marriage changes their attachment to the family, estate shifts accordingly (Gray, 1964).

In societies with unilineal descent groups (matri- or patrilineages) the major property rights are often vested in those individuals who make up a local segment of a lineage. The kin group through time typically holds rights of use to the main resource—land—among farming peoples (Gray and Gulliver, 1964). Land is not a saleable commodity, nor is it owned in any outright sense, but is held in trust from the ancestors, passed on to descendants, and in the present allocated to kin and affines to use. The head of the domestic group and the head of the kin group or segment of it administer the kin land on behalf of the group and at the same time are likely to control and care for the ancestral shrines and sacred objects, as well as representing the group to the outside world and holding jural authority over group members.

The distinction between individual and lineage property is not always easy to make. Individuals have legitimate claims to use group property and kin group members exercise claims on other members' goods, at opportune times making demands upon them, which may be ignored with impunity (Kopytoff, 1964).

The divisions of tasks by age and sex tend to be well defined and vary in different areas. Africa has been described broadly as the region *par excellence* of female farming, in which many of the tasks connected with food production and processing are left to women (Boserup, 1970). Shifting cultivation is pervasive, with small plots being cultivated for a few years and then abandoned. The strict sexual division of tasks is accompanied by a similar sexual division of property. Most objects of personal use are sex-typed and transmitted from generation to generation between females or males, and husbands and wives have separate property rights (J. R. Goody, 1976). This lack of community of goods is witnessed at death when one spouse does not inherit rights in the other's property (J. R. Goody, 1973).

Another important difference between societies in Africa and elsewhere is that in Africa in non-Muslim communities inheritance of property by children of both sexes is rare and parental property is not passed on to daughters at marriage through the dowry. A man's property is transmitted at death only to males of his own lineage or clan, and women's property is passed on to their sisters and daughters. Since personal property is usually minimal, however, it is mainly a question of individuals' rights in kin-group property and the position of property manager passing on to a brother, own son, or sibling's son.

Again, in contrast with societies on other continents, African marriage is characterized by widespread payment of bridewealth (J. R. Goody 1973: 50). This is property of various kinds which passes from the kin of the groom to the kin of the bride. Such transfers reallocate the reproductive power of women and have been viewed as a kind of prospective childwealth.

These patterns of inheritance and marriage transfers are linked in the African context with the lack of linguistic and functional differentiation between the nuclear family and the unity and solidarity of sibling groups. They are also more commonly found in societies with less marked economic and social status differentiation (ibid.)

Given a situation of relative abundance of the basic resource, land, and the prevalence of shifting agriculture, there is no great pressure to confine transmission of basic resources within the narrow limits of the conjugal family. Rather, descent groups provide the series of possible heirs. Indeed, the whole descent group holds rights in the land in perpetuity. It is only the position of senior manager of the family estate that is passed on at death. Kin-group property cannot be alienated by adoption, marriage, or sale, and wills are uncommon.

In the kinds of situation under discussion it is labour, not land, that is the scarce factor in production, and it is not available on any market other than the marriage market and through transactions in children. Thus, polygyny helps to increase the size of the domestic group, and fostering children of kin can add to the numbers of household and farm members who are young and active and have special knowledge and skills. Noteworthy is the practice of fostering children of kin to provide recruits for specialist occupations among the Dagomba (Oppong, 1973); see also E. N. Goody (1978) regarding the phenomenon in West Africa as a whole. Other means of gaining labour are through mutual assistance and co-operative labour groups of kin and affines.

Prescriptive Altruism and Reciprocity among Kin

A critical aspect of kinship which requires special consideration is its morality and the fact that it cannot simply be reduced to economic and political components. Kinship in the contexts discussed here is the basis of long-term commitment, characterized by sharing without reckoning and by generalized reciprocity within kin groups. Such relationships are invaluable for helping to maintain the viability of insecure small units in precarious circumstances, in which long-term reciprocity, with no immediate calculation of the debt and repayment period, may make all the difference to survival (Bloch, 1973). Kin ties are moral in the sense that there is great tolerance of imbalance in the transactions; debts may last from one generation to the next. Brother dares not deny the request of brother to share resources, whereas relationships of affinity may involve careful calculations of cattle transferred and children born over several decades. The contrast is clear: sibling ties are much more moral than conjugal ties. Siblings are solidary, and any attempt to calculate what is owned is likely to be viewed with horror. Similarly, the unity of parents and children and thus the avoidance of confrontation or demands for a return for labour spent on parents or on children and the unconsidered expectation on the part of parents that children will care for them without counting the cost in their old age.

Thus, kin ties provide a bedrock for economic co-operation continuing into an uncertain future and providing an ideal basis for long-term planning in a potentially precarious and changing environment. The long-term, uncalculated exchanges of labour between kin in a system of fluid shifting cultivation enable farmers to adapt to changing labour demands and availability of labour, which is particularly fluid in shifting agricultural systems. That need for long-term security as well as short-term shifts in needs are answered by the morality of kinship (Bloch, 1973). Often the sanction for failing to behave morally—that is, for failing to respond without calculation to requests to share or give—is to be accused of witchcraft, a frequent occurrence within the kin group. Similarly, child-care and care of the elderly are claims that kin cannot deny, thus ensuring the continued ability of the larger kin group to cope with short-term crises. In sum, the morality of kin ties is of crucial importance to the long-term survival of the domestic group living in marginal circumstances. The need to incorporate such moral values into economic–demographic models of traditional family behaviour is likely to be increasingly recognized.

Kinship Systems and Descent Groups

All societies can be categorized according to the way they reckon significant descent ties—that is, whether they have or do not have corporate descent groups. In societies without corporate descent groups there are personal kindreds that individuals reckon in any line. In societies with descent groups, in contrast, some are unilineal, others are non-unilineal. The former include *patrilineages* and *matrilineages*. The latter are groups reckoning descent from an apical ancestor or ancestress in either the female or the male line (*uterine* or *agnatic*). These are *descending kindreds* or *septs* or *ambilineal descent groups*. A small number of societies have *unilineal descent groups* of both kinds, matrilineal and patrilineal. Patrilineal descent group systems are more common than matrilineal descent group systems. Yet, every major type of descent-reckoning system can exist within a small geographical area with only minimal differences in economic arrangements in the several systems (J. R. Goody, 1962*a*). On the one hand, matriliny has been associated with simple hoe agriculture rather than with hunting, advanced agriculture, or pastoralism. On the other, societies lacking unilineal descent groups are more common among hunters (and industrial societies) (J. R. Goody, 1976) and they are also found in more differentiated kingdoms with commoners and ruling and religious estates. A common feature of many of these lineage systems is their characteristic modes of segmentation, segments at different levels of inclusiveness being relevant to different forms of activity. Lineages are often corporate in the sense that they act and are treated for certain purposes as a single legal personality. They are also often permanent property-holding units into which new recruits are continually born. A lineage usually has a hierarchy of legitimate authority that may be localized or dispersed.

Classificatory Kinship Terminologies

Another common feature of African kinship systems is classificatory kinship terminologies, according to which a large number of kin belong to a small number of categories. Terms for lineal relatives (e.g. parents and children) are also used to refer to collateral relatives (e.g. parents' siblings and siblings' children). The inclusion of different sets of relatives within the same linguistic category implies similarities in their customary behaviour or in the social relations that individuals have with them.

An important behavioural aspect of the sibling group is that in certain circumstances one member may take the place of the other. Thus, in many African societies the place of the husband, father, or grandfather can be taken by his brother, just as the place of a wife or mother can be taken by her sister. So, for example, in the custom known as *sororate* the place of the deceased or barren wife is taken by her sister. In widow inheritance a brother may take over the conjugal and paternal roles of the deceased or, in the special case of *levirate*, beget children for the name of the dead man (Potash, 1986). Crisis fostering provides another example of the assumption by a sibling of a deceased brother's or sister's parental responsibilities. A sibling may also assume these responsibilities at divorce or when there is no 'crisis', simply in accordance with a custom of sharing children and their rearing among siblings or parents and grandparents.

An important feature of family relations is the social inequality between proximate generations. Individuals in the filial generation owe respect, obedience, and often also service and labour to parents and others in the senior generation (Radcliffe-Brown, 1950). Parents need to control the labour of the younger generation in all the operations needed to produce food with simple tools and in harsh climatic conditions. In such a relationship of control and subordination, latent conflict needs to be dissipated. In contrast, many African societies have a widespread custom of privileged familiarity between grandchildren and grandparents, and the solidarity of alternate generations is often mirrored in a kinship terminology that equates them.

Marriage and Bridewealth

Examination of various practices relating to marriage in Africa demonstrates the subtlety, complexity, and diversity of the institution in African societies, in contrast to the simpler institutions often found elsewhere. The Akan of Ghana, for example, have enumerated more than 20 forms of heterosexual relationships, which vary according to such factors as the amount of kin involvement. Traditional marriage forms in Africa have long called into question the Western assumptions that marriage must be between living individuals and between people of the opposite sex. Given that the basic purpose of marriage in Africa is to produce offspring who will be attached to a particular kin group through a man or a woman, marriage can occur between two women (one bearing the children and the other having the offspring recruited to her kin group) or between a woman and a ghost (with a living man designated to act as genitor) (Evans-Pritchard, 1951; Potash, 1986). Numerous ethnographic accounts of African marriage transactions have shown that marriage in many, if not most, African societies customarily involves a whole series of donations—bridewealth or brideprice, that is, gifts or services from the kin of the groom to the kin of the prospective bride. The prevalence and content of these gifts vary widely among societies, as do their implications.

Two elements in bridewealth payments have been distinguished (J. R. Goody, 1973). These include a prime, normally fixed gift that is the jural instrument of the transfer of marital rights and may be returnable upon divorce, and contingent gifts. The latter contain an element of barter and are considered to be the medium for the establishment of affinal relations. These are often spread over time and vary according to the status, wealth, and cordiality of the people involved. They allow the husband to gain extra rights and privileges *vis-à-vis* his wife and her kin. The quantity and value of the goods transferred have been viewed partly as a function of the degree of jural authority and number of rights gained by the husband. The quantity varies from a few cowry shells or palm wine at one extreme to a herd of cattle at the other. The range of people involved in the gift giving and receiving varies, as does the use to which the objects received are put and the specific sets of rights transferred through the transactions.

Payments vary according to whether they are repayable at death or divorce and whether they are fixed for all members of the society or depend upon the recipients' status. The groom and his kin may acquire rights in all children born to the bride (by whatever genitor) or may not even have the right to bring the bride or her children to live with them or to have any of the children recruited to their descent group.

Bridewealth needs to be distinguished from money spent on the wedding ceremony or money or gifts given directly by the groom to his betrothed. It constitutes a pool of resources that are not consumed at the wedding and are not handed to the wife but rather are controlled by the bride's male kin so that they can in turn obtain wives.

A Bundle of Conjugal Rights and Duties

The idea that marriage is a bundle of rights is analytically useful in the African context in that it demonstrates the necessity of separating the various elements that form a complex relationship yet are capable of separation, delegation, and joint enjoyment. For instance, sexual rights may be delegated, distributed among several people (as in polygyny), or split into a ritual and symbolic element and a physical element. Besides being jointly owned or shared, such rights may be subject to strict rules of inheritance or ownership. Ownership rights may be conceived as continuing *post mortem*, while heirs gain only usufruct. The view of marriage as a bundle of rights and corresponding duties facilitates examination of which rights are gained at different stages of marriage transactions and demonstrates that some rights involved in marriage are more enduring than others. Detailed accounting of the reallocation of rights and duties between spouses and their kin groups illuminates the processes of bargaining that may occur and the potential conflicts, and thus explains the necessity for avoidance and joking, as mechanisms for minimizing conflicts and hostility between affines. The whole process of establishing a set of conjugal rights and duties—that is, a socially and legally acceptable form of marital relationship—may last any length of time from a few minutes, hours, or days to several months, years, or even more than a lifetime in the extreme instance (Oppong, 1985*b*).

A man's rights to his wife may be acquired only gradually, by work and presents. The sexual right may be acquired before the right to co-residence or domestic services, or co-residence may be acquired before sexual rights. Sexual rights may be exclusive or not. Conception or childbirth may mark the commencement of a stable conjugal relationship. The husband may or may not have the right to prevent his wife from taking lovers or to claim damages for adultery. A woman's sexual rights to her husband are more restricted, though he may need her permission before taking another wife. Her economic and social rights in her husband's home and community are likely to increase over time and with the birth of children. The right to co-reside is not always a part of the conjugal bargain, nor is co-residence necessarily conterminous with the duration of marriage.

Just as kin groups control and manage the distribution of land to domestic groups, so they control the sexual activities and marriage transactions of members (Kopytoff, 1964: 103). Some sexual freedom among the unmarried youth is countenanced in many societies, but sexual relations of married couples tend to be carefully managed and scrutinized by senior kin, with the result that for many years of married life the majority of women are sexually inactive. Sexual abstinence is practised widely for up to two years or more following the birth of each child to ensure the development of the infant. This sexual abstinence on the part of wives is in some cases ensured by their physical separation from their husbands—for example, a woman may be sent to live with her kin for one or two years after giving birth, or she may be carefully observed and controlled within the household by co-resident seniors. Not only does this behavioural pattern space births, but also it serves to maintain social distance between husbands and wives and facilitates the smooth rotation of polygynous wives. Domestic and public ridicule may follow violation of these sexual constraints. This post-partum sexual taboo has been documented in 167 societies in sub-Saharan Africa and is virtually universal for the whole region (Schoenmaeckers, *et al.*, 1981). The persistence of the pattern requires tight social control and is associated not only with polygyny and the social distance of spouses but also with the strength of ties between infants and their mothers and between women and their kin, especially when it involves prolonged periods of residence with the latter (Erny, 1981).

At the centre of African marriage transactions is the establishment of procreative rights. In many ethnic groups, if a woman proves barren her kin return the bridewealth or provide another woman, who will bear children. Inheritance of widows is a widespread custom, which provides not only clear examples of the sibling group's unity, since (classificatory) brother replaces brother or sister replaces sister, but also evidence of the importance of procreation for women and men. Hence, traditional and widespread practices exist for providing substitute spouses for either husbands or wives, so that their reproductive cycles will not be impaired and the desired series of births will be maintained (Radcliffe-Brown, 1950: 64). In some cases absolute equivalence in marriage exchanges is enforced. Two women are exchanged in marriage, and if one proves to be more fertile than the other, the group of the fertile woman is entitled to appropriate as many of her children as will compensate for the other's infertility. Or if divorce occurs and only one of the women has borne children, they may return with her to the mother's brother (Bohannan, 1965).

Exchange of valued goods and services or women for rights in women and their procreative powers are thus typical of these small-scale pre-industrial societies, in which people—especially family members—are the source of economic and social security, prestige, and psychological satisfaction. In such contexts, in which human fertility is at a premium and reproductive potential so highly valued, they are exchanged only for an equivalent return—if not another woman as a bride, then the means to obtain one. Thus, the exogamous kin group can itself achieve the same goal of reproductive increase.

Polygyny

All marriages are potentially polygynous, and a large proportion eventually becomes so. The estimated average of 150 wives per 100 married males is achieved not through an imbalance in the sex ratio, but rather by the longer marriageable span of females, who enter into marriage at a much earlier age than men, often in their early teens or soon after reaching puberty. Dorjahn (1954: 299) calculated, for example, that if the age at first marriage for women is 16 years and that of men is 25, there will be a surplus of 26 per cent of marriageable women.

Most polygynous households are characterized by some kind of formal rotation of conjugal rights, both culinary and sexual, the two often being linked. Polygyny is associated with separate rooms for husbands and wives and separate eating arrangements. Separate rooming arrangements have been demonstrated to be associated with less intimacy and more aloofness between men and their wives and children (Whiting and Whiting, 1975). They are most common in societies with medium levels of economic development—that is, agricultural rather than hunting and gathering societies. The separateness of spouses within the household is far more common in Africa, where it reaches 70 per cent, than in other regions of the world.

Relationships forged by marriage and transacted through a series of exchanges of goods and rights in people are potentially fraught with hostility and aggression, yet must remain overtly friendly. Hostile feelings are typically prevented or dissipated by avoidance or joking. Relationships of avoidance are typical between grooms and their parents-in-law, and through playful teasing and joking brothers-in-law may turn potential enmity into friendship (Radcliffe-Brown, 1940).

In many societies divorce is an important option for women who wish to withdraw from an unattractive conjugal situation and may be an important strategy for achieving greater autonomy. In some societies it occurs at the instigation of wives of all ages. In other societies it is a common practice among younger or older age groups. Older women may withdraw from publicly acknowledged marital relationships and live subsequently with kin. Such behaviour is observed in African societies regardless of the kind of descent reckoning. For example, in Ghana terminal separation of spouses is common among the Dagomba and Akan, and in old age Ga women are more likely to be living with kin than with their husbands (Sanjek, 1983).

Women in African families have several traditional means of diminishing any tendencies towards domination by their husbands. These means include maintaining strong ties with kin, who may support them in quarrels with their husbands and provide a place of refuge; maintaining access to land, crops, and other resources; and membership in women's extra-domestic groups. In addition, women may achieve independence and even dominance in their own right, both as household heads over their own kin, especially in matrilineal situations, and as senior women in the households of male kin.

Infant and Child-care

The first phase of infancy is characterized by close body contact with the mother and prolonged breast-feeding. The infant is often wrapped in a cloth close to the mother's body and is never left alone; the mother's breast is continually available. Gradually the mother is replaced by others, children and adults, who carry the baby on their back or hip. In this upright position and surrounded by a variety of familiar people, the African infant shows early developmental precocity. This precocity is not apparently the outcome of individual, personal stimulation by the mother, but rather due to early exposure to a variety of stimuli. (For a review of child-care practices and development in traditional rural African societies, see Erny, 1981.)

During this period of breast-feeding the mother is often separated from her husband or at least does not sleep with him, concentrating on the infant's care. Thereafter weaning comes abruptly, usually in the second year. The trauma of weaning typically leaves the child feeling abandoned (ibid.). The child may be sent to live with another female relative for a period. Normally the mother resumes sleeping with her husband at this time, and the child is plunged into the life of the group among other children in the home and close by. The relative neglect that the child now experiences may lead to an increased incidence of sickness or to malnutrition, anorexia, and even death in the post-weaning period. As the mother becomes more and more distant and inevitably involved with a subsequent pregnancy and infant, the child is forced to seek security and solidarity in the multiple parental and sibling figures typically in and near his or her domestic group. In spite of the roughness of weaning and the division of the mother's attentions among several offspring, for the child the relationship with the mother is generally the closest of all. Mother–daughter ties are especially strong.

Children are encouraged from an early age to take an active part in domestic and agricultural tasks. Participation in group activities for the common good, not individual accomplishment, is stressed, although different values are emphasized according to the type of subsistence base of the local economy (Barry, Child, and Bacon, 1959).

A child's personality and talents are generally thought to be the result of chance and are therefore accepted as they are, no attempt being made to change them (Erny, 1981: 137). But children are taught useful skills and learn to do tasks in the home and on the farm by watching, imitating, and participating with other children and adults in real situations. They also learn through imitative play. Among the most important values children internalize are self-control in speech and action and deference and respect to elders. Thus, they learn to keep silent and be politely composed and passive (Whiting, 1961). Expressions of feeling are inhibited even between parents and children as well as between husbands and wives (Whiting and Whiting, 1975; Erny, 1981).

The prevalence of fostering by non-parental kin varies from ethnic group to group. In some as many as 30 or 40 per cent of children may grow up in this way. Where all children in a domestic group receive more or less similar treatment from the adults present, they do not necessarily suffer deprivation. Many advantages of this practice have been enumerated. It provides children to households where children of a particular age or sex are lacking. It serves to link kin in households that may be scattered or far apart. It may provide grandparents with a substitute for the daughter they lost when she married. It may equalize the numbers of children in the homes of more and less prolific kin. It provides a home for a child after the mother experiences the crisis of widowhood or divorce. It provides recruits for specialist professions when they are needed and possibly recruits them from sisters' as well as brothers' children. Viewed from the perspective of the observer of traditional African family life, it provides an example *par excellence* of how role players are substituted within the system and how any propensity for intense and individualized emotional bonds is minimized. Because children have many parental figures and adults are parents to numerous children they did not beget or bear, a child lost through the tragedy of infant mortality is soon replaced and children are spared the insecurity of having only two parents in a precarious world (cf. Stone, 1977).

Concluding Comments

No useful analysis of African family systems can be undertaken using European concepts of marriage, household, parenthood, kinship. The simple addition of polygyny or 'extended household/family' to the repertoire of concepts is in no way adequate. A rich array of ethnographic evidence calls attention to why this is so. Some of this material has been referred to here. It is necessary to shift to a mode of analysis in which systems of roles are considered (parental, conjugal, kin of various kinds, etc.) and their associated prescribed norms, resources, activities, rights and responsibilities (Oppong and Abu, 1985). The modes of recruitment to permanent groups on the basis of descent have been examined and the typical functions of such groups, and domestic organization and the way individual roles are articulated within these and how they are connected to and feed into the enduring descent group systems. Certain characteristic features of these systems have been emphasized.

In earlier studies I have demonstrated why these considerations must be taken into account in any attempt to understand contemporary demographic processes in Africa, including change or lack of change in family-size values, fertility, and birth-control practices. For example, new home economists' models of household behaviour have been shown to be inappropriate for Africa (Oppong, 1982). Anthropological methods, however, have made an essential contribution to an understanding of fertility change (Oppong, 1985b); and a series of Ghanaian empirical family studies stretching over two decades have shown how changes of various kinds in traditional African family systems can be conceptualized, documented, and related to changing aspects of demographic regimes (e.g. Oppong, 1973; 1974; Oppong and Abu, 1987; 1988). In these studies two critical examples of role substitution are examined: that between kin and that between spouses for various types of domestic activities. These role substitutions have been related to family-size aspirations, achievements, and contraceptive practice and have helped researchers to conceptualize and interpret such phenomena found in models of demographic change as women's status, the costs and opportunity costs of children, and the quality of child care (Oppong, 1983).

These studies demonstrate not only that it is necessary to understand how traditional African family systems function in order to document and understand change but also that without such insights it will be impossible to plan for or bring about change. Thus, more studies are needed now of how African families and descent groups are continuously adapting to changing political, economic, and demographic circumstances.

References

Aries, P. (1962), *Centuries of Childhood: A Social History of Family Life*, Vintage Books, New York.

Barry, H. I., Child, L., and Bacon, M. K. (1959), 'Relation of Child Training to Subsistence Economy', *American Anthropologist*, 61 (1), 51–63.

Bloch, M. (1973), 'The Long and the Short Term: The Economic and the Political Significance of the Morality of Kinship', 75–87 in J. R. Goody and M. Fortes (eds.), *The Character of Kinship*, Cambridge University Press, Cambridge.

Bohannan, P. (1965), 'The Tiv of Nigeria', in J. L. Gibbs (ed.), *Peoples of Africa*, Holt, Rinehart, and Winston, New York.

Boserup, E. (1970), *Woman's Role in Economic Development*, St Martin's Press, New York.

Carroll, J. (1981), 'The Role of Guilt in the Formation of Modern Society: England 1350–1800', *British Journal of Sociology 32*, (4), 459–507.

Coppinger, R. M., and Rosenblatt, P. C. (1968), 'Romantic Love and Subsistence Dependence of Spouses', *Southwestern Journal of Anthropology*, 24 (3), 310–19.

Dorjahn, V. (1954), 'The Demographic Aspects of African Polygyny', Ph.D. thesis, Northwestern University, Evanston, Ill.

Erny, P. (1981), *The Child and His Environment in Black Africa: An Essay on Traditional Education*, Oxford University Press, Nairobi and New York.

Evans-Pritchard, E. E. (1951), *Kinship and Marriage among the Nuer*, Oxford Clarendon Press, Oxford.

Fortes, M. (1938), 'Social and Psychological Aspects of Education in Taleland', *Africa*, Supplement to 1 (4), 1–64.

Fortes, M. (1970*a*), 'Pietas in Ancestor Worship', in M. Fortes, *Time and Social Structure and Other Essays*, London School of Economics Monographs in Social Anthropology, University of London, Athlone Press, London and New York.

—— (1970*b*), 'The Structure of Unilineal Descent Groups', in M. Fortes, *Time and Social Structure and Other Essays*, London School of Economics Monographs in Social Anthropology, University of London, Athlone Press, London and New York.

—— (1970*c*), *Time and Social Structure and Other Essays*, London School of Economics Monographs in Social Anthropology, University of London, Athlone Press, London and New York.

Frank, O., and Dakuyo, M. (1985), 'Child Survival in Sub-Saharan Africa: Structural Means and Individual Capacity', Working Paper, No. 122, Center for Policy Studies, Population Council, New York.

Goody, E. N. (1978), 'Some Theoretical and Empirical Aspects of Parenthood in West Africa', in C. Oppong (ed.), *Marriage, Fertility, and Parenthood in West Africa*, Australian National University Press, Canberra, vol. i. 227–73.

Goody, J. R. (1962*a*), 'The Fission of Domestic Groups among the Lodagaaba', in J. R. Goody (ed.), *The Developmental Cycle in Domestic Groups*, Cambridge University Press, Cambridge and London.

—— (ed.) (1962*b*), *The Developmental Cycle in Domestic Groups*, Cambridge University Press, Cambridge and London.

—— (1973), 'Bridewealth and Dowry in Africa and Eurasia', in J. R. Goody and S. J. Tambiah (eds.), *Bridewealth and Dowry*, Cambridge University Press, Cambridge.

—— (1976), *Production and Reproduction: A Comparative Study of the Domestic Domain*, Cambridge University Press, Cambridge and New York.

Gray, R. (1964), 'Introduction', in R. Gray and P. H. Gulliver (eds.), *The Family Estate in Africa: Studies on the Roles of Property in Family Structure and Lineage Continuity*, Routledge and Kegan Paul, London.

Gray, R., and Gulliver, P. H. (eds.) (1964), *The Family Estate in Africa: Studies on the Roles of Property in Family Structure and Lineage Continuity*, Routledge and Kegan Paul, London.

Hagen, E. E. (1962), *On the Theory of Social Change: How Economic Growth Begins*, Dorsey Press, Homewood, Ill.

Kopytoff, I. (1964), 'Family and Lineage among the Suku of the Congo', in R. Gray and P. H. Gulliver (eds.), *The Family Estate in Africa: Studies on the Roles of Property in Family Structure and Lineage Continuity*, Routledge and Kegan Paul, London.

Lesthaeghe, R. J., Ohadike, P. O., Cocher, J., and Page, H. G. (1981), 'Child Spacing and Fertility in Tropical Africa: An Overview of Issues', in H. J. Page and R. J. Lesthaeghe (eds.), *Child Spacing in Tropical Africa: Traditions and Change*, Academic Press, New York and London.

Levine, R. A. (1964), 'The Gusii Family', in R. Gray and P. H. Gulliver (eds.), *The Family Estate in Africa: Studies on the Rules of Property in Family Structure and Lineage Continuity*, Routledge and Kegan Paul, London.

—— (1982), 'Fertility and Child Development: An Anthropological Approach', Paper presented at the Annual Meeting of the American Association for the Advancement of Science Symposium: Child Development and International Development: Research and Policy Interfaces, Washington, DC.

Oppong, C. (1973), *Growing up in Dagbon*, Ghana Publishing Corporation, Accra.

—— (1974), *Marriage among a Matrilineal Elite: A Family Study of Ghanaian Senior*

Civil Servants, Cambridge Studies in Social Anthropology, No. 8, Cambridge University Press, Cambridge. Reprinted in 1981 as *Middle Class African Marriage*, Allen & Unwin, London.

—— (1982), 'Family Structure and Women's Reproductive and Productive Roles', in R. Anker, M. Buvinic, and N. Youssef (eds.), *Women's Roles and Population Trends in the Third World*, Croom Helm, London.

—— (1983), 'Women's Roles, Opportunity Costs, and Fertility', in R. A. Bulatao and R. D. Lee (eds.), *Determinants of Fertility in Developing Countries: A Summary of Knowledge*, vol. i, Academic Press, New York and London.

—— (1985*a*), 'Marriage', in A. Kuper and J. Kuper (eds.), *A New Social Science Encyclopedia*, Routledge and Kegan Paul, London.

—— (1985*b*), 'Some Aspects of Anthropological Contributions to the Study of Fertility', in G. M. Farooq and G. B. Simmons (eds.), *Fertility in Developing Countries: An Economic Perspective on Research and Policy Issues*, Macmillan, London.

—— (1987), *Sex Roles, Population, and Development in West Africa: Research and Policy Issues*, James Currey, London.

—— and Abu, K. (1985), *A Handbook for Data Collection and Analysis on Seven Roles and Statuses of Women*, International Labour Organization, Geneva.

—— —— (1987), *Seven Roles of Women: Impact of Education, Migration and Employment on Ghanaian Mothers*, International Labour Organization, Geneva.

—— —— (1988), 'The Seven Roles Framework-Focused Biographies and Family Size: A Ghanaian Study', in T. C. Caldwell, A. G. Hill, and V. J. Hull, *Micro-Approaches to Demographic Research*, Kegan Paul International, London and New York.

Potash, B. (ed.) (1986), *Widows in African Societies: Choices and Constraints*, Stanford University Press, Stanford, Calif.

Radcliffe-Brown, A. R. (1940), 'On Joking Relationships', *Africa*, 13 (3), 195–210.

—— (1950), 'Introduction', in A. R. Radcliffe-Brown and C. D. Forde (eds.), *African Systems of Kinship and Marriage*, Oxford University Press, London and New York.

—— and Forde, C. D. (eds.) (1950), *African Systems of Kinship and Marriage*, Oxford University Press, London.

Sanjek, R. (1983), 'Female and Male Domestic Cycles in Urban Africa: The Adabraka Case', in C. Oppong (ed.), *Female and Male in West Africa*, Allen & Unwin, New York.

Schoenmaeckers, I., Shah, H., Lesthaeghe, R. J., and Tambashe, O. (1981), 'The Child Spacing Tradition and Post Partum Taboo in Tropical Africa: Anthropological Evidence', in H. J. Page and R. J. Lesthaeghe (eds.), *Child-Spacing in Tropical Africa: Traditions and Change*, Academic Press, New York.

Stone, L. (1977), *The Family, Sex and Marriage in England, 1500–1800*. Harper and Row, New York.

Vercruijsse, E. (1974), 'Composition of Households in Some Fanti Communities: A Study of Frameworks of Social Integration', in C. Oppong (ed.), *Domestic Rights and Duties in Southern Ghana*, Legon Family Research Papers, No. 3, Legon Institute of African Studies, Legon, 35–56.

Weisner, T. S. and Gallimore, R. (1977), 'My Brother's Keeper: Child and Sibling Caretaking', *Current Anthropology*, 18 (2).

Wéry, R. (1987), 'Resources and Relations in Bamako: A Study of Domestic Organisation', in C. Oppong (ed.), *Sex Roles, Population, and Development in West Africa: Research and Policy Issues*, James Currey, London.

Whiting, J. W. M. (1961), 'Socialisation Process and Personality', in F. L. K. Hsu (ed.), *Psychological Anthropology: Approaches to Culture and Personality*, Dorsey Press, Homewood, Ill.

—— and Whiting, B. B. (1975), 'Aloofness and Intimacy of Husbands and Wives: A Cross Cultural Study', *Ethos*, 3 (2), 183–207.

7 The Role of the Family in the Process of Entry to Marriage in Asia

LITA J. DOMINGO AND ELIZABETH M. KING

Cross-national analyses of age at marriage have shown that although universal marriage generally characterizes Asian societies, significant changes in the traditional pattern of early marriage have been registered. The changes are evident not only among countries experiencing high rates of economic growth such as the Republic of Korea but also in less developed countries such as Nepal and Pakistan. According to D. P. Smith (1980: 3), within five years ending in 1978, the singulate mean age at marriage (SMAM) for females increased by about 0.3 of a year (to 23.2) in the Republic of Korea, by 0.1 (to 17.1) in Nepal, and by more than one year (to 19.8) in Pakistan. Utilizing census and survey data from 14 countries, P. C. Smith (1980) demonstrates that this transition commenced at various times and at varying speeds. He notes that the 'mosaic of Asian nuptiality levels is structured spatially' (1980: 71). The lowest age at which a noticeable proportion of females marries in South Asia is 10.2 years. In South-east Asia and in East Asia the corresponding estimates are 13.1 and 18.4 years. Although by 1970 the proportion ever married in the childbearing ages varied substantially across the countries, all 14 of the countries examined showed a decline in this ratio, suggesting a trend towards later marriages. Smith further reports that delayed marriage has been as much a rural as an urban phenomenon.

A unique perspective on this transition phenomenon is offered by a comparison of the nuptial patterns of two generations. Using data from the Asian Marriage Survey, King, *et al.* (1986) show the cohort trend of rising age at marriage among women from Indonesia, Pakistan, and the Philippines. They found that the fraction of women who were married by age 15 was about 60 per cent and 43 per cent of women born in 1930 or earlier in Pakistan and Indonesia, respectively. The corresponding figure for the Philippines was 10 per cent. Among younger women—say, those born between 1951 and 1960—fewer than 10 per cent in Indonesia and fewer than 5 per cent in the Philippines were married by age 15.

We wish to thank Dr. John B. Casterline for sharing his ideas on the subject and Ms. Corazon P. Narvaez and Ms. Eileen M. Sarmiento for their assistance in the preparation of the data. We are also grateful for partial support from a Hewlitt Foundation grant to the Labor and Population Programme of the RAND Corporation and for support from the Demographic Research and Development Foundation, Inc.

This observed transition has several implications that make nuptiality an important policy variable. In Asia, marriage often signals the initiation of the process of family formation, as little childbearing occurs outside it. This reasoning has opened a route for policy intervention that can be an effective supplement to family planning. Its value as a policy variable is likewise enhanced by the fact that the timing and frequency of marital unions affect not only subsequent fertility but also the potential roles a woman may occupy during her lifetime. With this broad appeal for policy, it is therefore important to understand fully the process of entry to marriage so that the kinds of interventions that can be implemented are better specified.

In this chapter we seek explanations for recent changes in nuptial patterns in Asia, utilizing a theoretical framework that draws its major elements from recent expositions using the family as the pivotal institution as well as from those that focus on aggregate shifts brought about by economic development and demographic changes that bear on the availability of marriage partners. From this discussion a set of propositions will be drawn and empirically tested with data from the Asian Marriage Survey.

Conceptual Models

Past efforts at understanding this shift towards later ages at marriage and the variability of nuptiality patterns among and within nations have led to useful generalizations and resulted in the development of useful typologies. But a major limitation of these efforts is that often only aggregate data are available. Nevertheless, these efforts have helped specify some of the broad mechanisms underlying nuptiality changes. For example, Dixon's (1971) framework, which identifies feasibility, availability, and desirability as factors, allows the analysis of a spectrum of issues including those that are demographic or economic (e.g. occupational structure, absorptive capacity of the economy), and social (e.g. undesirability of remaining unmarried or childless). P. C. Smith's (1980) dichotomy of factors—the 'traditional village matrix' and 'modernizing' influences—provides an alternative approach. Smith found modernizing factors, specifically female literacy and urbanization, to have a positive effect on age at marriage. This same effect is alluded to in the study by King, *et al.* (1986), which shows that growth in educational attainment over time and shifts away from traditional occupations are associated with later marriage of younger cohorts. Others too have tried to explain individual variations in nuptiality in terms of socio-economic attainment and background characteristics and have drawn the same general conclusion that modernizing forces delay entry to marriage (e.g. Chamratrithirong, 1978; Von Elm, 1978; Domingo, 1982). Although the effect of these modernizing factors has been validated and revalidated with different data sets, these theoretical constructs and analyses fall short of representing the dynamic process of entry to marriage owing to lack of data on explanatory variables other than schooling, work experience, and parental characteristics.

Lack of appropriate data is not the only constraint in nuptiality analysis. A more adequate framework is needed that would transcend the static typologies and reflect the dynamism of the nuptial decision process. In such a framework the family would be the pivotal institution. The family is particularly relevant to the decision to marry in Asia because it has a strong influence on individual members' behaviour.

Caldwell's (1976) restatement of the demographic transition theory provides convincing arguments for examining variations in marriage timing decisions within the context of intergenerational flows of wealth. The fundamental thesis of this theory is that fertility behaviour in both pre-transitional and post-transitional societies is economically rational within the context of socially determined economic goals and within the bounds set largely by biological and psychological factors. Viewing the family as at the institutional centre of society, Caldwell posits a kind of development threshold or 'great divide' between traditional and modern family systems, a reversal of the long-standing traditional pattern of within-family intergenerational transfers of wealth and resources to parents from children.

Cherlin, *et al.* (1985) suggest that Caldwell's wealth flow framework can be expressed in the degree to which marriage is by free choice or constrained by older kin. Focusing primarily on the value of daughters to parents, they identify four sets of values, noting that the setting will determine which values are stressed. Where daughters are valued for their reproductive capacity, early marriage is preferred. Where daughters are valued primarily for their productive contributions to the family, late entry to marriage is to the parents' advantage. Where marriages are considered important in forming alliances, early marriage enables families to seize opportunities from such alliances as soon as possible. If the 'affective individualism' of daughters is valued, the resulting marriage timing may be moderately late because daughters may have to go through a lengthy search for a spouse.

The degree of influence a family has on its individual members is determined largely by how much the family controls the resources and provides for the needs of its members. Parents, therefore, should have considerable influence over the younger generation. To understand the dynamics behind this relationship between generations, Ryder (1984) highlights the processes of socialization and social control that ensure that the will of the society is served by its individual members. Acceptance of the terms of the social contract by members of the younger generation may be due in part to their expectation that their interest will be served in like manner by subsequent generations.

It is clear from these recent explorations of the family that a fuller understanding of changes in individual behaviour can be achieved only if they are viewed within a dynamic framework involving family interrelationships as well as family responses to opportunities and constraints brought about by the wider process of development.

Yet Another Theoretical Framework: Focus on the Family

In this section we discuss a conceptual framework for analysing nuptiality that focuses on the family's behaviour and links this to aggregate phenomena. We start by reviewing existing aggregate-level hypotheses.

One hypothesis (labelled A in Figure 7.1) states that economic change may bring about a rise in the work opportunities of women, and that this in turn delays marriage. Economic development, which includes a change in industrial composition, often creates a demand for new labour skills or labour shortages in certain areas or skills. As has been the case in economies such as Hong Kong and the Republic of Korea, an important repercussion of these shifts has been a rise in the demand for female labour. An increase in the work opportunities of women and consequently in female wages affects family labour allocation by increasing the labour-force participation of married and of young, unmarried women.

This description of aggregate change in nuptiality abstracts from the complexities of the macro-process. Economic development and the resulting social change do not occur simultaneously in all areas but instead generally take place unevenly over time and space. One would expect shifts to occur first in urban areas or other better-endowed areas before spreading to rural areas.[1] Thus, the influences of economic change on the labour-market opportunities of women and their nuptial patterns are likely to be similarly spatially distributed. Through the process of diffusion of social change, however, even families and individuals residing outside the realm of economic progress may be affected. The strength of the social change in the 'leader' areas and the speed of the diffusion process determine how quickly these families alter their values affecting nuptiality.[2]

A second hypothesis about aggregate change (labelled B in Figure 7.1) is based on demographic shifts. These shifts may consist of changing sex ratios and birth cohort sizes that cannot sustain existing nuptial patterns of, say, very early marriage for women and later marriage for men. The effect of such shifts on the availability of marriage partners may not be obvious to families and individuals immediately. But failure to adjust nuptial patterns quickly will result in failure to marry; these are members of the 'squeezed' generation. With learning and adjustment, new nuptial patterns emerge.

These two frameworks do not capture the changes within the family that result from aggregate phenomena. These aggregate phenomena are likely to affect aspects of family politics and economy—the allocation of labour within the family, the value of daughters relative to sons, the socio-economic position

---

[1]   An exception is if a sufficiently higher social status is accorded to observing traditional nuptial practices. Moreover, some nuptial practices may be less costly to change than others.

[2]   This process is similar to that involved in the dissemination of fertility control. Among individual women it is said that those who are more highly educated are likely to be more susceptible to change and thus act as 'leaders'.

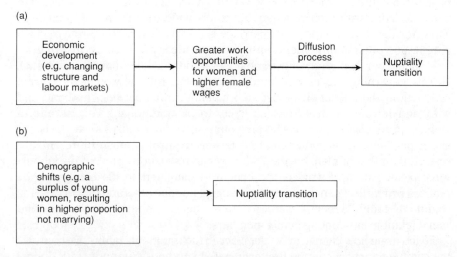

Fig. 7.1 Aggregate Hypotheses for Nuptiality Transition

of the nuclear family in the extended family system, and expectations of parents for future generations. These effects on the family in turn would modify its view of nuptiality.

The family may view nuptiality in several ways. Nuptiality is an important mechanism by which the family extends itself into future generations. It is also a means by which the family may form and strengthen its linkages with other family units within the same generation for the purpose of making social alliances or securing additional family labour for market or home production. The relative importance of these functions may change with macro-changes and imply a corresponding nuptiality transition.

In the following sections we sketch the mechanisms by which change occurs in nuptial patterns. We start with the premises of a model that, although simple, contains most elements of existing theories of nuptiality. The model emphasizes the links between nuptiality and other family behaviour, and between aggregate socio-economic phenomena and the family.

We define a traditional family as that in which nuptial decisions are made primarily by family elders and not by the individual who marries. Thus, the choice of marriage partner and the timing of marriage are made in large part with the view of serving the family's or the elders' interests. (This assumption, however, does not preclude the possibility that the individual's interest is also served.) If the primary purpose of marriage is progeny, it makes sense for the family to encourage early marriage for either sons or daughters and to ensure fecund marriage partners for them. If its principal goal is to harness additional family labour for, say, farm production, then it makes sense for the family to push for daughters to marry early (given that married daughters are expected to continue living with their parents), but to dissuade sons from early marriage. Thus, for the traditional family, marriage is a social institution through which parents and other family elders control the resources provided by offspring.

In such a family it is not only nuptial views and practices that are traditional. Norms governing the use of family labour, the role of women in market production, the allocation of decision-making power between husband and wife, and fertility control are also likely to be traditional.[3] The latitude of women, particularly of those who are young and unmarried, to make decisions about production, reproduction, and fertility control is much more circumscribed than that of men. Further, when social restrictions prevent the labour-force participation of women, the benefit of daughters to the family may be realized primarily when they marry. Changing nuptial views and practices in the traditional family depends therefore upon changes in family economics and social relationships among family members.

To illustrate how change may take place in the traditional family, we consider the stimulus to change in the first aggregate hypothesis. Suppose work opportunities for women expand and female wages rise. Change may occur within the same generation, or it may come only in the next generation. Among traditional families directly affected by such economic stimuli, those that will benefit most and suffer the least social and economic costs are more likely to respond by allowing their female members to enter the labour-market or by increasing the work hours of those already employed. Social tensions are likely to occur both within the family and between the family and the community owing to this change or if market work conflicts with social norms restricting the behaviour of women.

Value of Daughters

Since our interest is in nuptiality, we focus on daughters and changes in the roles and values that parents see in them. Suppose that in the traditional family described above the value of daughters lies primarily in the match they make in marriage. Parents and family elders may deem it extremely important to control the outcome of their daughters' marriages. For example, it may be in the interest of parents to arrange early marriages for their daughters to extend the period during which the benefits of a propitious marriage can be reaped. Aggregate phenomena that affect the possible benefits that daughters bring to the family are likely to influence also parents' views about having control over their daughters' marriages. However, parents will be unwilling to give up control over those marriages unless they find alternative means of control over their daughters' resources.

In Asian families the ties that bind sons to their parents both socially and

---

[3] For example, the 'purdah' system in South Asia which prevents women from working in jobs that involve interaction with male co-workers clearly limits work opportunities for women.

economically tend to be strong. Examples are Chinese families in which sons are expected to reside with their parents after marriage and to provide support for parents in their old age (Greenhalgh, 1985). Such ties commonly function to provide economic support for ageing parents or sometimes to ensure continuity of parents' enterprises such as a farm or a business. In some cases these informal contracts between sons and parents are designed to be mutually beneficial, with sons expecting to receive greater resources from parents and parents expecting to receive support from sons in the future. In other cases these informal contracts may be quite exploitative in that sons transfer greater resources to their parents than they receive. Sons may be willing to bear this responsibility if they can expect their own offspring to extend support to them in the future. Their confidence in the future in turn depends on the strength of social control over the younger generation.

Parents who want to delay their daughters' marriages may not be able to do so beyond some age, yet may wish to continue receiving support from the daughters. Under such circumstances, if parents can apply ties and social control to daughters even after the daughters marry (as with sons), they may be more willing to surrender control over their daughters' marriages. However, it may be difficult for parents to achieve that goal in those cultures in which daughters who marry virtually cease to be members of their parents' families and become members only of their husbands' families. If parents are able to delay sufficiently their daughters' marriages, having social control to ensure future support from daughters is not too important.

Human Capital

As socio-economic development proceeds, the types of income opportunities open to women may require greater human capital (e.g. education or training). Thus, the cost to parents of benefiting from their daughters' work would include not only social friction but also the economic cost of increasing their daughters' human capital. Unless parents can partake in the future benefits of their daughters' human capital or are able to recoup education or training costs, daughters will have to incur the associated costs of higher human capital up front. Social contracts between daughters and parents thus become more important as greater human capital is needed for female labour-force participation. Or, if future transfers of income from daughters are risky, parents may push for later marriage for their daughters so that they themselves can reap the benefits of the increased human capital sooner.

As parents become willing to defray all or part of the costs of increasing the human capital of daughters, their allocation of family resources between sons and daughters becomes more equal. Indeed, another result of aggregate socio-economic change may be a narrowing of the gap in the relative status of women and men within the family with respect to decision-making and access to resources.

Fertility

One would also expect the changes in family dynamics outlined above to have implications for the fertility goals and outcomes of daughters. Fertility is likely to decline as age at marriage rises. This hypothesis is consistent with observed trends in Asian countries in which past fertility decrease has been associated primarily with later age at marriage of women. As we have already noted, however, reproduction may be the principal goal of early marriage in the traditional family, for various reasons. Children are an important source of family labour in their youth or adulthood; they are also looked upon as insurance against the risk of ill health and as a source of economic support in their parents' old age. As long as children serve these functions and no better alternative exists for parents (such as efficient capital markets or health insurance), women will not be willing to delay marriage at the cost of jeopardizing their reproductive goals. Hence, daughters of marriageable age, looking into their future, may themselves forgo the work opportunities available to them in order to marry and bear children.

Empirical Evidence

From the discussion above we derive four propositions that we will attempt to test using both the Asian Marriage Survey (AMS) and findings from recent studies based on the survey. Ideally, a test of these propositions requires longitudinal data on marriage values, expectations, and outcomes of particular demographic groups as well as on macro-social and -economic variables. An alternative, though imperfect, test is to compare countries at different stages of socio-economic development. An important limitation of the latter is that the socio-cultural foundations may be so different as to make comparisons difficult. One may ask, for example, whether Pakistan at a higher level of development would ever resemble the Philippines. Perhaps a more appropriate test is to compare Pakistan's urban areas with its rural areas. Given the limited data available, in the following exploratory analysis we rely mainly on inter-country and inter-regional comparisons.

The Asian Marriage Survey

One feature of the AMS that is most useful for this analysis is that it contains data on the parents of the respondents. Furthermore, the respondents were asked about their educational and marital aspirations for their own children. The data enable us to use information about three generations to test the following four propositions:

1. The pattern of early marriage for women is more prevalent in societies where the primary benefits of daughters to the family come from the social and economic alliances they form with other families or from their reproductive outcomes.

2. Aggregate shifts that expand the economic activities of women in a traditional society enhance the productive value of daughters to the family and lessen parental pressure for their early marriage.

3. In societies where daughters are valued for their productive contributions to the family, parents are more likely to give up control over their daughters' marriage decisions. In exchange, they form social contracts with daughters that (similar to those with sons) ensure the transfer of future potential resources back to themselves. Delay in entry to marriage extends this resource flow to the family.

4. Parents are more willing to allocate family resources to daughters where social contracts with daughters are successful. Such co-operation results in greater freedom for daughters to choose when and whom they marry, which in turn generally results in a longer period of search for a mate.

The AMS was conducted in Indonesia, Pakistan, the Philippines, and Thailand among married women between the ages 15 and 45 and among a sample of their husbands.[4] In each country, samples of households were systematically drawn to represent three distinct socio-economic groups—a rural sample, an urban lower-class or 'squatter' sample, and an urban middle-class sample. The rural samples were obtained by selecting one village or a small cluster of villages in each country's major language area.

In Pakistan the rural and urban samples were drawn from the Punjab, a province that strongly reflects Muslim customs and culture. The province's capital city of Lahore provided the two urban samples, and a small number of villages (*mouzas*) in two adjoining districts provided the rural sample. The samples were drawn from a total of 20 census enumeration blocks in the urban area and from 10 villages in the rural districts of Kasur and Sheikhupura. In Indonesia the urban sample was drawn from Semarang, which is the administrative capital of the populous province of Central Java. The rural survey site was a hill village about 30 kilometres south of Semarang. In the Philippines the urban survey areas were several villages (*barangays*) in the districts of Pandacan, Paco, and Santa Ana in the capital city of Manila. The three contiguous barangays of Donación, Sulukan, and Marungko in the municipality of Angat in Bulacan Province were selected as the rural survey site. The province of Bulacan adjoins Manila to the north.

A common questionnaire was administered that covered a wide range of topics, including socio-cultural aspects of marriage, family of orientation, and aspirations for children. The survey, therefore, yielded a rich body of data on

---

[4] Thailand was not included in the analysis.

marriage, especially with its attention to cultural variables and individual life-history events, topics that hitherto had not been adequately treated in demographic surveys.

Family Alliances and Early Marriage

The AMS countries represent a continuum with respect to timing of marriage. At one end are the Punjabi and Javanese women, who marry early, while at the other end are the Thai and Filipino women, who tend to marry late. From Table 7.1 it is likewise clear that one feature that distinguishes the Punjabi women (and to a certain extent the Indonesians) from the others is the very important role played by parents in mate selection. Virtually all of the village respondents indicated that their parents had chosen their spouses for them. In these societies the main actors in the marriage decision are the older kin, who are motivated to control the nature of transfers between families. Juxtaposing these two patterns lends support to our first proposition.

These observations are consistent with ethnographic material for South Asia and Pakistan that emphasize the patriarchal control over resources and the important role of women as signifiers of alliance between families. As Fricke, Syed, and Smith (1986) point out, 'marriage process' variables significantly affect marriage timing. These processes include the degree of kinship distance between families before marriage, dowry values, the relative landed status of families, and the direction of wealth flows of marriage. On the basis of the issues of property transfer and knowledge of the woman's family, Fricke, *et al.* hypothesized that the youngest ages at marriage would be found in marriages between previously unrelated families, followed by those within the *biraderi* or patriline. Marriage between *rishtadari* and *vartan* groups (related persons outside the *biraderi*, and persons linked only by friendship and exchange relationships, respectively) would generally occur at the latest ages and at similar ages of wife and husband because of the structural similarity of property transfer and faith in a family's standing between groups. This hypothesis received support as controlling for the marriage process variables and selected background data. The earliest marriers, categorized by relationship, were those whose marriages were contracted by strangers (16.5 years), followed by those married within the patriline (16.9 years). The latest marriers were those who married non-patrilineally related kin or into *vartan* groups (17.7 years). In addition, Fricke, *et al.* show that the value of the dowry is positively associated with marriage age. Aside from signifying the transfer of property from the wife's natal home to her husband's, the authors assert that it serves, in part, to enhance the value of a daughter and also to offset her devaluation from biological ageing.

Although a substantial majority among the Pakistani women reported they had had no say in the selection of their mates, this practice may be slowly changing. More than 17 per cent of the better-educated and possibly more

TABLE 7.1. Mean Age at Marriage and Percentage Distribution of Selected Indicators of Mate Selection and Courtship, by Country, Demographic Characteristics, and Socio-economic Status

Age and indicator	Pakistan			Indonesia			Thailand			Philippines		
	Rural	Urban lower-class	Urban middle-class	Rural	Urban lower-class	Urban middle-class	Rural	Urban lower-class	Urban middle-class	Rural	Urban lower-class	Urban middle-class
Mean age at marriage	17.2	18.2	20.1	16.3	17.2	18.4	21.9	20.1	22.5	21.4	21.4	22.7
Role of parents in mate selection												
Parents' decision	98.7	90.5	78.7	52.8	38.6	26.2	11.1	11.5	13.5	1.4	1.0	2.4
Parents' decision with daughter's approval	1.3	7.8	17.4	20.0	9.6	18.0	17.9	7.9	11.8	2.2	2.4	1.6
Daughter's decision with parents' approval	0.0	1.0	1.6	18.9	27.1	45.5	14.6	11.4	17.4	34.2	22.0	36.0
Daughter's decision	0.0	0.8	2.2	8.3	24.7	10.3	56.4	69.2	57.4	62.2	74.6	60.0
Frequency of meeting with husband prior to marriage												
Never	50.8	52.6	50.0	36.3	24.8	8.3	2.9	1.9	1.5	0.0	0.0	0.4
Once	2.3	2.8	5.5	6.9	10.1	6.2	1.4	1.1	1.3	1.6	2.9	2.0
A few times	12.1	16.2	13.2	21.2	26.9	33.0	44.4	32.1	35.2	15.4	27.2	9.4
Often	34.8	28.4	31.3	35.6	38.2	52.5	51.3	64.9	62.0	83.0	69.9	88.2
Formal engagement												
Yes	59.7	63.7	56.8	98.8	90.6	91.7	12.8	19.2	54.4	39.7	43.3	55.9
No	40.3	36.3	43.2	1.2	9.4	8.3	87.2	80.8	45.6	60.3	56.7	44.1
Number of other men who courted respondent												
None	na[1]	na	na	90.2	86.5	75.9	18.4	16.5	24.5	3.2	5.7	4.1
One	na	na	na	8.6	11.5	17.1	6.1	10.0	9.6	5.4	13.8	7.8
Two or more	na	na	na	1.2	2.0	7.0	75.5	73.5	65.9	91.3	80.5	88.2

[1] not applicable. Pakistani respondents were not asked whether they had been courted by other men.

Source: Cheung, *et al.*, 1985: 298.

modern women in the urban-middle sample said they had had some participation in deciding whom they would marry by approving their parents' choice. If this urban pattern is indicative of the direction that will be taken in rural areas as development occurs and as women receive more education, then it may be expected that Pakistani women will gradually be making more decisions for themselves. The pace at which this change occurs will depend largely on the rate at which women become part of the development process.

The Expanding Economic Activities of Women and the Changing Value of Daughters

The changing role of women in the economy referred to in our second proposition is indicated by the increase not only in their level of participation in the work-force but also and more specifically in their involvement in non-farm activities. Increased participation of women may be inferred from Table 7.2, which compares the pattern observed for mothers and sisters of the respondents. The data provide clues to shifts in the types of work participation of women over time. These shifts, however, confound the effects of changes in the aggregate demand from female labour as well as cohort differences in the levels of human capital of mothers and daughters. Table 7.2 demonstrates the growing importance of non-agricultural work in the Philippines and Indonesia. This change is likewise evident in both the urban and rural sectors. For example, whereas only 13 per cent of the mothers in rural areas of the Philippines had blue-collar occupations, about one-third of their daughters were employed in those occupations. With increased opportunities for non-agricultural work even in the rural areas, more women may be drawn into the labour-market, where their services could be better compensated. In Indonesia the same increase in blue-collar occupations among daughters is observed, although to a lesser degree (4 per cent to 9 per cent), whereas in Pakistan there is virtually no change in the 2 per cent level of participation by the two generations.

From these broad patterns it may be inferred that with greater participation by women in the non-traditional, non-farm occupations, the productive value of the younger generation increases. Looking at the case of the Philippines, which is characterized by late marriage, it would be interesting to examine to what extent family influence accounts for the delayed marriage phenomenon because early marriage could curtail the flow of benefits from the wages of working daughters to their families. The productive value of daughters underlying such influence may actually complement the value of their 'affective individualism' (Cherlin, *et al.*, 1985), which may be translated into such activities as the pursuit of higher education and labour-force participation. These activities give the daughters fuller control over their own lives, including mate selection and the timing of marriage. The Pakistan experience, in contrast, implies that with daughters' low levels of participation in gainful work, their productive value ranks lower than, say, their alliance value.

TABLE 7.2. Percentage Distribution of AMS Respondents' Siblings (15 Years Old and Older) and Mothers, by Socio-economic Status, Country, and Type of Occupation

Country and type of occupation	Respondent's sisters			Respondent		
	Urban middle-class	Urban lower-class	Rural	Urban middle-class	Urban lower-class	Rural
Pakistan						
With occupation	11.0	6.0	4.2	1.5	3.6	4.6
White-collar	7.6	2.1	0.4	1.0	0.7	0.0
Blue-collar	3.4	3.9	1.8	0.0	2.6	1.7
Farm	0.0	0.0	2.0	0.5	0.2	2.9
With no occupation	88.9	94.1	95.8	98.5	96.4	95.4
(Number)	(437)	(725)	(560)	(204)	(457)	(350)
Indonesia						
With occupation	34.9	39.1	68.9	47.0	50.8	88.0
White-collar	18.9	17.6	24.2	25.7	18.9	36.3
Blue-collar	8.5	11.9	9.2	5.1	5.9	4.3
Farm	7.4	9.7	35.5	16.3	26.1	47.5
With no occupation	65.1	60.9	31.1	53.0	49.2	22.0
(Number)	(639)	(455)	(802)	(486)	(456)	(579)
Philippines						
With occupation	42.0	37.5	55.1	34.4	35.5	33.1
White-collar	30.1	15.5	16.0	20.3	11.6	13.5
Blue-collar	10.2	18.4	32.5	12.5	17.0	13.0
Farm	1.7	3.5	6.5	1.6	6.9	6.6
With no occupation	58.0	62.5	44.9	65.6	64.5	66.9
(Number)	(773)	(593)	(981)	(320)	(318)	(392)

Source: King, *et al.*, 1986: 23.

The involvement of daughters in economic activities, especially in those that would take them out of their homes and provide monetary income, enhances their value to their families. The family interest is served not only through the economic rewards shared with the other members but also through prestige derived from gainful work. Given their productive worth, coupled with their increased status within the family, daughters perhaps earn some amount of independence from parental control. One indication of that independence may be the freedom to choose their marriage partners. A simple cross-tabulation of women's occupations before marriage with the mate selection variable from the AMS provides some support for this hypothesized relationship (Table 7.3). In Indonesia, where 45 per cent of the women reported that their parents had played a major role in choosing their spouses, a substantial proportion of the

TABLE 7.3. Participation of Daughters in the Choice of Husbands, by Country, and Daughters' Occupations before Marriage

Participation in choice and occupation before marriage	Indonesia		Pakistan		Philippines	
	%	(No.)	%	(No.)	%	(No.)
All women						
Chose husbands with parents' approval						
Farm	13.5	(148)	0.0	(44)	48.0	(25)
Blue-collar	26.2	(367)	0.7	(147)	36.1	(402)
White-collar	42.4	(33)	3.8	(26)	41.0	(175)
Housework	26.7	(419)	0.4	(753)	26.8	(260)
Chose husbands alone						
Farm	4.0	(148)	0.0	(44)	48.0	(25)
Blue-collar	22.1	(367)	0.7	(147)	61.2	(402)
White-collar	21.2	(33)	3.8	(26)	54.9	(175)
Housework	11.2	(419)	0.8	(753)	69.6	(260)
Rural women						
Chose husbands with parents' approval						
Farm	14.3	(126)	0.0	(36)	40.9	(22)
Blue-collar	20.4	(157)	0.0	(32)	37.1	(256)
White-collar	33.3	(12)	0.0	(1)	35.7	(42)
Housework	17.8	(247)	0.0	(278)	25.0	(64)
Chose husbands alone						
Farm	3.2	(126)	0.0	(36)	54.6	(22)
Blue-collar	7.0	(157)	0.0	(32)	61.3	(256)
White-collar	33.3	(12)	0.0	(1)	59.5	(42)
Housework	9.7	(247)	0.8	(278)	65.6	(64)

Source: AMS.

urban middle-class women who had worked in blue-collar occupations prior to marriage said they had chosen their husbands alone (24 per cent) or with their parents' approval (39 per cent). Farm workers, who were most likely to have worked on their families' farms or with their families, reported less independence in their choice of husbands than did women in other occupations. In fact, proportionately more housekeepers than farm workers had participated directly in the choice of their husbands. In Pakistan very small proportions of women reported having a hand in the selection of their husbands. Given the low work participation among these women, the proportions shown are probably unreliable. As expected, the level of independence exhibited by Filipino women in mate selection exceeded that of women in the other two countries. The occupational categories, however, do not show the distinct advantage of the women who had held jobs over those who had merely helped with housekeeping. The selection of husbands may have become almost entirely, if not entirely, the privilege of Filipino women and is generally not conditioned by their productive role in the family.

Another aspect of the effects of aggregate changes on women may be seen in improvements in the educational attainment of women. Cohort differences in educational levels documented in national statistics reflect individual families' responses to changes in educational opportunities and economic benefits from education. Higher educational attainment indicates parents' growing commitment to the education of their children. An important consideration is that, with changes in the occupational structure, education increasingly determines labour-force participation. The increasing trend across birth cohorts in the three countries, which is similar to that observed from census data, is documented in the study by King, *et al.* (1986). A substantial fraction of females in the oldest birth cohort (those born in or before 1930) left school after completing grade six. This drop-out rate fell rapidly for younger cohorts, with younger Javanese women staying in school longer than contemporary Punjabi women. The youngest cohort (born after 1965) appears not to have done better than the next older cohort; this is largely because, during the survey, some of them were too young to have completed school. In the Philippines, although the trend has been towards higher education levels, the change across cohorts has been less dramatic than in Indonesia and Pakistan.

These patterns observed in the national level mirror the changes occurring within the families. King, *et al.* (1986) report in Pakistan, for example, progress from mothers to daughters: in 48 per cent of urban-middle families, 100 per cent of mothers had zero years of schooling, compared with less than 16 per cent of daughters. In rural families 86 per cent of daughters had not completed their schooling, compared with 99 per cent of mothers. In Indonesia and the Philippines the rise in education over time is indicated by the higher mean number of years of schooling for daughters than for mothers. King, *et al.* further observe the persistence of disparities across the socio-economic samples in these countries. Young women in the urban areas achieved more education than their rural counterparts, and in Indonesia the urban–rural gap had widened. However, a positive trend is that gender differences had been reduced, especially in the Philippines.

The educational advancement of daughters must have resulted partly from the increasing participation of women in productive activities. Corresponding changes within the family may have likewise occurred. In the allocation of family resources for the education of children, for example, the daughter's potential for production could positively influence parental decisions. This is perhaps part of what is reflected in Table 7.4. When the respondents were asked what they thought was the minimum amount of education that children would need to make a 'satisfactory living', most of the Filipino and Indonesian women, regardless of their residence or socio-economic status, gave the same answers for boys and girls. Rural and urban lower-class Pakistani women favoured

TABLE 7.4. AMS Respondents' Opinions of the Amount of Education Required for Boys Relative to Girls

Education for boys relative to girls	Percentage distributions of responses		
	Indonesia	Pakistan	Philippines
All socio-economic groups			
Boys higher	16.4	56.1	4.8
Boys and girls equal	82.6	39.9	95.0
Girls higher	1.0	4.1	0.2
(Number)	(1,587)	(1,011)	(1,041)
Rural			
Boys higher	17.6	64.4	5.6
Boys and girls equal	80.7	29.9	94.4
Girls higher	1.7	5.7	0.0
(Number)	(601)	(351)	(395)
Urban-low			
Boys higher	17.0	55.5	4.9
Boys and girls equal	82.4	40.8	94.4
Girls higher	0.6	3.7	0.6
(Number)	(489)	(456)	(324)
Urban-middle			
Boys higher	14.5	43.1	3.7
Boys and girls equal	85.1	54.9	96.3
Girls higher	0.4	2.0	0.0
(Number)	(497)	(204)	(322)

Source: AMS.

higher education for boys than for girls; but more than half of the urban-middle respondents gave the same estimate for both sexes, possibly indicating changing attitudes regarding the provision of opportunities for the advancement for daughters even in that traditional society.

Parental Control through Social Contracts

Our third proposition suggests that with the changing value of daughters, instead of parents exercising direct control, social contracts that ensure that the will of the family is served are made between children and parents. It is conceivable that part of the parents' side of the arrangement is the provision of education for their children. The children are expected in turn to support their parents, especially with their improved skills for productive work. Among the terms imposed by this contract could be the delay of marriage by daughters, not only to enable them to complete the desired level of education but also to ensure that the parents benefit from their daughters' economic activity.

From the patterns on mate selection described above, it may be stated that it is in the Philippines and Thailand where the AMS revealed the least parental control over daughters. That those countries likewise showed higher levels of educational attainment than Pakistan further implies that parents had been investing more in their daughters' education in those countries. The AMS data do not, however, contain the information necessary to test our third hypothesis. Instead, we cite findings from the National Demographic Survey (NDS) conducted in the Philippines in 1983, where the ever-married women respondents were asked whether or not they had given support to their parents before and after they married. Relating their responses to their ages at marriage, Domingo (1985) reports the appearance of a direct relationship between giving support to parents and age at marriage; that is, those who reported having done so tended to marry later (Table 7.5). Moreover, proportionally more of the late marriers supported their parents prior to marrying. This pattern lends support to our third proposition, as some delay in entry to marriage may have been effected through compliance with the terms of the social contract between daughters and their parents. The delay in marriage may be a necessary condition since, as the Philippine data also show, the proportion of women providing support to their parents declined after marriage from 28 per cent to 10 per cent. Perhaps the mechanism still involves adherence to the traditional expectation that daughters will support their parents; but rather than through direct parental control, it is achieved through developmental inputs that ultimately benefit the younger generation.

TABLE 7.5. Percentage Distribution of Ever-Married Women by Whether or Not They Gave Support to Parents before Marriage and by Timing of Marriage: Philippines

Gave support to parents before marriage?	Timing of marriage			Total	Number
	Early (< 18)	On time (18–24)	Late (25+)		
% distribution by row					
Yes	16.9	61.3	21.7	100.0	(1,221)
No	27.2	57.9	14.8	99.9	(3,129)
% distribution by column					
Yes	19.6	29.2	36.4	27.9	
No	80.3	70.6	63.5	71.7	
Total	99.9	99.8	99.9		
(Number)	(1,060)	(2,567)	(731)	(4,363)	

Source: Domingo, 1985.

Success of Social Contracts and Greater Freedom of Choice for Women

To test the fourth proposition, that parents are more willing to allocate family resources where social contracts with daughters are successful, we focus on the pattern of responses given to the AMS question about whether or not the respondents and their husbands would choose their daughter's spouse. This question was asked of those who had unmarried daughters 10 years old or older. More than 60 per cent of the samples from the three countries were therefore excluded from this analysis. On the basis of current practice, we expected the Philippines to have the largest proportion of respondents saying that they would not choose their daughters' future spouses. This expectation was borne out by the data, as almost all the women interviewed (90 per cent) said they would not be the main decision-makers (Table 7.6). The demographic and socio-economic differentials in the percentages giving this response suggest that this attitude may have evolved through time. One clue is the lower percentages among rural versus urban respondents and among older women (those 40 years old and older) compared with younger ones. It is possible that greater freedom for daughters comes with parents' realization that the family's interest is served in ways other than through making sure that daughters marry men the parents choose.

The high proportions observed for Indonesia clearly indicate the pattern of decline in parental control over daughters. This sign of change is likewise in evidence in Pakistan, where 22 per cent of urban middle-class respondents said they would allow their daughters to choose their husbands, compared with 5 per cent and 8 per cent of rural and urban lower-class women, respectively. More women who had had at least some secondary education than those who had not also expressed their intention of diverging from the traditional practice of arranged marriages. Some of those who had married later and who had white-collar occupations likewise expressed this non-traditional attitude. It should be underscored, however, that the women expressing this modern intention are still in the minority. The majority of Pakistani women had had their husbands selected by their parents, and that experience seems to have strongly influenced their attitudes towards their own role in the selection of their daughters' husbands. Six of the 10 women who approved their parents' choice and 2 of 8 who chose their husbands together with their parents reported that they would choose their daughters' husbands. These numbers are of course very small and do not warrant generalization.

One hypothesis that relates to the fourth proposition is the positive influence of mothers' characteristics on the daughters' choices. It may be argued that mothers' labour-force participation, education, and marriage and their assessment of the benefits derived from those activities bear heavily on family decisions such as the amount of schooling for daughters or the timing of daughters' marriages. Some empirical support for this hypothesis is provided by

TABLE 7.6. AMS Respondents Who Would not Choose Their Daughters' Spouses, by Residence and Socio-economic Indicators

Indicator	Indonesia		Pakistan		Philippines	
	%	(No.)	%	(No.)	%	(No.)
All respondents	82.5	(610)	9.6	(385)	89.7	(321)
Residence and socio-economic status						
Rural	76.5	(226)	4.6	(130)	85.0	(140)
Urban-low	88.5	(165)	7.9	(178)	93.3	(89)
Urban-middle	84.0	(219)	22.1	(77)	93.5	(92)
Education (years)						
0	78.7	(202)	3.2	(251)	*	(4)
1–3	80.4	(87)	*	(5)	94.3	(35)
4–5	75.6	(86)	11.1	(36)	84.6	(65)
6	92.1	(101)	*	(5)	92.2	(90)
7–9	89.9	(79)	26.7	(45)	82.4	(51)
10	81.4	(43)	25.0	(24)	94.1	(34)
11	*	(8)	*	(19)	92.7	(41)
Who chose respondent's spouse						
Parents	78.7	(249)	8.2	(354)	*	(1)
Parents with R's approval	69.8	(53)	*	(10)	*	(3)
R and parents	79.4	(63)	*	(8)	*	(2)
R with parents' approval	87.7	(163)	*	(0)	93.9	(99)
R alone	93.0	(57)	*	(3)	87.6	(209)
Forced	95.2	(21)	*	(6)	*	(5)
Current age						
15–19	*	(0)	*	(1)	*	(0)
20–9	86.7	(60)	*	(27)	*	(12)
30–9	81.8	(325)	10.0	(199)	90.0	(188)
40+	81.7	(224)	8.2	(158)	87.6	(121)
Age at marriage						
<15	*	(14)	3.2	(62)	*	(10)
15–17	*	(28)	6.6	(152)	89.7	(58)
18–19	85.7	(42)	13.5	(83)	91.3	(69)
20–1	84.3	(83)	12.2	(49)	87.1	(85)
22–4	81.9	(105)	25.0	(28)	92.1	(63)
25+	82.9	(105)	*	(11)	88.9	(36)
Current occupation						
Farm	74.3	(61)	*	(28)	81.2	(32)
Blue-collar	76.3	(152)	7.1	(70)	92.2	(77)
White-collar	*	(20)	*	(6)	91.1	(57)
Housework	87.5	(305)	10.1	(278)	89.0	(127)

Note: * Percentage not calculated because of small sample size (N < 30).

Table excludes respondents who did *not* have unmarried daughters 10 years old or older (62 per cent in Indonesia, 62 per cent in Pakistan, and 69 per cent in the Philippines).

Source: AMS.

King, *et al.* (1986). Examining the determinants of the level of daughters' education, they show that, in Indonesia, mothers' education had a significantly positive effect. This effect was larger in the urban middle-class area than in the urban lower-class and rural areas. For example, a 10 per cent rise in mothers' education would raise daughters' education by 1.2 per cent in urban middle-class families, by 0.7 per cent in urban lower-class families, and by 0.37 per cent in rural families. In the Philippines the effect of mothers' education was largest in the urban middle-class sample and smallest in the rural sample. In Pakistan, mothers' education had no discernible effect on daughters' education except in the urban middle-class sample. If the observed trend towards higher education and increasing participation of women in the work-force persists, it is likely that these observed influences of the older generation's characteristics on the younger will acquire greater significance.

Summary and Conclusion

Nuptiality in Asia cannot be fully understood by using theoretical frameworks that assume primacy of individual choice in the timing of marriage and selection of marriage partners. Although greater freedom for the individual exists in some countries, in many others the nuptial choice is a family decision. In this chapter we have discussed the elements of a framework that considers how the family may respond to aggregate changes that influence existing marriage practices and how traditional nuptial practices may give way to modern ones. In our proposed framework nuptiality is not independent of other outcomes for offspring, such as educational attainment and type of occupation. The factors that influence nuptiality are just as likely to affect these other outcomes. Hence, the nuptiality transition in Asia may best be evaluated and predicted if analysed together with these outcomes.

Utilizing data from the Asian Marriage Survey and other studies, we tested four propositions derived from our theoretical framework. The nuptiality experience of Pakistan lends support to our first proposition, which relates early marriage to the important role the daughters play in the formation of social and economic alliances between families. With development and the expansion of women's opportunities for education and labour-force participation, the role that women play in the family expands to include economic production. As reflected by data from the three AMS countries analysed, the observed shifts at the aggregate level are also evident within families as the experience of mothers and daughters are compared. The AMS data show that these shifts are likewise accompanied by more freedom in daughters' choice of husbands. This is especially evident in Indonesia, where nearly half of the non-agricultural working women differed from the average by having directly participated in the decision.

To test empirically the effectiveness of socialization and the formulation of contracts between parents and children is admittedly a difficult task. One indicator that we thought could help operationalize this complex concept was the provision of support to parents. We cited findings from the Philippines showing a positive relationship between parental support prior to marriage and delay in entry into marriage. We view the Philippine experience of delayed nuptiality as partly resulting from the daughters' honouring their social contract with their parents. The success of this arrangement results in parents' granting their daughters more freedom in their nuptiality decisions. With data from the AMS on what respondents perceived their role would be when the time came for their own daughters to marry, we documented the continued practice of freedom of choice among the Filipino women and the changing attitude of second-generation mothers among the majority of the Javanese. The pattern for the Pakistani women appears consistent with their own experience of having had arranged marriages, although some segments of that sample reflected a tendency to deviate from this practice.

This chapter demonstrates that the observed nuptiality transition in Asia reflects dynamic changes within the family as it responds to changing opportunities and constraints in the economy. These aggregate changes have had some effect on resource allocation within the family, and the direction has been favourable for daughters as they are increasingly valued for their productive contributions and not just for their reproductive capacity and for the formation of alliances. Although the traditional expectation persists that members serve the good of family, daughters are increasingly fulfilling that obligation through non-traditional means by providing income and, to a certain extent, prestige. This change has resulted in the loosening of traditional parental control. With continued support from parents in their daughters' development process, it is likely that more Asian daughters will eventually enjoy autonomy in various aspects of decision-making and thus will have more control over their lives.

References

Caldwell, J. C. (1976), 'Toward a Restatement of Demographic Transition Theory', *Population and Development Review*, 2 (3/4), 321–66.

Chamratrithirong, A. (1978), 'Thai Marriage Pattern: An Analysis of the 1970 Census Data', paper presented at the Ninth Summer Seminar in Population, East–West Population Institute, East–West Center, Honolulu.

Cherlin, A. J., Smith, P. C., Fricke, T. E., Domingo, L. J., Adioetomo, S. M., Chamratri-thirong, A., and Syed, S. H. (1985), 'Family Influence on the Timing of Marriage: Evidence from Four Asian Societies', Paper presented at Workshop on Changing Marriage and the Family in Asia, Pattaya, Thailand, 21–5 February.

Cheung, P., Cabigon, J., Chamratrithirong, A., McDonald, P. F., Syed, S., Cherlin, A., and Smith, P. C. (1985), 'Cultural Variations in the Transition to Marriage in Four Asian Societies, in *International Population Conference, Florence, 1985*, vol. iii, International Union for the Scientific Study of Population, Liège.

Dixon, R. B. (1971), 'Explaining Cross-Cultural Variations in Age at Marriage and Proportions Never Marrying', *Population Studies*, 25 (2), 215–33.

Domingo, L. J. (1982), 'Pre-adult Independence: A Life State Analysis on Women of the Philippines', Ph.D. thesis, Harvard University.

—— (1985), 'Cultural Determinants of Nuptiality: Some Empirical Evidences', 1983 National Demographic Survey Paper, No. 10, Population Institute, University of the Philippines, Manila.

Fricke, T. E., Syed, S. H., and Smith, P. C. (1986), 'Rural Punjabi Social Organization and Marriage Timing Strategies in Pakistan', *Demography*, 23 (4), 489–508.

Greenhalgh, S. (1985), 'Sexual Stratification: The Other Side of "Growth with Equity" in East Asia', *Population and Development Review*, 11 (2), 265–314.

King, E. M., Peterson, J. R., Adioetomo, S. M., Domingo, L. J., and Syed, S. H. (1986), *Change in the Status of Women across Generations in Asia*, RAND Corporation, Santa Monica, Calif.

Ryder, N. B. (1984), 'Fertility and Family Structure', in *Fertility and Family: Proceedings of the Expert Group on Fertility and Family*, United Nations, New York.

Smith, D. P. (1980), 'Age at First Marriage', in *Comparative Studies Cross National Summaries*, 7, April 1980, World Fertility Survey, London.

Smith, P. C. (1980), 'Asian Marriage Patterns in Transition', *Journal of Family History*, 5 (1), 56–96.

Von Elm, B. R. (1978), 'Determinants of Age at First Marriage: A Study of West Malaysia', Paper presented at the Annual Meeting of the Population Association of America, Atlanta, Ga.

8 Celibacy, Solitude, and Personal Autonomy: Individual Choice and Social Constraints

ELIZABETH JELIN

To write on celibacy is not an easy task, especially if the aim is to approach it from a positive rather than a residual point of view. Celibacy is usually conceived as that state of the individual in which, although he or she has reached a certain age, no mating has occurred. The Random House Dictionary of the English Language (1966 edition) defines celibacy in this negative or residual manner: '1. state of being unmarried; 2. abstention by vow from marriage; 3. abstention from sexual relations.'

The social norm has always been that at one point in their life course, individuals enter some kind of stable relationship with a member of the other sex, and offspring are the prescribed result of this mating. There have always been accepted exceptions—priests or virgin maids to be offered in sacrifice to the gods—mostly linked to religion. Seen in this light, celibacy is the negative state, one that is the result of not fulfilling socially prescribed norms.

This is also the prevalent view of celibacy in the social sciences. Most writers on the subject accept without questioning the view that marriage is the 'normal' or 'natural' state. Thus, in a recent journal article published in a special issue devoted to spinsterhood, Hufton (1984: 33) asserts that 'All women lived in societies in which marriage and motherhood were regarded as the norm, spinsterhood and infertility as a blight, and in which the notion of the family economy, of the family as a composite working unit permitting the sustenance of the whole, was axiomatic.'

But there is more to this approach. Marriage and motherhood are conceived as the 'normal' state, especially for women, and spinsterhood and bachelorism as anomalous. Thus, an article on spinsterhood in Japan in the same journal concludes by comparing Japan and Western Europe in the following way:

the question posed in this paper is the wrong one. It should not be 'Why are there no spinsters in Japan?' but 'Why are there spinsters in Europe?' Marriage must be inevitable in most preindustrial societies. It is not Japan that is the anomaly, but Western Europe. What perverse economic conditions or religious ideologies forced women to give up their natural and fulfilling roles as wives and mothers and coerced them into barren lives as spinsters? (Cornell, 1984: 338)

From such a perspective, celibacy is a curse, a social fault, something that should be avoided, an intrinsically undesirable state of affairs, and much more so for women than for men.

To what extent is this view a projection of the values of the researcher? To what extent is it a description of a state of affairs so universal and 'natural' that no culture has been able to alter it? This chapter attempts to approach the issue of celibacy in a different way, looking at the changing place of marriage and of celibacy in social and cultural structures. Futhermore, it attempts to place the issue in a wider context of understanding personal autonomy and solitude in various socio-cultural settings.

At the individual level of analysis, this means taking a life-course perspective focusing on the transition from a single to a married state. It implies looking at the ways in which this transition takes place, both the actual practices and the culturally prescribed norms that govern them. It also involves relating this transition to the timing of other events in the life course, such as schooling, work, or household formation (Modell, Furstenberg, and Strong, 1978; Balan, Browning, and Jelin, 1973).

At the institutional level, family systems have to be examined, to explore how celibate and non-celibate members, both men and women, are located in family structures and come to participate in the intra-family division of labour and roles. At the macro-social level, overall value systems and patterns of societal relations—power relations, conflict, and solidarity—are embedded in the ways in which the demographic statistics present the aggregate results of societal processes. Every society has expected, 'normal' social patterns. And in each there is room for exceptions. All societies have prescribed ways to handle cases that do not follow the dominant pattern, creating mechanisms to compensate for 'failures' and for 'accidents' that alter the smooth functioning of the expected life-course patterns of transition. For instance, there are culturally prescribed ways to deal with orphans, and there are inheritance rules for childless persons (Goody, Thirsk, and Thompson, 1976). Bourdieu (1976) analyses the development of marriage strategies to counteract the effects of certain fertility patterns that do not allow for the culturally 'correct' operation of inheritance patterns. Celibacy can have a place in structured patterns of social behaviour linked to it. However, when interpreted in the context of the trends towards individuation and autonomy, its social meaning is altered; from being the exceptional experience it may become one possible pattern of behaviour within a more pluralistic, mainstream set of norms.

Some Demographic Considerations

From a demographic, life-course perspective, celibacy is an initial state, from which people exit. That is, children are born celibate, and after a certain period of time they begin to move into the category of 'married'. The timing of this change varies from culture to culture: in some societies the normative selection of partners and marriage take place at birth, or even before. Of course, actual mating has biological restrictions based on sexual maturity, but patterns of 'early' and 'late' marriage have been detected and studied extensively in historical and contemporary demography (Hajnal, 1965; Dixon, 1971; 1978).

Most demographers have been interested in celibacy and nuptiality because of these states' explanatory role in fertility behaviour. Given the interest in understanding population growth or decline and the interrelationships among the basic demographic variables (fertility, mortality, migration), nuptiality and age at marriage have been studied to measure their effects on fertility. Under conditions of no use of contraceptives, for instance, later age at marriage implies lower marital fertility. Societies may shift their prevalent pattern of nuptiality (increasing or decreasing the age at marriage or, more rarely, changing the incidence of marriage) to adapt to mortality trends, if they are to keep a certain pattern of population growth.

However, population homeostasis is not a sufficient explanation of societal patterns of behaviour. To understand nuptiality in particular, one must consider social and cultural norms from their historical origins. The well-known European pattern of late marriage and high celibacy rates contrasts sharply with the 'non-European' one of early and almost universal marriage; between the two extremes is the 'Eastern European' type (Hajnal, 1965). Although convergent trends have been detected during the twentieth century, 'Hajnal's three types could still be distinguished with respect to both the timing and prevalence of male and female nuptiality' by the 1960s (Dixon, 1978: 451).

These three patterns are a crude but efficient indication of the operation of cultural patterns in the determination of nuptiality and celibacy practices. That is, the practices are part of the cultural family system and of the norms governing the formation of households. In so far as family systems also change historically and respond to economic and political circumstances, it is necessary to consider these general societal dimensions to understand varying meanings of celibacy and marriage.

On the specific subject of celibacy, the basic question is, what makes people move out—that is, marry? Some of the proximate dimensions that have to be considered are known: Dixon (1978) refers to the feasibility of marriage, to its desirability, and to the availability of mates. These dimensions involve, first, the relationship between marriage and economic conditions; secondly, the cultural norms governing marriage patterns and alternative role options for men and women; and thirdly, sex ratios combined with the cultural patterns affecting the preferred age difference between mates. Much cross-cultural research is needed to understand the ways in which these dimensions operate in different cultural contexts.

Regarding the economic considerations, as Dixon (1978: 449) points out, 'The feasibility of marriage depends on how much economic security is considered necessary to found a new family by the norms of a particular social class; crucial here is the gap, if any, betweeen ideal and actual levels.' This statement implies that beyond the inter-class differences and the cross-cultural ones, marriage rates vary with shifts in the relative well-being of different social classes. Thus, in times of recession and economic crisis, nuptiality tends to decrease temporarily because many young people delay their marriages in response to the discrepancy between expected behaviour and available resources.[1]

Cultural norms influence patterns of nuptiality within each of the major cultural areas of the world. Two fundamental cultural processes are taken into consideration in this chapter because they have direct bearing on the subject at hand: the historical process of individuation and the changes in the social position of women.

A final determinant of celibacy is the proportion of males to females in a society. Although sex ratios put a clear limit on the proportion of people of each sex who can marry, the availability of mates is part of the socio-cultural world that defines homogamy and exogamy, the accepted age differences between mates, and other conditions of mate selection. For instance, historically there have been cases in which societies have handled 'marriage squeezes' by shifts in ages at marriage (Ermisch, 1981; Modell, Furstenberg, and Strong, 1978) and by shifts in the boundaries of the group that define homogamy and exogamy.

Celibacy, however, is a topic of research about which little is known. What are the social patterns followed by people while being celibate and by those who never marry?[2] In other words, what are the social positions of the bachelor and the spinster in different societal contexts? Put another way, the questions to be dealt with here are: First, what is the social and cultural nature of celibacy, given the changing practices, norms, and values attached to individuality and family belonging? Is celibacy synonymous with being 'unmarried', or is it one of the various forms of the 'unmarried' state? Second, and related to the first, what are the conditions of the process of 'moving out'? That is, which are the prevailing patterns of marriage and family formation? Here again, historical changes have been highly significant, linked to shifting economic conditions, cultural norms, and family codes. A third major issue is the different ways in which all these patterns affect women and men and the historical transformation of the position of men and women *vis-à-vis* celibacy and marriage.

[1] Recent data for Argentina indicate a decline from 206,000 registered marriages in 1975 to 159,000 in 1982, a period of economic and political crisis. The downward trend was reversed in 1983 (175,000 marriages) and 1984 (185,000 marriages), the reversal coinciding with the transition to democratic rule, still under conditions of an extreme economic crisis.
[2] It should be clear by now that the state of celibacy can be abandoned even in old age. Demographic definitions that put limits on age at marriage (for instance, age 50) are based on empirical generalizations indicating the low probability of marriage after that age.

Individualism and Solitude in Western Civilization

It is a well-known fact that the process of emergence of the individual is a historical one, initiated in the West and extending world-wide from there. Individual choice, recognition of sexual desire, and, most importantly, a gradual and slow social acceptance of behaviour responsive to biological and psychological forces are at the root of significant shifts in the social patterns of celibacy and marriage. Perhaps the most significant of these is the gradual shift towards a social norm that prescribes marriage by personal choice, based on love. Writing on the historical processes that made the modern family, Shorter (1977) devotes a full chapter to 'romance':

The most important change in nineteenth- and twentieth-century courtship has been the surge of sentiment. Two things happened. People started to place affection and personal compatibility at the top of the list of criteria in choosing marriage partners. These new standards became articulated as romantic love. And secondly, even those who continued to use the traditional criteria of prudence and wealth in selecting partners began to behave romantically within these limits. (p. 152)

Although patterns of courtship changed—for example, recognition of sentiment increased—they have not become random.[3] The process has been one of shifting mechanisms of selection and recruitment: instead of being arranged by families, today's marriages are based on personal choice. Of course, personal choice is not free from social constraints, at least of two sorts: parents and relatives exert great pressure on those contemplating marriage, especially when the chosen mate does not meet their standards; and socialization processes mold personal sentiments and the social places where mates can meet.[4]

The changes described here imply also a major historical development in understanding sexuality and its relation to modern solitude, that solitude that derives not from alienation or rebellion, but from recognizing oneself as different from others.

La soledad de la diferencia, de una vida interior que no es mero reflejo de la de los otros es, del mismo modo, histórica. ... El sentido de separación, de diferencia, ... es una experiencia tremendamente confusa en la sociedad moderna. Una de las causas de esa confusión consiste en que nuestras ideas sobre la sexualidad, como indice de la

---

[3] It is important to differentiate courtship from dating. 'Courtship leads to marriage; dating is undertaken purely for amusement' (Lasch, 1977: 56).

[4] Recognition of the effect of 'the social' on the construction of subjectivity and on the definition of the realm of private life has been a major contribution to revised interpretations by the social sciences of the institution of the family. On the one hand, the French tradition of the 'histoire des mentalités' and Foucault's studies on the history of sexuality (Aries, 1962; Foucault, 1978) have established the basis for the analysis of how social and political forces shape individual realities and their images. Donzelot (1979), for example, has shown how the family is placed in relation to 'the social'. On the other hand, this revision has been nurtured by the development of feminist rethinking of the social and cultural boundaries between private and public life (Elshtain, 1982; Rapp, 1978; Thorne and Yalom, 1982; Jelin, 1984).

conciencia de si, nos dificultan la comprensión del porqué nos apartamos de otros indivíduos de la sociedad. (Sennet and Foucault, 1982: 48)

The solitude based on difference, on interior life that is not a mere reflection of the life of others, is likewise historical. ... The feeling of isolation, of difference, ... is a highly confusing experience in modern society. One of the reasons of such confusion is that our ideas about sexuality, as an indicator of our self-consciousness, hinder our understanding of the reasons why we detach ourselves from other individuals in society (my translation).

The body and sexuality become the final arbiters of 'truth':

Parte de la moderna tecnología del yo consiste en utilizar el deseo del cuerpo para saber si una persona está siendo sincera o no. '¿De verdad?' '¿Eres honrado contigo mismo?' Son preguntas que la gente ha intentado contestar plasmando lo que el cuerpo desea: si tu cuerpo no lo desea, entonces no estás siendo honesto. La subjetividad se ha mezclado con la sexualidad: la verdad de la conciencia subjetiva se concibe en términos de simulación corporal controlada. (Sennet and Foucault, 1982: 48)

Part of the modern technology of the self consists of using the body to know whether a person is being sincere or not. 'Truly?' 'Are you honest with yourself?' These are questions that people have attempted to answer establishing what the body wants: if your body does not desire it, then you are not being honest. Subjectivity has come to be intertwined with sexuality: the truth in subjective consciousness is conceived in terms of controlled simulation of the body (my translation).

Furthermore, individuation includes the recognition that 'culture itself requires us to think of ourselves as able to look at our lives and actions from, among others, the point of view of the self-legislator' (Schneewind, 1986: 72). In turn, this recognition implies the emergence of personal autonomy, in the sense of the ability to make decisions about oneself based on information and knowledge as well as on the recognition of our own desires (ibid. 64–75). On the other hand, if this inner personal self-reliance is at the core of modern life, internal deep solitude is unavoidable. In that case, social solitude—the un-attached person, with a lessened presence of family and partner in everyday life—may become a normal occurrence. When inner sentiment is the measuring rod for truth, formal external credentials and sanctions lose their privileged position in guiding and legitimizing behaviour, and marriage licences and religious ceremonies may give way to a multiplicity of ways in which men and women get together to share their intimacy. Casual encounters, open and stable homosexual relations, communal everyday life, and all other imaginable forms become possible, replacing the traditionally sanctioned 'civil and religious marriage'.

Is Celibacy a Condition with No Comeback?

From an individual life-course perspective, long-term demographic trends have implied two basic changes: a considerable increase in life expectancy and a decrease in the time span devoted to reproduction. These two changes imply that a much longer period can be devoted to other activities during the lifetime. As various historical studies have shown, however, these demographic shifts have not been accompanied by a wider spacing of life-course transitions (Demos and Boocock, 1978; Hareven, 1978). What can be observed in the West is a secular decline in age at first marriage (Dixon, 1978), leading to a clustering of three major life-cycle transitions in a very short time: finishing school (which is occurring at later ages, given the expansion of the educational system), entering the labour-force, and the first stage of family formation.

What are the other activities to be carried out during the rest of the lengthened life? The long-term historical answer has to be 'recycling': educational retraining for adults; possibilities of shifting careers in mid-life; divorce and regaining singleness, or remarrying.

To a large extent, central Western societies have been adapting their cultural values and their social institutions to these trends. If this adaptation has not been a complete success, at least it implies an explicit recognition of the issues involved and a discussion of ways and policies to cope with them. In that light, and perhaps with some cynicism, the crisis of the welfare state and the growth of the neo-liberal individualistic ideology are responses to the issues raised by the conditions of increased life expectancy.

Within this context of a changing life-cycle structure, celibacy and marriage have shifting social meanings, in so far as the decision to marry no longer implies a life-long commitment. The ideal Christian marriage is at one extreme of the continuum; in it, the transition from celibacy to marriage is a total one, involving almost all areas of life—sexuality, reproduction, co-residence, and, in the Western tradition, emotional and economic companionship to counteract the effects of individuation. Furthermore, the family, that 'haven in a heartless world', is the space for the merging of individualities, the space where solitude disappears (Lasch, 1977). The model also implies that only death can change this state of affairs. Much of the literature on the family and on the marriage transition has been written with this model as the measuring rod of reality. And the model is in crisis at present.

The universal trend is towards greater diversity in life-course patterns of singleness and nuptiality. It is not so much a change in the major demographic measures of celibacy: except for the cross-cultural convergence shown by Dixon (1978), there are no great changes in age at first marriage and in celibacy rates. Rather, it is the changes taking place later in life, especially those linked to growing divorce rates and growing numbers of single-person households. In that context the traditional notion of celibacy loses social salience and visibility. The category 'single', meaning simply 'unmarried'—a category that allows for multiple entries and exits during a lifetime—gains in social relevance.[5]

---

[5] Two of the basic trends in household composition are the increase in female-headed and in single-person households. Both are related to the shifting patterns of marriage and divorce, as well as to increased life expectancy. Among others, Ross, Sawhill, and MacIntosh (1975), Buvinic and

Greater flexibility may also imply a change in the temporal organization of the transitions involved in marriage. Whereas, in the Christian view, marriage implies the onset of monogamous sexual intercourse and procreation, plus marital co-residence, today the onset of sexual intercourse is becoming increasingly independent of marriage, and pregnancy is becoming an inducement for marriage (Carmichael, 1987). Residential patterns are also becoming more flexible, especially in affluent central Western countries, where single youngsters abandon their parents' homes when entering higher education or the labour-force, rather than at marriage. Socialist countries may also offer alternatives for young people's residence, especially for students.

Women, Celibacy, and Independence

The image of the European (English) suffragist—that is, the woman who was actively and publicly struggling for the recognition of the rights of women during the first decades of the twentieth century—is usually that of an educated person (very likely a teacher) who had passed the ideal age for marriage and opted to remain single, defending her independence and economic autonomy. Marriage and economic dependence seemed at that time bound together. If a woman wanted to gain or maintain a certain degree of autonomy, it was usually at the social cost of remaining a spinster (Vicinus, 1972; also Anderson, 1984; Freeman and Klaus, 1984; Hareven and Tilly, 1981).

But there was a time (in many places) before then, when it was hard for a woman even to dream of autonomy and independence, or of attaining a higher education. Memoirs and autobiographies abound with references to the limitations women experienced in their opportunities for education and employment. Women were by 'nature' subordinate in a patriarchal system, first to their fathers, then to their husbands. Marriage was a 'natural' step in the process of ageing, socially inevitable, culturally expected. Not to marry required a very special reason and justification, or even a calling. Among them were devotion to religion and, by extension, social services and caring for others, relatives or non-relatives. Spinsters were given a social space and a role in the social division of labour: they were in charge of philanthropic tasks, they were governesses and assumed other educational roles, and they were nurses and caretakers of the sick.

Hufton (1984) describes the way spinsters lived in England and France during the eighteenth century and their position in society. Whereas celibate males commanded full wages on which they could survive, women's much lower incomes made it impossible for them to be economically independent. Their

Youssef (1978), Youssef and Hetler (1983), and Merrick and Schmink (1983) have dealt explicitly with female-headed households. There is also a growing literature on single-person households (e.g., Michael, Fuchs, and Scott, 1980; Pampel, 1983; Roussel, 1983; Borsotti, 1983).

economic insecurity explains the practice of 'spinster clustering', which was an alternative to living with relatives or seeking work that provided accommodations.

Given the prevalent approach to the subject of spinsterhood, it is to be stressed that, at certain times and places, remaining single was acceptable and possible: 'What is, in the end, as remarkable as the proportions of spinsters is the plethora of explanations for remaining single, the number of goals that, apparently, took precedence over marriage' (Watkins, 1984: 323).

Social conditions and constraints on women have been changing drastically, especially during the last decades. Women's employment opportunities and a diminishing income gap explains in part why some women delay marriage or do not marry (Davis, 1984). They also help to explain the increase in divorce rates. If women had to marry or remained married because they needed economic support, increasing economic independence would affect both marriage and divorce. But greater economic independence may have also led to higher marriage rates, for the reason that marriage decisions are no longer irreversible and can be changed by women as well as men.

... other things being equal, the wider the gap between the sexes in occupational skills, wages and promotion opportunities, the more likely it is that women will be discouraged from employment and seek marriage. The narrower the gap, then, the more likely it is that women will view their employment as a genuine alternative to marrying for economic support. (Dixon, 1978: 465)

Economic independence of women is perhaps the best indicator of breaking with the ideology that prescribes the role of woman = wife = mother. Taking on other roles may imply at one point the need to make a choice between alternatives. Later, it may involve an attempt to combine them. If, on the one hand, this implies often a double burden of work on married women, on the other it is based on the growing realization that decisions and choices can be reversed.

The association between decisions about family formation and the position of women is quite strong. In spite of the changes that are taking place all over the world, there are still great differences between countries and regions in the position of women, and these affect the patterns of celibacy and nuptiality.

Celibacy and Nuptiality in Latin America

In a sweeping overview, Latin America can be characterized as a cultural area that combines familism and statism. In the Latin American cultural tradition, the patriarchal family is seen as the natural unit for everyday life. The household is the basic unit of reproduction; within it, gender and generational relations are hierarchical, with a clear division of labour and of domains of activity. Women are in charge of the domestic activities, which are associated with the private sphere of reproduction and maintenance of the family; men are in charge of the tasks associated with the public sphere of social and political life.

Familism has had very different effects on the position of women and of men. For women, it has meant subordination; for men, a pattern of personal relationships based on kinship solidarities that carries over into the public sphere of politics and productive activities. The male pattern of relationships accounts for the 'clientelistic' and 'paternalistic' relations in traditional public life in Latin America. For both men and women, family identity is basic to self-identity and to construction of a social place.

The Latin American societies are, and have been from early in their history, class societies. Capitalist development imposed itself upon other forms of social and economic organization. Ethnic identities and considerations had to be recast and reshaped in class terms (Stavenhagen, 1969). Moreover, the emergence of class societies was linked to the emergence of national states, in which a strong state apparatus has impinged upon the daily lives of their populations. There are few recognized institutional alternatives to the state and the family. Although cultural norms are slowly changing, little cultural room exists for individual choice outside these institutions.

Strong familism entails a clear norm prescribing marriage and children, especially for women. As is well known, Latin America is a region where consensual unions are widespread; and practices vary regarding civil marriage, religious marriage, and both (Berquó and Loyola, 1984). Beyond differences in legislation—for instance, the absence of divorce laws in Argentina, which led to high numbers of consensual unions in the case of second marriages—not much is known about the social meanings attached to each of these modalities.

Little information on the subject of celibacy and nuptiality is available. Camisa (1978) studied nuptiality patterns in 14 Latin American countries. In spite of the limitations of her data and consequently the uncertain reliability of the estimates (which were based on an analysis of three cohorts of women 15–19 years of age in 1950, 1955, and 1960), her paper shows large inter-country variations in nuptiality rates and in the prevalence of legal versus consensual unions (Table 8.1).

In-depth studies in Mexico show that legal unions have been increasing considerably in recent decades, from 48 per cent in 1930 to 75 per cent in 1975 (Quilodrán, 1974). Recent analyses also show considerable inter-class differences in celibacy; thus, celibacy rates for women vary from 1.8 per cent in the 'new petite bourgeoisie' to 11.3 per cent among peasants and farm workers (Ojeda, 1987).

For Brazil, available data and analyses point to the complexities of the social practices of marriage and celibacy. A recent study of the evolution of nuptiality between 1960 and 1980, for example, indicates considerable stability in the distribution of the population by marital status (Souza e Silva, 1986). There have been both a decrease in the age difference at first union between men and women, and a decline in celibacy, more visible among men.

TABLE 8.1. Nuptiality and Celibacy in Latin America (by percentage)

Country	Legal marriages	Consensual unions	Adults celibate
Argentina	82.4	9.5	8.1
Brazil	80.1	6.0	13.9
Chile	83.4	3.9	12.7
Colombia	66.4	14.2	19.4
Costa Rica	72.6	12.2	15.2
Dominican Republic	48.5	35.7	15.9
El Salvador	40.3	41.3	18.4
Guatemala	41.1	46.7	12.2
Honduras	40.8	43.9	15.3
Mexico	76.3	12.7	11.1
Nicaragua	57.7	30.1	12.2
Panama	45.5	39.2	15.4
Paraguay	63.2	21.1	15.7
Venezuela	55.4	25.0	19.5

Note: Data are based on the average of three female cohorts of ages 15–19 in 1950, 1955, and 1960.

Source: Camisa, 1978: Tables 6, 7.

The sex differences in the trends make it necessary to study separately men's and women's marital choices and constraints. As Berquó (1986) eloquently shows, the excess of women in the categories of widows and divorced is large and growing. Celibacy is also higher for women than for men (Tables 8.2 and 8.3). When analysing these patterns in combination with a decline of almost one year in the age difference between men and women during the twenty-year period under consideration, it is clear that, as they age, women are more likely to

TABLE 8.2. Marital Status, by Sex: Brazil, 1960 and 1980

Status	Females		Males	
	1960	1980	1960	1980
Single	30.7	31.5	37.4	37.9
Separated, divorced	3.2	3.5	1.7	1.5
Widowed	8.8	8.1	2.5	1.8
Married	57.3	56.9	58.4	58.8

Source: Berquó, 1986: Table 1.

TABLE 8.3. Age at Marriage and Percentage Celibate,
by Sex: Brazil, 1960 and 1980

Item	Females		Males	
	1960	1980	1960	1980
Average age at marriage	22.2	22.6	25.8	25.3
Percentage celibate	8.7	8.1	6.2	6.1

Source: Berquó, 1986: Table 2.

experience solitude; hence, the title of Berquó's paper, 'Piramide da solidao?' In this, single, divorced, and widowed women share the same lot.[6]

What is the social setting for single women in Latin America? Subordination of women has traditionally been very strong. Their subordinate position has implied relatively low rates of labour-force participation, the concentration of women in a few service occupations, and poor wages and employment opportunities, especially for women with children (Jelin, 1978; CEPAL, 1985). Recognition of women's roles in the public sphere is limited. If women perform well in outside work or in politics, this does not excuse them from their 'true' role as wives and mothers. Even though divorce is slowly gaining in legitimacy and social acceptance, a single or divorced woman has few chances of being self-supporting or able to lead a satisfactory everyday life.

Yet, there have been important changes: the increase in women's labour-force participation, an increase in their education, a decrease in fertility, an increase in divorce. These trends, however, have no clear and lineal effects. They may mean different things for educated, urban, middle-class women and for those who are rural or urban lower-class. For the educated, marriage and family formation are slowly but increasingly a manifestation of options and choice, linked to the general Western process of individuation and search for personal autonomy. Although social acceptance of this new behaviour of women is slow, and not encouraged, nevertheless it is growing.

For rural and urban lower classes, as in pre-industrial Europe, the institutional setting is not prepared to handle single people on their own, especially women. Perhaps the most prevalent pattern for single women is to leave their parental homes to become live-in domestic servants. This act often involves also a move from the countryside or a small town to an urban area. In such cases, the women's subordination to their parents is replaced by their subordination to a patron. Only slowly are domestic servants in Latin American cities gaining some

---

[6] A further analysis of nuptiality by race indicates that it is the Black Brazilian women who have the highest celibacy rates and the most restricted marriage opportunities (Berquó, 1987).

recognition of their rights. Most of the women hope to marry and in that way to improve their positions.

It is not customary for bachelors or spinsters to leave their parental homes before marrying, except to migrate. Divorced persons perhaps have more freedom to choose their place of residence, but they may experience little social support from informal networks.

In spite of all these restrictions, there has been a slow increase in single-person and female-headed households, following a trend that is also evident in other areas of the world. The association of these households with poverty is well established. Again, singleness still seems to be more a curse than a positive alternative to marriage.

What inferences can be drawn from the Latin American experience? First is the need to consider explicitly cultural and class contexts in relation to family formation patterns. Within the region, great variations exist in the norms and practices associated with household formation, despite the centrality of familism. Cultural norms may be at odds with behavioural patterns, creating tensions and contradictions that can have important long-term effects. Thus, the impact of the economic crisis in much of the region has led to new patterns of behaviour developed to cope with uncertainty and hardship, which may be at variance with expected and prescribed forms of action. In low-income urban sectors, there are indications of changes in traditional gender roles. Women are the ones who carry the burden of meeting their families' survival needs, and this change has led them into new activities and patterns of social interaction (de Barbier and de Oliveira, 1985). The changing patterns of behaviour among women have effects on their position within the family and on their marital behaviour. It is still to be seen whether these changes are short-term responses to a crisis situation or, more likely, longer-term adaptations that signal greater female solitude.

Whether by choice or because of desertion by men, the mother–child unit is becoming the social reality of the reproductive unit. The growing number of unmarried mothers may be due to a desire to have some family life in spite of the difficulties of establishing a conventional nuclear family. Brazilian data indicate a considerable increase between 1960 and 1980 in the proportion of single women who have had at least one child, from 3.0 per cent to 7.5 per cent. In the age category of 35–44 the proportion of single women with children has increased from 10.4 per cent to 22.4 per cent.[7] To what extent are we witnessing new ways in which women are establishing their options in life?

Why solitude and not autonomy? The self-reliance that women exercise for daily survival may be linked to increasing autonomy and choices to greater equality and freedom, at least for middle- and upper-class women. But for women less well-off economically it may be the result of a more perverse process. In both cases, the destruction of the traditional patterns of social organization and division of labour among the genders implies an increasing

---

[7] Personal communication from Elza Berquó, who has suggested that single motherhood may be a reaction to solitude.

burden for women. They have to take care of their families but are left to themselves. Thus, their lot today is not freedom and autonomy, but rather hardship and solitude. How these two outcomes, autonomy and solitude, mesh in the Latin American experience, and what their effects are on the expectations of the more recent cohorts are basic questions for future research.

References

Anderson, M. (1984), 'The Social Position of Spinsters in Mid-Victorian Britain', *Journal of Family History*, 9 (4), 377–93.

Aries, P. (1962), *Centuries of Childhood: A Social History of Family Life*, Vintage, New York.

Balan, J., Browning, H. L., and Jelin, E. (1973), *Men in a Developing Society: Geographic and Social Mobility in Monterrey, Mexico*, University of Texas Press, Austin, Tex. and London.

Berquó, E. (1986), 'Piramide da solidao?' Paper presented at the Fifth National Meeting of the Associacǎo Brasileira de Estudes Populacionais (ABEP).

—— (1987), *Nupcialidade da populacǎo negra no Brasil*, Núcleo de Estudos de Populacǎo, Universidade Estadual de Campinas, São Paulo.

—— and Loyola, M. A. (1984), 'União de sexos e estrategias reproductivas no Brasil', *Revista brasileira de estudos de populacao*, 1 (1/2), 35–98.

Borsotti, C. (1983), 'Hogares unipersonales en Argentina', CENEP, Buenos Aires (mimeo.).

Bourdieu, P. (1976), 'Marriage Strategies as Strategies of Social Reproduction', in R. Forster and O. Ranum (eds.), *Family and Society*, Selections from the Annales: Économies, Sociétés, Civilisations, Johns Hopkins University Press, Baltimore, Md.

Buvinic, M., and Youssef, N. H. (1978), *Women-Headed Households: The Ignored Factor in Development Planning*, International Center for Research on Women, Washington, DC.

Camisa, Z. (1978), 'La nupcialidad de las mujeres solteras en la América Latina', *Notas de población*, 6 (18), 9–75.

Carmichael, G. (1987), 'Bust after Boom: First Marriage Trends in Australia', *Demography*, 24 (2), 245–64.

Comisión Económica Para América Latina (CEPAL) (1985), *Las mujeres latino-americanas en los ochenta*, CEPAL, Santiago, Chile.

Cornell, L. L. (1984), 'Why Are There No Spinsters in Japan?' *Journal of Family History*, 9 (4), 326–39.

Davis, K. (1984), 'Wives and Work: Consequences of the Sex Role Revolution', *Population and Development Review*, 10 (3), 397–417.

de Barbieri, T., and de Oliveira, O. (1985), *La Presencia de las mujeres en América Latina en una década de crisis*, UNAM and El Colegio de México, Mexico.

Demos, J., and Boocock, S. S. (eds.) (1978), *Turning Points: Historical and Sociological Essays on the Family*, University of Chicago Press, Chicago and London.

Dixon, R. B. (1971), 'Explaining Cross-cultural Variations in Age at Marriage and Proportions Never Married', *Population Studies*, 25 (2), 215–33.

—— (1978), 'Late Marriage and Non-marriage as Demographic Responses: Are They Similar?' *Population Studies*, 32 (3), 449–66.

Donzelot, J. (1979), *The Policing of Families*, Pantheon Books, New York.

Elshtain, J. B. (1982), 'Antigone's Daughters', *Democracy*, 2 (2), 46–59.

Ermish, J. F. (1981), 'Economic Opportunities, Marriage Squeezes and the Propensity to Marry: An Economic Analysis of Period Marriage Rates in England and Wales', *Population Studies*, 35 (3), 347–56.

Foucault, M. (1978), *The History of Sexuality*, Pantheon Books, New York.

Freeman, R., and Klaus, P. (1984), 'Blessed or Not? The New Spinster in England and the United States in the Late Nineteenth and Early Twentieth Centuries', *Journal of Family History*, 9 (4), 394–414.

Goody, J. R., Thirsk, J., and Thompson, E. P. (eds.) (1976), *Family and Inheritance: Rural Society in Western Europe, 1200–1800*, Cambridge University Press, Cambridge and New York.

Hajnal, J. (1965), 'European Marriage Patterns in Perspective', in D. V. Glass and D. E. C. Eversley (eds.), *Population in History: Essays in Historical Demography*, Aldine Publishing Co., Chicago.

Hareven, T. K. (ed.) (1978), *Transitions: The Family and the Life Course in Historical Perspective*, Academic Press, New York.

—— and Tilly, L. A. (1981), 'Solitary Women and Family Mediation in America and French Textile Cities', *Annales de Démographie Historique*, 253–71.

Hufton, O. (1984), 'Women without Men: Widows and Spinsters in Britain and France in the Eighteenth Century', *Journal of Family History*, 9 (4), 355–76.

Jelin, E. (1978), *La mujer en el mercado de trabajo urbano*, Estudios CEDES, Buenos Aires.

—— (1984), *Familia y unidad doméstica: Mundo público y vida privada*, Estudios CEDES, Buenos Aires.

Lasch, C. (1977), *Haven in a Heartless World: The Family Besieged*, Basic Books, New York.

Merrick, T. W., and Schmink, M. (1983), 'Households Headed by Women and Urban Poverty in Brazil', in M. Buvinic, M. A. Lycette, and W. P. McGreevey (eds.), *Women and Poverty in the Third World*, Johns Hopkins University Press, Baltimore, Md.

Michael, R. T., Fuchs, V. R., and Scott, S. R. (1980), 'Changes in the Propensity to Live Alone: 1950–1976', *Demography*, 17 (1), 39–56.

Modell, J., Furstenberg, F. F., Jr., and Strong, D. (1978), 'The Timing of Marriage in the Transition to Adulthood: Continuity and Change', in J. Demos and S. S. Boocock (eds.), *Turning Points: Historical and Sociological Essays on the Family*, University of Chicago Press, Chicago and London.

Ojeda, N. (1987), 'Unpublished Tabulations', University of Texas, Austin, Tex.

Pampel, F. C. (1983), 'Changes in the Propensity to Live Alone: Evidence from Consecutive Cross-sectional Surveys, 1960–1976', *Demography*, 20 (4), 433–47.

Quilodrán, J. (1974), 'Evolución de la nupcialidad en México, 1900–1970', *Demografía y economía*, 8 (1), 34–49.

Rapp, R. (1978), 'Family and Class in Contemporary America: Notes Toward an Understanding of Ideology', *Science and Society*, 42 (3), 278–300.

Ross, H. L., Sawhill, I. V., and MacIntosh, A. R. (1975), *Time of Transition: The Growth of Families Headed by Women*, Urban Institute, Washington, DC.

Roussel, L. (1983), 'Les Ménages d'une personne: L'Évolution recente', *Population*, 38 (6), 995–1016.

Schneewind, J. B. (1986), 'The Use of Autonomy in Ethical Theory', in T. C. Heller,

M. Sosna, and D. E. Wellbery (eds.), *Reconstructing Individualism: Autonomy, Individuality, and the Self in Western Thought*, Stanford University Press, Stanford, Calif.

Sennet, R., and Foucault, M. (1982), 'Sexualidad y soledad', *El Viejo Topo*, 47–54.

Shorter, E. (1975), *The Making of the Modern Family*, Basic Books, New York.

Souza e Silva, R. (1986), 'O panorama da nupcialidade brasileira no periodo 1960–1980', Relatorio final da pesquisa, Centro Brasileiro de Anaálise e Planejamento (CEBRAP), São Paulo (mimeo.).

Stavenhagen, R. (1969), *Las clases sociales en las sociedades agrarias*, Siglo XXI, Mexico.

Thorne, B., and Yalom, M. (eds.) (1982), *Rethinking the Family: Some Feminist Questions*, Longman, New York and London.

Vicinus, M. (ed.) (1972), *Suffer and Be Still: Women in the Victorian Age*, Indiana University Press, Bloomington, Ind.

Watkins, Susan Cotts (1984), 'Spinsters', *Journal of Family History*, 9 (4), 310–25.

Youssef, N. H., and Hetler, C. B. (1983), 'Establishing the Economic Condition of Women-Headed Households in the Third World: A New Approach', in M. Buvinic, M. A. Lycette, and W. P. McGreevey (eds.), *Women and Poverty in the Third World*, Johns Hopkins University Press, Baltimore, Md.

9 The Slavery Period and its Influence on Household Structure and the Family in Jamaica, Cuba, and Brazil

VERENA STOLCKE

A family unit within the ingenio was a foreign body, naturally rejected. (Moreno-Fraginals, 1978: 42)

The family was unthinkable to the vast majority of the population . . . the nuclear family could hardly exist within the context of slavery. (Patterson, 1967: 9, 167)

The child of a slave, if he knew his mother, often did not know who was his real father. In effect, even if not in the biological sense, his father was the white patriarch, the slave master. (Bastide, 1971: 104)

These quotations are a fair sample of how, until the mid-1970s, most students of slavery in the Americas saw slave family life. Forced transport to the plantations of the New World had torn Africans out of their familiar social and cultural environments; and the slaveholders, by their inhumanity and brutality, had thwarted any possibilities for the slaves to develop permanent new social relationships and a cultural identity and values of their own in their stead. Bondage disrupted marital and kin relationships and generated mother-centred households in which the father was marginal or absent, thereby undermining the Black male's sense of self. Moreover, marital instability and sexual promiscuity, as well as the disparity of sex ratios, depressed slave fertility so that the continuous decline of the slave forces made slaveholders in Jamaica, Cuba, and Brazil heavily dependent on the slave trade. This legacy of family disorganization still marks the Black family today.

In the mid-1970s two scholars, Gutman for mainland North America and Higman for the British West Indies, undertook to challenge the view that traced the contemporary disorganization of the Black family to the experience of slavery. The earlier, almost exclusive, emphasis on the constraints that had oppressed the slaves needed to be transcended to throw light on the choices that had been available to slaves to develop familial behaviour and ideals of their own. Family bonds and values were regarded as the most suitable indicators for measuring the existence of a cultural identity and integrity among the slaves. By the late 1970s a new, more differentiated, picture of the slave family in mainland North America and the British West Indies had emerged (Gutman, 1975; 1976; Higman, 1975; 1976a; 1976b; 1979).

As no comparative studies exist of the slave family, in this chapter I undertake to compare recent findings on slave families and their descendants in Jamaica, Cuba, and Brazil. To gain an adequate understanding of the influence slavery had on the Black family, it is necessary not only to examine the multiple forms of oppression suffered by the slaves and the social and cultural forms they were none the less capable of forging for themselves, but also to study mating patterns and family experiences of free non-Whites in their interaction with Whites. Slavery was a particularly harsh system of human exploitation which had a profound effect also on the societies that practised it and on free non-Whites. Slave societies developed characteristic colour–class hierarchies which were enforced by forms of legal and extra-legal coercion and exclusions that were designed to preserve White supremacy. These discriminations found expression also in particular sexual practices and family behaviour among free non-Whites. My aim is to identify some of the ways in which slaves and free Blacks shaped their mating patterns, values, and family forms under the socio-structural constraints of societies structured in a very fundamental way by race.

A few preliminary words of caution are in order, however. The literature on slavery and the slave family in mainland North America is vast, whereas students of slavery in the Spanish and Portuguese colonies have been slower to revise established ideas about the slave family.[1] No investigation of the slave family in the Americas can disregard the insights that Gutman and Higman have advanced. But there is the problem of the diffusion of theoretical paradigms. The revision of the traditional notions about the Black family in slavery and thereafter is not only the outcome of improved sources and methods of analysis. It forms part of a political debate over Black history and identity that needs to be taken into account. The role that mating patterns and family behaviour and values play in the definition of social identity is a delicate issue, and to draw the line between submission and resistance to oppression, which is a fine one, is an elusive task.

In addition, slavery in the New World was not a homogeneous phenomenon, although it has tended to be viewed as either one single or two contrasting modal types. Certain common traits cannot be denied—for example, that slavery was generally adopted in situations where land was plentiful but labour scarce—but adequate attention needs to be paid also to contrasts and diversities. The numbers of slaves transported to mainland North America, for example, were much smaller than the numbers brought to the Spanish and Portuguese colonies, and the demographic evolution of the slave populations was entirely

---

[1] Hall (1971) emphasizes the disintegrating effect of slavery on the slave family, whereas Scott (1985) refutes this position without, however, offering a systematic study of the slave family. For a demographic analysis of Cuban slavery see Moreno-Fraginals, 1977. For a review of the slave family debate, with special emphasis on Latin America, see Russell-Wood, 1978. Russell-Wood (1982) and Schwartz (1985) devote long chapters to discussing the hypotheses advanced by Gutman in the case of Brazil. For recent regional case studies on the slave family in Brazil see Slenes, 1987; del Nero da Costa, Slenes, and Schwartz, forthcoming; Metcalf, 1987; Ribeiro Fragoso and Garcia Florentino, n.d.; Gutiérrez, n.d.

different in the South. The English North American colonies are estimated to have received 399,000 slaves in the period between 1701 and 1870, whereas in the same period slave imports into Spanish America and Brazil were somewhat over one million and three million, respectively (Russell-Wood, 1982: 171).[2] None the less, by the 1830s, the United States had roughly one-third of the Black population in the New World, a development suggesting very different demographic dynamics which may have been connected with differences in family forms (Klein and Engerman, 1984: 208–9). Jamaica, Cuba, and Brazil also differed among themselves. All three countries were large slave plantation economies which produced crops for the international market, but their economic maturity and the share of Africans and their descendants in their populations varied. Despite a similar economic setting, different colonial realities had consequences for the timing and the way in which abolition occurred. Slaves were emancipated in Jamaica in 1833, and in Cuba in 1884. Brazil was the last country to abolish slavery, in 1888.

Family and Kin among the Slaves

One difficulty in comparing slave mating patterns and family types in Jamaica, Cuba, and Brazil is the varying extent to which research on familial behaviour among slaves has advanced in each case. By contrast with Higman's detailed quantitative analyses of slave household structure in the British West Indies and especially in Jamaica, a study of this type is still needed for Cuba, while Gutman's researches have prompted examination of his views on the development of an Afro-American familial culture in Brazil only recently. Another difficulty is the sparsity and diversity of quantifiable data available on slave family behaviour, which impose limitations on analysis specific to each case.

The point of departure for the recent re-examination of the slave family was the question of whether slaves were able under bondage to constitute families and preserve kin relationships that provided them with a protective force against slaveholders' abuses and exploitation. (See Yanagisako, 1979, for a discussion of the conceptual difficulties surrounding the terms 'family' and 'household'.) One general finding has been the diversity of slave household types prevalent in all three colonies. In Jamaica the proverbial unstable, matrifocal household of a woman with her children was only one family form among others on plantations and usually did not constitute the modal type. Nuclear family households composed of a man, a woman, and her children, extended family households, and units of unrelated or single individuals existed as well. Higman also found evidence of polygyny practised by some occupationally privileged male slaves, although it is presumably not easy, with available data, to distinguish institutionalized polygyny from more or less casual mating

---

[2] Russell-Wood (1982: 161) is sceptical about the hypotheses advanced by Gutman (1976).

arrangements. Moreover, a sizeable proportion of the households was composed of kin, and the majority of slaves who possessed family links lived in nuclear family households. As Higman (1976b: 534) concluded for Jamaica, 'although fewer than 25% of the slaves lived exclusively with identifiable kin, almost 50% lived in households approximating the elementary family'. A similar diversity of household forms has been found in Brazil. Kin relationships, in addition, extended well beyond the individual household (Schwartz, 1985: 394–406; del Nero da Costa, Slenes, and Schwartz, 1987). In Cuba and Brazil, which both have a Catholic tradition, slaves adopted the practice of ritual godparenthood, thereby creating networks of ritual obligations beyond the boundaries of the household. Godparents were acquired at baptism and chosen ideally from among people at least of equal but preferably of somewhat better social and racial status then the parents of the child. Masters, however, were not eligible for godparenthood (Schwartz, 1985: 406–12; Scott, 1985: 18; Higman, 1979: 45; Russell-Wood, 1982: 164–5).

That slaves did develop nuclear family households and were able to sustain kin relationships does not imply, however, that bondage had no effect on slave family experiences and forms. Demographic and economic factors such as the size and the sex ratio of the plantation slave force, the degree of creolization, and the type of crop raised on the plantation, as well as sexual abuses of White men, limited the slaves' ability to mate according to their own choice and to form lasting kin relationships.

Fresh shipments of Africans averaged about 60 per cent males and contained few slaves under 20 years of age (Craton, 1975: 268–9). As long as the slave trade continued there was always a large excess of male slaves who had no chance of finding themselves in the family households (Higman, 1975; Moreno-Fraginals, 1977; Schwartz, 1985). Africans also generally tended to possess fewer kin than did Creoles (Higman, 1975: 276). But although Africans were less likely than Creoles to find themselves in families, of the plantation slaves who lived in families the Africans were twice as frequently to be found in nuclear units as were the Creoles, among whom mother-centred households were more common (Higman, 1979: 52–3). From the point of view of the women slaves' mating and reproductive opportunities, however, a high index of masculinity favoured their mating and fertility. On coffee plantations in the Province of São Paulo in the nineteenth century the number of excess male slaves correlated positively with the marriage rate among women slaves (Slenes, 1987). In Jamaica a high sex ratio stimulated fertility in the rural population (Higman, 1976a: 120–1). One possible reason for this may have been that the larger the deficit of women slaves, the greater was the premium for males in stable mating relationships.

Africans were transported to the New World mainly for forced plantation labour. Of critical importance to slave family development, in addition to the disparate sex ratio, was the size of the slave-holding estate to which they were sold. Because plantation exogamy was often prohibited, possibly to avoid conflicts over ownership of slave offspring, large plantations provided larger populations from which to choose mates. The ethnic mating preferences noted especially on larger plantations in Bahia and the Caribbean are one indication that slaves enjoyed a measure of choice in mating (Schwartz, 1985: 391; Higman, 1979: 55). On large holdings, moreover, slaves tended to be less threatened by family fragmentation through sale than on small properties, although slaveholders' policies in the different countries varied in this respect (Higman, 1976b: 530; 1979: 50; Slenes, 1987; Schwartz, 1985: 379–412). In the Province of São Paulo, which had Church-sanctioned marriage rates among slaves higher than anywhere else in the country, on medium and large estates (those with more than nine slaves) the majority of slave women were married by the time they were over 35 years of age, whereas on small estates the marriage rate was very low for both sexes. Single mothers usually married soon after conception, so that childbearing and rearing occurred mostly after religious marriage, although most slave holdings in the Province of São Paulo were small or of medium size (Slenes, 1987; del Nero da Costa, Slenes, and Schwartz, forthcoming).[3]

Somewhat more difficult than determining what the mating patterns and resulting household types were at a particular time is establishing the unions' durability. But growing evidence suggests that sales of slaves and division of properties by inheritance did not everywhere lead to slave family disruption to the degree previously thought. In the British West Indies most of the nuclear family households among slaves appear to have been founded on long-term unions (Higman, 1975: 281–3). In Brazil, depending on the point in the economic cycle, family groups were often sold together rather than broken apart (Slenes, 1987: 7; Ribeiro Fragoso and Garcia Florentino, 1986: 16; but cf. Metcalf, 1987). On large coffee estates in São Paulo, consequently, the majority of children grew up in the company of both parents.

The prevalence of formalized marriages among the slaves is not a good indicator for assessing household types because nuclear households resulting from consensual unions are thereby neglected. But regional differences in formal marriage rates are quite marked and demand some explanation. The frequency of formal marriage among slaves distinguishes the Province of São Paulo from Bahia in Brazil as well as from Jamaica and Cuba. On medium and large plantations in the region of Campinas, Province of São Paulo, in 1872 an average 67 per cent of the slave women and 30 per cent of the slave men over 15 years of age had been formally married by the Church or were widowed (Slenes, 1987: Table 1, p. 13). In contrast, only 9 per cent of all slave women in Brazil in 1872 were wed (Slenes, 1973: 412–20); formal marriage rates were also much lower among plantation slaves in nineteenth-century Paraiba do Sul (Ribeiro Fragoso and Garcia Florentino, 1986: 4) and in eighteenth-century Bahia (Schwartz, 1985). In the British West Indies, legal marriage rates were also very

---

[3] In eighteenth-century Bahia, however, formal religious marriages among plantation slaves in the sugar cane zone seem to have been rare and rates of illegitimacy high (Schwartz, 1985: 354 ff.).

low, although figures are difficult to obtain, in part because researchers' attention has focused on mating patterns without distinguishing formalized marriages. In Cuba, however, only 10 per cent of slave women over 16 years of age were formally married in 1862 (Martinez-Alier, 1974: 59–60). Slenes has attributed these unusually high marriage rates on São Paulo coffee plantations to the stronger presence there of the Church. But there may also be an economic, crop-related reason for the high rates. A certain gender bias in the emphasis given to the sexual selectivity of the slave trade and the deficit of females has sometimes led researchers to underrate the economic value of women slaves. Female slaves worked especially in the fields to a considerable extent, whereas male slaves tended to have a wider range of occupations. Slave women's participation rates appear to have varied according to the labour demands of the crop (Mörner, 1980). In Brazil, for example, child and woman labour was known to have been valued very highly on coffee plantations, especially at harvest time. Coffee planters may have been, therefore, more favourably inclined than planters of other crops towards slaves' formalizing their unions in the Church, although this does not explain why slaves themselves wanted to marry in the Church. Significantly, Cuban sugar plantations had a much greater deficit of female slaves than did coffee plantations (174 and 124 male slaves, respectively, per 100 female slaves) in 1862 (Scott, 1985: 12). In the case of Brazil, however, this difference in slave sex ratios is less clear-cut, for example, between São Paulo coffee plantations in the second half of the nineteenth century (188 males per 100 females on estates with more than nine slaves) and Bahia sugar mills and cane farms throughout the eighteenth century (cane farms, 126; sugar mills, 199) (Slenes, 1987: 13; Schwartz, 1985: 348). In Jamaica, in turn, monocultural coffee plantations had an almost balanced sex ratio and experienced a natural increase of the slave population, although it was not so high as on estates that combined certain crops—e.g. pimento, livestock, and coffee (Higman, 1976a: 121–5). And in Paraná, Brazil, where small- to medium-scale subsistence agriculture and livestock breeding for local consumption predominated and women slaves played an important role as field hands, sex ratios were practically balanced early in the nineteenth century, although indices of masculinity were somewhat higher among Blacks than among mulattos and formal marriage and fertility rates rose with the size of slave holdings (Gutiérrez, n.d.; Graham, 1976). That is to say, crop-related variations in labour demand may have also influenced sex ratios, household structure, and fertility rates among slaves.

Higman was the first to test the traditional thesis on slave fertility, which linked levels of natural increase in the slave population with sex ratios, family instability, and casual mating practices in the Caribbean. He questioned the generally depressive effect the sex ratio was thought to have had on reproduction and showed that the most fertile women on Jamaican slave holdings were those who lived in household units with a mate and their children. The next most fertile women were those living in households with their offspring but without mates, whereas women living alone or with unrelated women or men showed very low fertility. In addition, Creoles tended to be more fertile than Africans, and miscegenation contributed to slave women's fertility. Other non-demographic factors such as breast-feeding and sexual taboos after birth, as well as voluntary abortion, may have reduced fertility, but the single most important factor affecting slave reproduction was high infantile mortality, estimated at between 25 per cent and 50 per cent of all live births on selected plantations in Jamaica (Higman, 1976b: 545; 1976a: 115–18). In other words, marital instability and casual mating did depress fertility, but unstable mating patterns were not dominant among slaves. In Paraná, Brazil, early in the nineteenth century, on the other hand, sex ratios were fairly balanced and the population was very young on account of a high birth rate, suggesting vegetative growth despite infantile mortality (Gutiérrez, n.d.), in contrast with sugar plantations in Bahia until the eighteenth century. There Africans predominated and the percentage of children was much lower than among slave and free Creoles, so that the slave population did not reproduce itself but was maintained through the slave trade (Schwartz, 1985: 349). In nineteenth-century São Paulo, medium and large coffee plantations, in turn, seem to have provided a much more favourable environment for regular sexual intercourse in stable families consecrated by the Church than did small estates, as indicated by the higher proportion of legitimate slave children on the former, although origin, colour, and marital status of slave women also influenced their fertility. Irrespective of size of holdings and sex ratios, African slave women married more often and when they did were more fertile than married Creole mulatto women, who were more predisposed to become single mothers and had more children than did Black single mothers (del Nero da Costa, Slenes, and Schwartz, 1987). Nothing certain is known about the form of slave families in Cuba, but, as elsewhere, progressive creolization of the slave population on plantations improved sex ratios and increased the proportion of children in the slave force (Moreno-Fraginals, 1977: 192; Higman, 1975). Although in Cuba the *barracón* symbolized slave plantations, those prison-like barracks were confined to the large sugar mills, and even within them slave family units were not entirely unknown (Scott, 1985: 17–20).

In those countries under consideration in which re-examination of the slave family structure has advanced most, the prevalence of nuclear family households besides other domestic arrangements such as mother-centred units, extended families, and units of single individuals of either sex has been established beyond doubt. Although important in itself, this reinterpretation of slave family types has some difficulties. Slaves did succeed in creating social and kin relationships of their own. But the respective influences of African traditions and of the constraints imposed by slavery in this process of adjustment are unclear (Higman, 1979). Nor are the content and meaning of these social bonds clear. Scholars have tended to extrapolate values from behaviour in their desire to establish the slaves' ability to influence decisions that affected their lives as proven by the reality and functioning of the slave family. The shift from a jural perspective focused on formal marriage among slaves to an analysis of household composition has failed to provide insights into the slaves' own motives for their choices and into the social, political, and symbolic meanings these had for them. It is acknowledged that family households are constituted by different types of mating, which, in turn, influence their composition, stability, and the mutual rights and obligations between the partners; but perceived differences— for example, between formal marriages and consensual unions—are ignored. Nor is the re-examination of earlier wisdom on the slave family exempt of a sexist bias. Nothing is said about the quality of intra-household relationships. The nature of household headship in the sense of intra-family patterns of dominance, which had occupied such a central place in the earlier thesis on the mother-centredness of the slave family, ceased to be an issue once the existence of nuclear family households had been established. Either male headship was taken for granted but the implications for women's position of this were ignored, or scholars introduced the confusing notion of 'double headedness' without specifying what this term actually meant as regards patterns of dominance (Russell-Wood, 1982: 181; Schwartz, 1985: 395; Yanagisako, 1979: 178).

The greatest difficulty in these re-examinations resides, however, in drawing the fine divide between coercion and choice in the shaping of slave family forms. In their endeavour to redress the earlier emphasis on disorganization, scholars have now focused their attention on slave family organization, thereby tending to neglect the master–slave relationship of extreme oppression (Russell-Wood, 1982; Gudemann, 1979).

Interracial Sex

As a Cuban proverb of the period asserted, it was as unlikely for a tamarind fruit to be sweet as for a mulatto girl to be a virgin ('No hay tamarindo dulce ni mulata senorita'). This proverb undoubtedly served as a moral justification for White men's sexual exploits. It none the less reflected a social reality. Non-White women were exposed to the sexual abuses of White men, which, as the proportions of mulattos in the populations demonstrate, frequently bore fruit. Interracial sexual intercourse, in addition, had far-reaching consequences for slave and free non-White women's family lives. The Bishop of Havana in the 1860s denounced it in no uncertain terms:

everywhere adultery and concubinage persist, largely between white men and mulattoe women, producing an excessive number of natural offspring, which, with the exception of a few who are recognized by their progenitors, it can be said, have neither family nor society, for this consists of no more than a mother. (Martinez-Alier, 1974: 125)

Ideally, slaves were to be kept segregated from the world of White masters, but in practice interracial sex blurred racial and social boundaries.[4] Mis-

[4] It is nowhere easy to establish the proportion of Mulattos in the populations because of the dynamics of race and the diversity of racial categories. None the less, it has been estimated that in

cegenation took place typically between slave and free non-White women and White men. Interracial sex was not haphazard but followed a distinct pattern informed by the racial hierarchy that prevailed. In colonial Bahia as in nineteenth-century Cuba, non-White women tended to mate with men who were at least equal or above them in the colour hierarchy, whereas non-White men mated with women who were on an equal or lower level (Schwartz, 1985: 391). And evidence from Jamaica shows that slaves with White fathers lived almost exclusively in households headed by mothers, grandmothers, or aunts (Higman, 1976b: 534–6).

Analysis of miscegenation tends to attribute its frequency to the disparity of sex ratios among Whites. White men without a partner are thought to have turned to slave or free non-White women for sex (Degler, 1971: 227). I have qualified this demographic explanation in the case of Cuba by pointing out the informal nature of interracial sex, which is not explained by the disparity in sex ratios (Martinez-Alier, 1974). Higman (1976a) also has challenged the view that seeks the grounds for interracial sex in White demography, suggesting instead that it was the sex ratio among slaves that, at least in Jamaica, accounted for the proportion of Coloureds in the slave population. The greater the excess of slave women, which was especially pronounced in the towns, the larger the Coloured slave population proved to have been. In urban areas female slaves formed the largest majority and White and free Coloured males were also present in considerable proportions. Since fewer slave mates were available, slave women were more ready to accept White men whose sexual exploits cannot, however, be attributed to a lack of White women because White sex ratios were also more balanced in the towns. Coloured males, on their part, tended to mate with Black slaves because they lost out to the Whites in competition for free Coloured females. As a result, in the late 1820s an estimated 10.7 per cent of all slave births in Jamaica were fathered by Whites who did not usually form nuclear family households with their non-White mates (Higman, 1976a: 143–53). Mother-centred households were also more common in towns because the Coloured population concentrated there, although they were by no means an exclusively urban phenomenon. Slave women on the plantations were equally subject to White men's sexual aggression. None the less, in the towns, where the majority of White men lived, non-White women were exposed to sexual advances by a proportionately larger number of them. Africans predominated among those slaves who formed nuclear households in town (Higman, 1979: 50–3).

Mother-centred households among slaves, as among the free non-White population, were then to a significant extent the result of interracial sex. Quantitative analyses of this sort do not reveal anything, however, about the

Jamaica about 10% of the slaves were 'Coloured' by 1832 (Higman, 1976a: 142; 1976b: 536). In Bahia there were never more than 10 per cent of *pardos* among descendants of Africans in the colonial period (Schwartz, 1985: 348–9); and in nineteenth-century Cuba as many as 50% of the free Coloured population may have been Mulattos (Knight, 1977: 263–4).

social processes and values involved in interracial sex, nor do they reveal non-White women's motivations, hopes, or options when confronted with White men's sexual advances, nor, finally, do they help to elucidate possible differences in attitude and experience between slave women and non-White women who were free. Beyond anecdotal evidence, no systematized information exists on slave women's experiences. Nor are studies available for Jamaica or Brazil that focus specifically on sexual relationships between Whites and free non-Whites.

'Each One with his Own Kind'

Slavery was much more than an extreme form of labour exploitation. It brought with it a racial ideology that transcended the world of the slaves. The society the slaveholders made was structured by a racial hierarchy that contaminated every sphere of life among those who belonged to it. This racial hierarchy served to underwrite the dominance of the Whites and coerced and discriminated against non-Whites, simply because of their origin, even when they were free. Precisely because of this racial ideology slavery exerted a profound influence also on the family life of free non-Whites.

In a study of marriage patterns, racial ideals, and sexual attitudes in nineteenth-century Cuba I have examined the forms taken by interracial sex and the values informing it (Martinez-Alier, 1974; see also Ramos, 1975). As distinct from Jamaica and Brazil, in Cuba interracial marriage was outlawed after 1810. (This difference itself demands analysis.) The massive introduction of slaves early in the nineteenth century had intensified the racial fears of Whites. The prohibition against interracial marriage reflected the Whites' hostility to interracial marriage but was also proof that this antagonism was not shared by all Whites (Martinez-Alier, 1974); some White men were keen enough to marry across the colour bar throughout the nineteenth century to apply for government licence to do so. None the less, interracial sex mostly took the form either of sporadic sexual exploitation of non-White women by White men or of more or less stable concubinage, neither of which established any formal social commitments on the part of the White men.

Interracial marriage was opposed by Whites because it threatened the slave order in a double sense. It challenged the 'social equilibrium' and public safety founded on the segregation of the races. It undermined the 'honour'—that is, the racial purity—of the White families that was the requisite in the private sphere of the dominant position of Whites in the racial hierarchy. Because nineteenth-century Cuba was rigidly stratified along racial as well as class lines, family origin and only secondarily personal achievement determined an individual's place within society. Acute anxiety over racial purity resulted in an obsessive preoccupation with heredity.[5] Social class and racial endogamy served to

---

[5] In relation to Brazil, Degler (1971) has argued that racial prejudice was merely a reaction to visible differences in colour, whereas in the United States it entailed a deep concern with genetic origin. But then it is not clear why miscegenation generally took place outside marriage, especially

safeguard family status and thereby the socio-racial hierarchy.[6] Because social status was construed in these racial-genetic terms, the protection in particular of the White women's sexual integrity played a central role in this ideological edifice.[7] By controlling their women's sexuality and mating, White men endeavoured to ensure their families' social and racial purity. Prevailing racial ideals viewed White women as the bearers of racial purity, so that informal and in particular interracial sex was a preserve of White men. (Revealingly, the stock argument to denounce the threat of a Black uprising was that Black men were about to rape White women.) Formal marriage was the rule between social equals among Whites of prominence, whereas informal mating and sexual relations occurred typically between unequals. Non-White women were the double victims of the colour–class hierarchy. They were the preferred objects of White men's sexual exploits and, because the latter shirked any responsibility for the consequences, often ended up living with their offspring in households without a man. If a more stable union resulted from their relations, however, rarely was it formalized. The household form resulting from interracial sex and the institutional form it took depended also upon the class status of the White men involved. Poor White men would occasionally marry non-White women, whereas for men of prominence even cohabitation was inconceivable. But because the dominant ideal was marriage, consensual unions were regarded as second-rate alternatives and non-White women who were engaged in such extra-marital unions were thought to lack sexual and social respectability. Moreover, because White men were mostly unwilling to assume any marital or parental responsibilities, the mother–child bond emerged as the primary socially significant relationship.

Despite the multiple abuses to which they were subjected by the Whites, free non-White women had, none the less, some options of which they did make use. Cirilo Villaverde in his 1882 novel *Cecilia Valdés*, a condemnation of Cuban slave society, tends to put the blame on non-White women for their lot. Cecilia, the heroine, is a light-skinned *parda* (mulatto woman) who is courted by a young White man of good family and rejects a *pardo* suitor because, as she herself admits, 'of course I like the whites better than the *pardos* . . . I would blush with shame if I married and had a throwback for a son.' Her White lover, who,

when it involved the middle or upper class. This was surely, the same as in nineteenth century Cuba, the way to exclude the racially-cum-genetically inferior offspring from upper-class privileges.

[6] It should be noted, however, that none of the three societies considered here was monolithic or based on caste. Dominant hierarchical racial ideals in Cuba were challenged by some groups, such as certain members of the Catholic Church who argued for intermarriage on the grounds that all people were equal before God irrespective of race, some progressive Creoles who saw in racial integration a precondition for political emancipation from the metropolis, and some poor White men who wanted to marry non-White women out of love or to have a woman to look after them (Martinez-Alier, 1974).

[7] The belief that sexual purity was a characteristic of women belonging to the dominant class was not confined to slave societies. The sexual prudishness of Victorian England is well known. Genetic ideologies of social status with similar consequences for women can be found also in societies that are not overtly racist (Stolcke, 1981).

unknown to the couple, is also her half-brother by the White father, ends up marrying a White woman of his own class and abandons Cecilia with a child.

An aspiration to be as light-skinned and to get as far away from slavery as possible did exist among non-Whites. Some non-White women attempted to improve their children's lot through 'whitening' (mating with a White man) in the hope, perhaps, that the father might eventually formalize the union. In the case of slave women in Brazil this strategy could enhance the chances of mother and offspring to obtain manumission, and the child's lighter colour would benefit him or her in general (Russell-Wood 1982: 181).

But there were also those who chose to affirm their own racial identity. The reaction of one mulatto mother, who rejected her daughter's White suitor when he requested her permission to co-habit with the daughter—'for her daughter was a virgin [and] she [wished] her to marry one of her own class'—exemplifies one form of resistance to White dominance. It is not clear in this case whether the mother opposed the consensual union because of its insecurity, whether she desired marriage (which would have been conceivable only with a man of her own race) for status reasons, or whether she was expressing her rejection of White supremacy. It was probably a combination of all three.

It is difficult, retrospectively, to establish the relative frequency of either attitude. Most non-Whites probably felt intense antagonism against Whites but attempted to adjust to their situation as best they could. A sign of the latent tensions present in the society was that, although Whites fathered mulattos, they regarded them with particular unease. Because mulattos were racially closer to the Whites, they were expected also to resent segregation most.

Dominant racial values operated also within the non-White community. The majority of non-White women, when they married at all, did so with partners of their own race and status. Differences in shade and in legal condition (free or slave status) influenced non-Whites' marriage choices. Endogamy of shade and condition predominated, parents rejecting candidates whom they regarded as inferior to their own children (Martinez-Alier, 1974: 91).

Finally, intraclass concubinage occurred, as elsewhere, among the lower strata of Cuban society, White and especially non-White. For example, in Vila Rica in Mina's Gerais, the capital of Brazil's gold mining district, in 1815 only 21.3 per cent of the White population and about 15 per cent of the non-White population were married. Marriage by the Church was a reality for only 16.6 per cent of the population over the legal age and for only 32.6 per cent of the heads of household (Ramos, 1975: 209, 218–19). Such unions would often be initiated by a couple who lacked the resources for a proper wedding and had no socio-economic status to protect, by setting up house together after eloping. Once they had offspring and had acquired some means, either they would wait no longer to formalize the union through marriage or the union might dissolve (Figueras, 1907).[8] The symbolic meaning with which formal marriage was

[8] Ramos (1975: 218–19) reports that women headed 45 per cent of all households (34.8 per cent of all slaves lived in matrifocal households). Such households may have had husbands or fathers

invested was socially less relevant for those who lacked the status that marriage served to consecrate. The deep social cleavages produced by slavery may have intensified this polarization of mating forms by race and class. The extra-marital nature of interracial sex may have further eroded dominant family values among the lower strata. Those values were never quite obliterated, however, precisely because of the symbolic meaning with which they were endowed.

Matrifocality Revisited

Post-slavery family studies in the Caribbean have focused mostly on the post-war period. They were inspired mainly by welfare concerns and, paralleling earlier studies on the slave family, they tend to identify lower-class family disorganization, in particular the noted prevalence of so-called matrifocal households,[9] as the source of all social ills. (To my knowledge no systematic study exists that traces permanences and changes in the family from abolition to the post-war period.) The early studies were detailed inventories of household types whose implicit point of reference was the Western nuclear family. In the latter part of the 1950s this static taxonomic approach gave way to a more dynamic model. The 'matrifocal' family ceased to be regarded as a symptom of the poor Blacks' social disorganization, being now attributed to contemporary socio-economic circumstances that were particularly adverse to them.

The first systematic community studies of family organization in the Caribbean were carried out by R. T. Smith (1956) in British Guiana and by Clark (1957) in Jamaica. Both authors argued that prevailing socio-economic circumstances produced economic insecurity and low social status of males. On account of their low racial status, which went together with low occupational status, men became marginalized throughout the developmental cycle of the family, their functions gradually being taken over by the wife–mothers instead (R. T. Smith, 1956: 221). A decade later M. G. Smith (1962) took issue with the 'intra-household' perspective of his predecessors. His intention was to establish for the Caribbean a typology of family forms which he saw as having developed during the slavery period. He made the important point that the mating system constituted the central formative principle of the family structure and argued that the 'matrifocal' family often resulted precisely from the unwillingness to set up a stable nuclear family. Furthermore, again in disagreement with R. T. Smith, who had denied any normative distinction between different forms of mating, he

present but were nevertheless perceived by the community as being headed by women. Ramos relates this phenomenon to a surplus of women as well as to a lack of jobs for men. Similar practices have been found more recently among the rural poor elsewhere in the Caribbean and Latin America (Bastien, 1961; Berquó and Loyola, 1984).

⁹ The term 'matrifocality' has been used to describe diverse situations, on the one hand a household in which the wife–mother acquired authority and control over resources at some point in its development cycle while the husband–father became marginalized, on the other a domestic arrangement without a male present.

maintained that marriage and concubinage constituted two different options which resulted in formally distinct family forms and types of parenting, adding yet another modality, namely extra-residential mating, which had much in common with Cecilia Valdés's experience.[10]

More recently, attention has been attracted in the study of household structures in the Caribbean and Latin America by the specific experience of women in the growing number of woman-headed households that are concentrated in low-paid and low-status groups. In Jamaica 33.8 per cent of households were headed by women in 1970 (Massiah, 1983: 18).[11] Woman-headed households in Brazil the same year amounted to 13 per cent, predominated in urban areas, and were still on the increase (Merrick and Schmink, 1983: 246–8). As has been suggested, the growing incidence of households headed by women was linked with forms of poverty produced by so-called economic development, which disadvantaged women heads of household most (Buvinic, Youssef, and Elm, 1978; Merrick and Schmink, 1983; Massiah, 1983). But economic processes do not occur in a cultural vacuum. They are mediated by existing social values and ideals. Gender hierarchies shaped the ways adopted to deal with the economic crisis as well as its consequences for the families.[12]

Household analysis *per se* usually fails to reveal the social values and symbolic meanings that underlie the forms identified. Rapp, Ross, and Bridenthal (1979) have pointed out the need to distinguish the 'family' as an aspect of ideology—that is, an *ideal* regarding relationships with kin and with non-kin and appropriate ways of reproducing them—from really existing household forms in her critique of biological reification common to conventional family studies. Taking up this distinction between family ideology and practice, I want to suggest that in a class society concrete household forms result, in effect, from the

[10] Simey had already referred to upper-class males' abuses of lower-class women in 1946 when he wrote that in the West Indies 'the exploitation of the women of the masses by the men of the upper classes has brought with it a general lowering of standards of behaviour which is now a part of a West Indian culture common to people of all races. The upper classes have set a bad example which it will take many generations to efface, and it is by no means certain that as middle class standards become more widespread in the population the situation will show any tendency towards improvement' (Simey, 1946: 100–1, quoted by R. T. Smith, 1982a: 117; see also R. T. Smith, 1987).

[11] As Youssef and Hetler (1983) have noted, however, the quantitative assessment of woman-headed households poses difficulties because definitions are lacking or unclear. Household headship as recorded in official surveys may refer, for example, to the person who controls the maintenance of the household or to the head of the household as reported by the respondent. But function and perception of function may be quite different. In addition, women-headed households are not undifferentiated, but may include a household with no male present at the time (as in the case of desertion, divorce, or death), a temporary union with a man who does not provide regular economic support, and a situation characterized by the temporary absence of the husband due to seasonal migration.

[12] The situation in post-revolutionary Cuba is, of course, quite different. In the early years of the revolution, the government carried out 'collective marriage' campaigns to marry couples who had so far lived in concubinage. Divorce seems to have increased markedly thereafter but the incidence of women-headed households is unknown. Cf. Youssef and Hetler, 1983; Stolcke, 1984; R. T. Smith, 1984.

interplay between dominant family ideals and conflicting class or group interests, rather than from biological facts.

Mating patterns constitute the formative moments of diverse household types. One issue then, is, to identify the conditions that give rise to different mating patterns. As Leach (1967: 19) put it so aptly, 'in a very fundamental way, we all of us distinguish those who are of our kind from those who are not by asking ourselves the question "Do we intermarry with them?"' In the Caribbean as in Brazil there persists a notion of 'different kinds' which has been reinforced by the socio-political meaning with which slavery invested race. Legal marriage as the dominant ideal regulating reciprocal rights between spouses is endowed with social prestige. In practice it is the appropriate form for colour–class equals who have family status to preserve and transmit. Mating between colour–class unequals continues to take the form of temporary or sporadic sexual unions which often result in single mothers living in households without a resident male and lacking socially recognized patrilateral bonds of the offspring.

Such sporadic sexual encounters also occur among low-status equals. Although they may be legalized later, these unions often dissolve, leaving the woman on her own to support herself and the offspring.[13] But nuclear family households founded on legal marriage entered into with an intent of permanency do, of course, also occur among low-status equals. Yet, under adverse economic circumstances the ideal of family stability and respectability may be more difficult to fulfil. The husband–father's socially defined role as breadwinner and household head may be jeopardized by his inability to comply with his family responsibilities on account of job instability and unemployment. Domestic authority may therefore shift to the wife–mother, who may eventually become the head of a household with or without the husband–father present. The severe economic crisis in Latin America in recent years appears to have produced this effect. None the less, it should be noted that the effect of adverse economic circumstances on household structure is mediated by prevailing ideals regarding gender roles (Stolcke, 1988: 208–41). A husband–father is expected literally to 'earn' his place of authority in the home, whereas the wife–mother's 'natural' place is in the home. If the male fails to fulfil his socially ascribed role as provider for the family, it is, therefore, felt that he has forgone his rightful place in the home. As a Brazilian proverb puts it, 'When the father leaves the home, the household trembles; when the mother leaves it, the house crumbles.' Yet, I want to stress that women assume household and child-care responsibilities under such harsh economic conditions not because the mother–child dyad is the ultimate (biologically) irreducible core of the family, but on account of prevailing cultural values and gender ideology.

Quite different are intracolour–class consensual unions among the poor—i.e., households formed extra-legally from the start—which could be found in

---

[13] In Jamaica 62.4% of the women who headed a household in 1970 had never married, 18.9% were married, 16.5% were widowed, and 2.2% were divorced or separated (Massiah, 1983: 19).

pre-revolutionary Cuba and exist in the West Indies and Brazil today and which reveal a certain disregard for dominant family ideals.[14] The relative frequency of consensual unions of this type may be related to the depth of perceived class inequality on the part of the poor. The greater social inequality is felt to be, the lesser sense it may make for the underprivileged to abide by dominant, 'respectable' family norms. But because these unions are not legalized, they may also tend to be more fragile and the males' role in them less permanent.

To sum up, in all these different mating options and the household structures that result from them, the critical point is the male–female relationship, whose content and permanence is a function of the degree to which those involved are willing or able to assume the reciprocal rights and obligations established by dominant family and gender norms (R. T. Smith, 1982a). Because gender ideology conventionally invests men, however, with the active, dominant role, it is they who in principle set the tone of the relationship even if this privilege may turn against them.[15] Marriage among the well-to-do entails a tight conjugal bond between the husband, invested with domestic authority, and the wife, who is conventionally subordinate and largely dependent upon him. Intracolour unions within the lower class exhibit, by contrast, three alternatives. Sporadic sexual relationships more often than not result in single mothers without a male. In turn, even in stable consensual unions the husband–wife bond is weaker than when marriage has occurred, and the male as the active element may leave. But even marriage does not either necessarily assure household stability, for economic insecurity, to which low-income groups are, by definition, especially prone, may undermine a husband's position within the household and lead to a breakup of the conjugal bond.

Has the legacy of slavery then any relevance for understanding present family forms? As I have attempted to show, mating patterns and household types are the result of the interplay of the colour–class hierarchy, family ideals, and gender ideology. More research is therefore needed on the values and meanings that inform specific household forms against the background of the colour–class hierarchy. Mating patterns and family forms have to do with the construction of social identity, and notions regarding social identity influence family ideals and behaviour. Even during slavery, race relations were ultimately class relations, race serving to legitimate and reinforce class inequality. In the post-emancipa-

---

[14] Berquó and Loyola (1984) have shown that in Brazil consensual unions have increased markedly since the 1960s, not only as an alternative to marriage in difficult or provisional circumstances, but also as an option that is becoming institutionalized. Such consensual unions can be found in all classes; but legal unions predominate among the well-to-do, whereas consensual unions are more frequent among the less privileged. In pre-revolutionary Cuba more than one-third of all unions were consensual, according to the 1943 census (Martinez-Alier, 1974: 140).

[15] This generalization does not apply to the new type of 'cohabitation' that has proliferated in advanced industrial countries in recent years. Although similar in form to the consensual unions discussed in this chapter, modern 'cohabitation' has a markedly different social and symbolic meaning. Consensual unions in Latin America occurred by default, as it were, of dominant family values. Cohabitation in Europe initially seems to have been an expression of rebellion by both partners against prevailing mating norms (Hopflinger, 1985).

tion period, similarly, rather than being a direct legacy of slavery, the social relevance of race, as well as family forms, has been mediated by the manner in which class relations have developed under specific historical circumstances.

References

Bastide, R. (1971), *As religiões Africanas no Brasil*, vol. i, São Paulo.
Bastien, R. (1961), 'Haitian Rural Family Organization', *Social and Economic Studies*, 10 (4), 487–510.
Berquó, E. S., and Loyola, M. A. (1984), 'União de sexos e estrategias reprodutivas no Brasil', *Revista Brasileira de Estudos de Populacão*, 1 (1/2).
Buvinic, M., Youssef, N. Y., and Von Elm, B. (1978), 'Women-Headed Households: The Ignored Factor in Developing Planning', Report Submitted to the Office of Women in Development, Agency for International Development, Washington, DC.
Clark, E. (1957), *My Mother Who Fathered Me: A Study of the Family in Three Selected Communities in Jamaica*, Allen & Unwin, London.
Craton, M. (1975), 'Jamaican Slavery', in S. L. Engerman and E. D. Genovese (eds.), *Race and Slavery in the Western Hemisphere: Quantitative Studies*, Princeton University Press, Princeton, NJ.
Degler, C. N. (1971), *Neither Black nor White: Slavery and Race Relations in Brazil and the United States*, Macmillan, New York.
del Nero da Costa, I., Slenes, R. W., and Schwartz, S. B. (forthcoming), 'A familia escrava em Lorena (1801)', *Revista Estudos Económicos*.
Figueras, F. (1907), *Cuba y su evolución colonial*, repr. 1959, Isla, SA, Havana.
Graham, R. (1976), 'Slave Families in a Rural Estate in Colonial Brazil', *Journal of Social History*, 9 (3), 382–402.
Gudeman, S. (1979), 'Herbert Gutman's *The Black Family in Slavery and Freedom, 1750–1925*', *Social Science History*, 3 (3/4), 56–65.
Gutiérrez, H. (n.d.), 'Demografia escrava numa economía não-exportadora: Paraná, 1800–1830 (mimeo.).
Gutman, H. G. (1975), *Slavery and the Numbers Game: A Critique of Time on the Cross*, University of Illinois Press, Urbana, Ill.
—— (1976), *The Black Family in Slavery and Freedom, 1750–1925*, Pantheon Books, New York.
Hall, G. M. (1971), *Social Control in Slave Plantation Societies: A Comparison of St. Domingue and Cuba*, Johns Hopkins Press, Baltimore, Md.
Higman, B. W. (1975), 'The Slave Family and Household in the British West Indies, 1780–1834', *Journal of Interdisciplinary History*, 6 (2), 261–87.
—— (1976a), *Slave Population and Economy in Jamaica, 1807–1834*, Cambridge University Press, Cambridge and New York.
—— (1976b), 'Household Structure and Fertility on Jamaican Slave Plantations: A Nineteenth Century Example', *Population Studies*, 27: 527–50.
—— (1979), 'African and Creole Family Patterns in Trinidad', in M. E. Crahan and F. W. Knight (eds.), *Africa and the Caribbean: The Legacies of a Link*, Johns Hopkins University Press, Baltimore, Md.
Hopflinger, F. (1985), 'Changing Marriage Behaviour: Some European Comparisons', *Genus*, 41 (3/4), 41–64.

Klein, H. S., and Engerman, S. L. (1984), 'Demografia dos escravos americanos', in M. L. Marcilio (ed.), *Populacão e Sociedade*, Vozes, Petropolis.

Knight, F. W. (1977), 'The Social Structure of Cuban Slave Society in the Nineteenth Century', in V. Rubin and A. Tuden (eds.), *Comparative Perspectives on Slavery in New World Plantation Societies*, New York Academy of Sciences, New York.

Leach, E. R. (1967), 'Characterization of Caste and Class Systems', in A. V. S. De Reuck and J. Knight (eds.), *Caste and Race: Comparative Approaches*, Little, Brown, Boston, Mass.

Martinez-Alier, V. (1974), *Marriage, Class and Colour in Nineteenth Century Cuba*, Cambridge University Press, Cambridge.

Massiah, J. (1983), *Women as Heads of Households in the Caribbean: Family Structure and Feminine Status*, Unesco, Paris.

Merrick, T. W., and Schmink, M. (1983), 'Households Headed by Women and Urban Poverty in Brazil', in M. Buvinic, M. A. Lycette, and W. P. McGreevey (eds.), *Women and Poverty in the Third World*, Johns Hopkins University Press, Baltimore, Md.

Metcalf, A. C. (1987), 'Slave Family Life in Eighteenth Century São Paulo: Evidence from Santana de Parnaiba', *Revista Estudos Económicos*.

Moreno-Fraginals, M. M. (1977), 'Africa in Cuba: A Quantitative Analysis of the African Population in the Island of Cuba', in V. Rubin and A. Tuden (eds.), *Comparative Perspectives on Slavery in New World Plantation Societies*, New York Academy of Sciences, New York.

—— (1978), *El ingenio: complejo económico social cubano del azúcar*, vol. ii, Havana.

Morner, M. (1980), 'Buy or Breed?—Alternative Sources of Slave Supply in the Plantation Societies of the New World', Research Paper, 23, Institute of Latin American Studies, Stockholm.

Patterson, H. O. (1967), *The Sociology of Slavery: An Analysis of the Origins, Development and Structure of Negro Slave Society in Jamaica*, MacGibbon and Kee, London.

Ramos, D. (1975), 'Marriage and the Family in Colonial Vila Rica', *Hispanic American Historical Review*, 55 (2), 200–25.

Rapp, R. (1978), 'Family and Class in Contemporary America: Notes toward an Understanding of Ideology', *Science and Society*, 42 (3), 278–300.

—— Ross, E. and Bridenthal, R. (1979), 'Examining Family History', *Feminist Studies*, 5 (1), 174–200.

Ribeiro Fragoso, J. L., and Garcia Florentino, M. (1986), 'Marcelino, filho de Inocencia Crioula, neto de Joana Cabinda: um estudo sobre familias escravas em Paraiba do Sul (1835–1872)' (mimeo.).

Russell-Wood, A. J. R. (1978), 'The Black Family in the Americas', *Societas—A Review of Social History*, 8 (1), 1–38.

—— (1982), *The Black Man in Slavery and Freedom in Colonial Brazil*, St Martin's Press, New York.

Schwartz, S. B. (1985), *Sugar Plantations in the Formation of Brazilian Society: Bahia, 1550–1835*, Cambridge University Press, Cambridge and New York.

Scott, R. J. (1985), *Slave Emancipation in Cuba: The Transition to Free Labor, 1860–1899*, Princeton University Press, Princeton, NJ.

Simey, T. S. (1946), *Welfare and Planning in the West Indies*, Clarendon Press, Oxford.

Slenes, R. W. (1973), 'The Demography and Economics of Brazilian Slavery, 1850–1888', Ph.D. thesis, Stanford University.

—— (1987), 'Escravidão e familia: padrões de casamento e estabilidade familiar numa comunidade escrava (Campinas, Seculo XIX)', *Revista Estudos Económicos*.

Smith, M. G. (1962), *West Indian Family Structure*, University of Washington Press, Seattle, Wash.

—— (1965), *Stratification in Grenada*, University of California Press, Berkeley, Calif.

Smith, R. T. (1956), *The Negro Family in British Guiana: Family Structure and Social Status in the Villages*, Routledge & Paul, London.

—— (1982), 'Family, Social Change and Social Policy in the West Indies', *New West Indian Guide* (Utrecht), 56 (3/4), 111–42.

—— (ed.) (1984), *Kinship Ideology and Practice in Latin America*, University of North Carolina Press, Chapel Hill, NC.

—— (1987), 'Hierarchy and the Dual Marriage System in West Indian Society', in J. F. Collier and S. J. Yanagisako (eds.), *Gender and Kinship: Essays Towards a Unified Analysis*, Stanford University Press, Stanford, Calif.

Stolcke, V. (1981), 'Women's Labours: The Naturalization of Social Inequality and Women's Subordination', in K. Young, C. Wolkowitz, and R. McCullagh (eds.), *Of Marriage and the Market: Women's Subordination in International Perspective*, CSE Books, London.

—— (1984), 'The Exploitation of Family Morality: Labor Systems and Family Structure on São Paulo Coffee Plantations, 1850–1979', in R. T. Smith (ed.), *Kinship Ideology and Practice in Latin America*, University of North Carolina Press, Chapel Hill, NC.

—— (1988), *Coffee Planters, Workers and Wives: Class Conflict and Gender Relations on São Paulo Plantations, 1850–1980*, St Martin's Press, New York.

Villaverde, C. (1882), *Cecilia Valdés o la Loma dē Angel*, Las Americas Publishing Company, New York.

Yanagisako, S. J. (1979), 'Family and Household: The Analysis of Domestic Groups', *Annual Review of Anthropology*, 8, 161–205.

Youssef, N. H., and Hetler, C. B. (1983), 'Establishing the Economic Condition of Woman-Headed Households in the Third World: A New Approach', in M. Buvinic, M. A. Lycette, and W. P. McGreevey (eds.), *Women and Poverty in the Third World*, Johns Hopkins University Press, Baltimore, Md.

10 The Slavery Period and its Influence on Family Change in the United States

RICHARD H. STECKEL

The slave family that developed in the United States was an amalgam created from diverse African origins, slave-owner business interests, slave-owner perceptions of appropriate forms of family organization that were shaped by their own experiences with Western European family norms, and accommodations reached between slave-owners and slaves on acceptable cultural practices. The nature and form of this family were constantly evolving with changes in the relative importance of the African slave trade and changes in the crops, methods, and geographic locations of planter activity. Thus, it is difficult to depict the slave family; one must qualify any discussion by time period, region, plantation size, main crop, and condition of the plantation (whether newly created and stable, or in transition as a result of death of the owner or bankruptcy).

This chapter focuses on developments from the early 1800s to 1860. Commonly called the 'ante-bellum' period, this era was the most dynamic in southern agriculture before the Civil War. At the beginning of the period the Atlantic slave trade was legal, production was concentrated on farms with fewer than 15 or 20 slaves located primarily in the piedmont and coastal areas of the Atlantic coast states of the South (Maryland, Virginia, North Carolina, South Carolina, and Georgia), and, with the exception of pockets of rice and sea island cotton cultivation along the coasts of South Carolina and Georgia, tobacco was the dominant crop. By the 1850s production had shifted substantially to the Gulf Coast states of Alabama, Mississippi, Louisiana, and Texas; cotton was the dominant crop; the typical plantation had more than doubled in size; and the Atlantic slave trade had been abolished for nearly 50 years. This was also the era of the abolition movement in the Western Hemisphere. The institution of slavery came under increasing attack in the United States during and after the 1830s, and abolitionists charged, among other things, that the Black family was a victim of the peculiar institution. Specifically, they alleged that slaves had little control over partner selection and fertility, that slave-owners indiscriminately separated family members on the auction block, and that slaves endured extraordinarily harsh material conditions of life. In short, abolitionists maintained that slaves were deprived of the Western European, nuclear family norm that was characteristic of the free population in the United States.

Although historians of the subject discount the claims of abolitionists as exaggerated or fantastic, the ante-bellum debate defined many issues for modern research. This chapter examines the lines of argument, beginning with the background of the ante-bellum slave family, and then focuses on the dynamics of change in categories of centrifugal forces that weakened the family and centripedal forces that strengthened the family.

Background

The age distribution of slaves who were sent from Africa to the Western Hemisphere was highly skewed towards those in their teens and twenties, a majority (perhaps two-thirds) were males (Curtin, 1969: 19, 28, 41, 46; Steckel and Jensen, 1986), and little or no effort was made for those transported in the Atlantic slave trade to preserve family relationships that may have existed in Africa. Thus, the overwhelming majority of newly imported African slaves had no family connections in the United States. Those connections were formed gradually as recently imported slaves learned a new language, made acquaintances with existing slaves, formed unions, and had children.

The share of slaves in the population who underwent the cultural adjustment to life in North America was influenced by two factors. One was the volume of imports from Africa. The number of imports grew irregularly from a few hundred per year during the late 1600s to about 5,000 per year during the mid-1700s, and reached a peak of over 10,000 per year during the 1790s and the early 1800s (Fogel and Engerman, 1974: 25). There is some uncertainty over the amount of smuggling that occurred after the closing of the legal Atlantic slave trade after 1807; plausible estimates range from roughly 1,000 per year (Curtin, 1969: 74; Fogel and Engerman, 1974: 25) to approximately 5,000 per year (McClelland and Zeckhauser, 1982: 46–9). Even the figure in the upper range was reasonably insignificant for population growth, however, because the total slave population in the United States was about 0.9 million in 1800, 2 million in 1830, and 4 million in 1860. The factor that more than offset imports as an influence on social and cultural development was a high rate of natural increase. Unlike slave populations elsewhere in the Western Hemisphere, slaves in North America had an excess of births over deaths, and by the early to mid-1700s the rate was sufficiently high to double the population every 25 to 30 years. As early as 1750 less than 40 per cent of the slave population had been born in Africa, and by 1830 the figure was less than 10 per cent (Fogel and Engerman, 1974: 23). Therefore, linguistic and cultural obstacles to the formation and operation of families were largely overcome by the beginning of the ante-bellum period.

Centrifugal Forces

Conditions that led to tension on the slave family from the early 1800s to the Civil War include selection of partners on other farms and the inter-regional movement of the slave population to larger units in the South-west. Accompanying this geographic transition was a movement towards work routines that influenced parent–child relationships. Miscegenation and the breakup of plantations also influenced family effectiveness and stability. The discussion begins with the legal setting in which these elements operated.

The Law of Slavery

Those Blacks who were imported into North America in the years immediately following the first shipment in 1619 probably had the status of indentured servants. By 1660, however, terms defining and enforcing slavery under English law were operational and nearly all of those imported from Africa after that date arrived as slaves. The US Constitution dealt with fugitive slaves and the Atlantic slave trade, but the existence and other details of the institution were primarily matters for the states (discussions of this subject are available in Stampp, 1956: 192–236; Friedman, 1973: 192–201; Tushnet, 1981). Congress banned slavery in the North-west Territory in 1787, but the constitutionality of this measure was never tested in the Supreme Court, and the extension of slavery to newly created states and territories was a topic of recurring debate in American politics for over 70 years. Legislative schemes of gradual emancipation and court interpretations of state constitutions eliminated slavery in the northern states beginning in 1781, and by the early 1800s slavery had a viable political future only within the South. Although each state fashioned slave codes, the laws and court interpretations were remarkably similar in part because residents in newly created states sought familiarity in the legal system. In addition, the desire to cope with recurrent economic change prompted slave-owners to seek total control over their slave assets. Thus, slaves were identified as property and had almost no rights before the law. Specifically, slave marriage and the family were not recognized or enforced in the slave codes, but individual slave-owners created a type of 'plantation law' that endorsed and regulated these institutions.

The Setting in which Partners were Selected

The laws of slavery indicate that slave-owners had wide latitude in the management of their chattel. Since the codes did not prohibit owners from selecting mates and enforcing cohabitation, some abolitionists charged that plantations operated as 'breeding' farms. However, evidence at the aggregate level contradicts the widespread existence of this activity; slave prices more than doubled between the early 1840s and 1860 while birth rates of the slave population declined (Phillips, 1918: 371; Steckel, 1985: 3). Higher child–woman ratios in the eastern states of the South have been interpreted by some as an indication that 'breeding' was practised within this region. Farms identified in the manuscript schedules of the 1860 census as having high ratios of women to men and large numbers of children have been cited as evidence of the selective existence of this activity (Sutch, 1975). Yet account books recording these operations have never been found. Moreover, slaves spent most of their available time working in the fields, and sales of slaves accounted for no more, on average, than a trivial portion of a farm's income (Fogel and Engerman, 1974: 78–86). In addition, the costs of forcing slaves to cohabit against their will, in the form of shirking their field work, could easily have outweighed the monetary benefits of additional children (Steckel, 1985: 203–6). Finally, the high mortality rates of slave infants and children contradict the idea that owners gave high priority to pro-natal policies.

It is impossible to establish reliably the degree to which slave-owners may have selected partners and enforced cohabitation arrangements. The available evidence suggests that it was rare. Nevertheless, the possibility that it could have occurred was a source of tension on the family.

Marriage across Plantations

If the conclusion is essentially correct that slave-owners established no more than indirect inducements for family formation, such as housing and other material goods, then slaves were substantially free to seek partners on the farm, provided the partners were not close relatives. Which relatives may have been eligible cannot be determined in general, but studies of birth lists and inventory lists indicate that slaves ordinarily did not marry someone as close as a first cousin (Gutman, 1976: 88). Although owners could have purchased slaves in hopes that a union would result, and in some instances may have done so, arrangements whereby slaves could marry outside the plantation (to someone who had a different owner) was the only practical solution to this problem, particularly on small units.

Table 10.1, which is based on testimony from witnesses on behalf of former slaves who were seeking Civil War pensions, shows that approximately one-half of the slaves were involved in these arrangements and that the incidence of these marriages ranged from about 69 per cent in counties where the median size of holding was less than 25 slaves to about 8 per cent in counties where the median size of holding exceeded 75 slaves. The fact that it took time and energy to commute—usually the man travelled—under these arrangements in part explains the inverse correlation of frequency with plantation size (Steckel, 1985: 228). Also important was the need to maintain discipline. Large plantations ordinarily had many rules and regulations, and slaves who commuted became aware of different rules and customs, which undermined authority.

Biological and geographic restrictions on eligible partners implied that slaves

TABLE 10.1. Percentage of Marriages in
which the Husband and Wife had Different
Owners, Classified by Median Plantation
Size in the County of Residence in 1860

Plantation size (no. of slaves)	Marriages	
	%	Number
1–24	69	49
25–74	40	35
75+	8	12
All sizes	51	96

Source: Civil War pension files.

may have waited several years to find a suitable partner, and in some cases may have never found a partner. This difficulty was noted by slave-owners who discussed rules for the successful management of a slave plantation in southern agricultural journals (Breeden, 1980: 239–45). If a partner was found on another unit, then the family members risked separation if one of the owners moved or the farm was otherwise dissolved. Arrangements by which one of the owners or a different owner in the same neighbourhood bought one of the slaves may have lessened the risk of separation. As Table 10.1 shows, the risks were greatest for unions involving slaves on small farms, which were located primarily in the upper states of the South (Maryland, Virginia, North Carolina, Kentucky, and Tennessee).

Inter-regional Migration

The extent to which family members were separated by the inter-regional slave trade is one of the most controversial subjects on the topic of slavery in the United States. There is little doubt that separations occurred and that the possibility of separation must have caused anxiety among slaves, particularly when a plantation was relocated or dissolved. Fogel and Engerman (1974: 48) argued that 84 per cent of the slaves involved in the westward movement migrated with their owners, but Gutman and Sutch (1976a) rejected the methods underlying that conclusion and emphasized instead that a slave had a high probability of being sold at least once during his lifetime. Carstensen and Goodman (1977) also argued against the methods and conclusions of Fogel and Engerman.

I have nothing new to offer on the overall magnitude of separations. However, Table 10.2 shows that whatever the extent of separations, they were much more

TABLE 10.2. Age Distribution of Slaves Destined for Gulf Coast
Ports, by State of Origin (percentage)

Age	Males		Females	
	Virginia, Maryland	South Carolina, Georgia	Virginia, Maryland	South Carolina, Georgia
<10	9.25	8.78	15.96	11.36
10–14	9.83	12.83	14.02	14.85
15–19	21.29	14.78	38.91	19.23
20–4	36.11	18.85	16.40	13.76
25–9	13.20	15.37	6.26	10.60
30–4	4.69	10.20	3.43	8.30
35–9	2.39	6.72	1.82	6.55
40–4	1.68	5.00	1.90	5.81
45–9	0.80	3.03	0.57	3.35
50+	0.77	4.45	0.73	6.18
Total	100.01	100.01	100.00	99.99
N	(3,265)	(12,760)	(2,475)	(11,357)

Source: Slave manifests.

likely to have occurred among those originating in the upper states of the South.
The data in the table, which pertain to shipments in the coastwise trade, show
that slaves destined for Gulf Coast states (Alabama, Mississippi, Louisiana, and
Texas) had an age distribution that more closely resembled that of the entire
slave population if the area of origin was the lower Atlantic coast states. About
30 per cent of the slaves originating from South Carolina or Georgia were 30 or
more years of age, but fewer than 10 per cent fell into this age category if they
originated from Maryland or Virginia. One may conclude that slaves who
moved in an east–west line were more likely to have moved as a family.

The concept of human capital can be used to explain the contrasting age
distributions. It has been shown that farmers were likely to move along east–
west lines during the early and mid-1800s, probably because they acquired
latitude-specific skills in crops, seeds, livestock, soil, and vegetation types, and
in the production of goods made at home (Steckel, 1983). Because older slaves
originating from the border states were accustomed to working in tobacco and
mixed farming, they had to be retrained for work in the cotton fields of the
South-west. Ordinarily it was not profitable to retrain older slaves. Slaves
originating from South Carolina and Georgia, however, tended to raise cotton
and did not require retraining.

Miscegenation

The 1860 census reported that 10.4 per cent of slaves and 13.2 per cent of the 'free Coloured' population were mulattos. In 1850 the corresponding figures were 7.7 per cent and 11.2 per cent. Since no Whites were slaves and a child from a mixed union assumed the legal condition of the mother, it is clear that sexual contacts occurred between White men and slave women. Because the census did not specify the definition of a 'mulatto' in terms of the shares of Black and White ancestry, it is impossible to deduce the extent of contacts or the possible degree of 'sexual exploitation' from these data. Under the assumption that census enumerators used a definition of one-eighth or more African ancestry to designate a mulatto, Fogel and Engerman (1974: ii. 101–11) developed a model showing that the fraction of slave births that were fathered by White men between 1850 and 1860 could have been as low as 0.61 per cent to 13.87 per cent and was probably as low as 1 per cent to 2 per cent. Gutman and Sutch (1976*b*) disputed the assumptions and the conclusions of Fogel and Engerman's model and emphasized instead that ex-slaves interviewed during the 1930s reported that 4.5 per cent had a White father. Gutman and Sutch also observed that the number of contacts between Whites and slave women would have been much higher than the share of births fathered by Whites.

Although estimates of the number of slave children fathered by Whites are suggestive, these figures do not measure its overall impact on the slave family. It seems clear, however, that these contacts made family life difficult for some, if not many, young adult slaves. A study of the incidence of mulatto children reported in the slave schedules of the 1860 census shows that contacts were greater among slaves located in urban areas, in the exporting states, on small farms or plantations, and particularly in counties that had large numbers of White men (Steckel, 1980*a*). The last point suggests that many contacts were initiated by Whites who lived off the farm or plantation.

Work Routines and Parent–Child Relationships

In recent years the field of economic history has witnessed the emergence of a substantial body of literature that utilizes human heights or stature as an index of health and living standards. This work was initiated by questions over the age at menarche and general health of American slaves (Trussell and Steckel, 1978; Steckel, 1979) and encouraged by work in auxology (the study of physical growth), which showed that height by age, growth rates, the age at which adult height is reached, and adult height 'reflect accurately the state of a nation's public health and the average nutritional status of its citizens' (Eveleth and Tanner, 1976: 1; see also Tanner, 1978; 1981).

When Congress abolished the Atlantic slave trade in 1807, provisions were made for regulating the coastwise transfer of American slaves. Specifically, ship captains were required to prepare duplicate manifests that described each slave originating in an American port by name, age, sex, height, and colour (Wesley, 1942). Comparisons of the cargo with the manifest at the port of destination were made to prove that the slaves were not smuggled to the United States from Africa. Table 10.3 shows slave heights estimated from a large sample of these data. The fact that Europeans, Americans of European descent, and Americans of African descent who grow up under relatively good circumstances have approximately the same growth patterns and adult height (Eveleth and Tanner, 1976: Appendix) indicates that it may be useful to compare slave heights with modern height standards for Europe and North America. Columns 4 and 7 of Table 10.3 show the centiles of these standards achieved by slaves at various ages. The young children were extraordinarily small (below the first centile); comparisons with developing countries show that young children from urban areas of Bangladesh and the slums of Lagos, Nigeria, for example, were taller and probably had an environment for growth superior to that of American slave

TABLE 10.3. Estimated Slave Heights Compared with Modern Standards

Age	Males			Females		
	Estimated height (cms)	Modern standard (cms)	Centile of modern	Estimated height (cms)	Modern standard (cms)	Centile of modern
4.5	90.7	105.0	0.2	91.2	103.8	0.5
5.5	97.6	11.5	0.4	97.9	110.3	0.9
6.5	104.0	117.6	0.7	104.0	116.4	1.3
7.5	109.9	123.4	1.0	109.5	122.2	1.5
8.5	115.4	128.8	1.3	114.7	127.8	1.6
9.5	120.6	134.3	1.4	119.7	133.5	1.5
10.5	125.6	139.3	1.9	124.6	139.5	1.4
11.5	130.6	144.7	2.4	129.9	146.1	1.8
12.5	135.7	150.3	2.9	135.6	152.5	1.2
13.5	141.2	156.8	3.1	141.8	157.9	0.8
14.5	146.9	164.0	2.2	147.8	161.1	1.6
15.5	152.8	170.1	1.1	152.5	162.0	5.8
16.5	158.2	173.5	1.2	155.5	162.2	13.4
17.5	162.7	174.5	3.8	157.3	162.2	20.3
18.5	165.9	174.7	9.2	158.1	162.2	24.5
19.5	167.9	174.7	15.4	158.5	162.2	26.8
20.5	169.1	174.7	20.0	158.6	162.2	27.8
Adult	170.6	174.7	27.1	158.8	162.2	28.4
N		(10,634)			(10,839)	

Sources: Slave manifests and Tanner, Whitehouse, and Takaishi, 1966. See Steckel, 1986c; 1987 for additional discussion.

children (Steckel, 1986*b*). However, catch-up growth during and after adolescence propelled the slaves to roughly the twenty-eighth centile as adults.
Moreover, measurements of eighteenth- and nineteenth-century populations in
Europe and the United States and of populations in developing and developed
countries in the twentieth century show that the slave growth profile was
unusual; ordinarily children and adults in the same population attain approximately the same centile of modern standards (Steckel, 1986*c*; 1987).

Growth and health on one hand and mortality on the other are opposite sides
of the same coin. Table 10.4 shows estimates of mortality rates for slaves
derived from plantation birth and death lists and for the entire population of the
United States from 1830 to 1860 derived by fitting model life tables. Nearly
three-quarters of the live births for the entire United States and about one-half
of those for slaves survived to age 5. The excess mortality of slaves diminished at
later ages and was approximately zero at ages 20 to 24.

Why were slave children so small and mortality rates so high? The slow
growth and poor health of slave children can be traced to poor pre-natal
conditions (Steckel, 1986*a*; 1986*b*). Determinants of these conditions include
diet, work, and disease; but the rapid growth of slaves during and after
adolescence suggests that diets were reasonably good for working adults and
that poor conditions should focus on work and disease. Slave women worked
long hours at physically demanding tasks, and ordinarily they had little relief
from work before the fifth month of pregnancy. Data on pounds of cotton
picked by pregnant and non-pregnant women (Table 10.5) show that during
seasonal peaks in the demand for labour pregnant women ordinarily continued
working hard until delivery and then returned to the fields within a few weeks.
Diseases of the mother, which were frequent during the 'sickly season' of late
summer and early autumn, also thwarted foetal growth. Birth weights were
probably low for many slave newborns and contributed to high neo-natal
mortality rates.

TABLE 10.4. Mortality Rates per Thousand for
Slaves and the Entire Population of the United
States, 1830–60

Age	Slaves	United States
0	350	179
1–4	201	93
5–9	54	28
10–14	37	19
15–19	35	28
20–4	40	39

Sources: Steckel, 1968*a*; Haines and Avery, 1980: 88.

The scanty evidence available on breast-feeding practices in the ante-bellum South suggests that slaves terminated breast-feeding within one year of birth, whereas southern Whites continued for more than one year (Steckel, 1986*a*). Moreover, the data on cotton-picking rates (Table 10.5) show that slave women quickly resumed a heavy work schedule after delivery. Because infants remained in a nursery (usually under the care of women too old for field work), supplemental feedings began within one or two months after birth. The supplements were high in starch and often contaminated, and both conditions fostered disease. Plantation records commonly listed 'cholera infantum' and 'diarrhoea' as causes of infant death.

Although acquired immunities increased and mortality rates declined after infancy, little catch-up growth occurred before adolescence, probably because diets remained low in protein and deficient in minerals such as iron and calcium. Slaveowners prescribed rations of meat, for example, in terms of working hands (Breeden, 1980: 89–113). Children entered the labour-force, initially performing light tasks, at around the age of 10. The realization of catch-up growth during and after adolescence, despite the additional claims on the diet made by physical activity, suggests that working slaves had reasonably good diets for the effort required of them.

What are the implications for our understanding of the slave family of the unusual pattern of slave health and growth? It seems clear that parents had little time to spend with their young children. Working slaves ate breakfast and lunch in the fields and probably had dinner after the non-working children had eaten in the evening. Mealtime was not an activity during which parents shared food and discussion with their younger children. When not working, such as on Sundays, parents apparently did not give their children food, or at least did not

TABLE 10.5. Daily Cotton-picking Rates before and after Giving Birth

Time period	Rate (lbs.)	Percentage
9–12 weeks before	73.2	83.4
5–8 weeks before	69.2	78.8
1–4 weeks before	67.0	76.3
Week of birth and week after	31.3	35.6
2–3 weeks after	8.6	9.8
4–7 weeks after	58.9	67.1
8–11 weeks after	80.6	91.8
Other weeks	87.8	100.0

Source: Calculated from Metzer, 1990: 27–8. The results are based upon weekly picking records of 15 female slaves on the Leak plantation, located in Mississippi, who gave birth a total of 28 times between 1841 and 1860. The calculations assume that each woman was 25 years old.

give them enough food, from their own supplies to promote catch-up growth. It is not known whether slave parents believed that young children did not need meat, or whether they were prohibited from giving it. However, it can be shown, from the costs of additional meat and the returns in the value of taller slaves, that it was not profitable for slave-owners to feed slaves enough meat to cover probable protein deficits (Steckel, 1986c).

Although slave-owners have been accused of slave 'breeding', evidence at hand suggests that their policies were actually anti-natal. Poor pre-natal care, abbreviated breast-feeding routines, and poor diets caused large losses. American slavery was foremost a system for the production of field crops. Slaves too old for field work, rather than parents, were the primary agents of socialization. A tragic legacy of this system may have been that parents who lived in nuclear families after the Civil War were ill-equipped through lack of experience to train their young children.

Centripedal Forces

Slaveowner Incentives

Although freedom to buy, sell, and use assets in a dynamic economy may have led slave-owners to seek total control of their slaves, they also had incentives to stabilize the labour-force by minimizing jealousy and conflicts over partners and by promoting attachments to the plantation. Marriage and the family were condoned for this purpose.

Table 10.6 presents evidence on the stability of unions from the records of ongoing plantations for which the owner generally recorded the names of both parents. (For further discussion of these records and of records for which the fathers' names were sporadically recorded, see Steckel, 1980b.) The first line in the table shows that 144 fathers and 130 mothers were involved in births 1 and 2. If there had been no switching of partners, then exactly the same number of fathers would have produced the second births in the pair as had produced the first births, namely 130. Therefore 14 women had a different father for the second birth. The average ratio of fathers to mothers for the first pair was 1.108, which was nearly twice as high as the next highest ratio. Column 4 in the table shows that switching generally declined after the first pair of births. The exception to the downward trend as family size increased was between births 3 and 4, which would have occurred approximately five to seven years after the first birth.

The last column in Table 10.4 shows the ratio of fathers to mothers that would have occurred on the basis of mortality rates of the husband and remarriage by all widows. Beyond the pair 3, 4, new partners were so infrequent that an important share of widows did not remarry and therefore actual fertility was below attainable fertility at older ages. Slave widows may have had little incentive to remarry because the owner supported the family with shelter, clothing, and most of its food.

TABLE 10.6. Numbers of Mothers and Fathers, the Ratio of Fathers to Mothers, and the Expected Ratio of Fathers for Various Pairs of Births

(1) Number Births	(2) Number of mothers	(3) Number of fathers	(4) Expected ratio $((3) \div (2))$	(5) Expected ratio of fathers
1, 2	130	144	1.108	1.026
2, 3	96	99	1.031	1.028
3, 4	81	86	1.062	1.029
4, 5	58	58	1.00	1.030
5, 6	42	43	1.024	1.036
6, 7	31	31	1.00	1.036
7, 8	27	27	1.00	1.040
8, 9	18	18	1.00	1.044
9, 10	15	15	1.00	1.047
10, 11	11	11	1.00	1.052
11, 12	8	8	1.00	1.056
12, 13	6	6	1.00	1.061
13, 14	2	2	1.00	1.066
All pairs	525	548	1.044	

Source: Birth lists of 13 plantations. See Steckel, 1980*b* for details.

Slave Society

Evidence on age at menarche and age at first birth indicates that most slave girls abstained for a period of time after they were sexually mature (Trussell and Steckel, 1978). Menarche ordinarily occurs within 1 to 1.5 years after the peak of the adolescent growth spurt. According to the data cited in Table 10.3, the peak occurred at age 13.3, and if one to two years are allowed for the average waiting time to conception caused by adolescent sterility, and one year is allowed for the interval from the onset of regular sexual activity to first birth, then slave women could have had children by ages 16.3 to 17.8, on average. Yet the average age at first birth was 19.8 to 21.6 years, depending on plantation size (Steckel, 1985: 103–4). Most plantations had so few Whites that some co-operation or policing of sexual relations must have occurred by slaves.

It is noteworthy that rules and regulations usually specified that slaves seek and obtain the permission of their owners before marrying. One reason that owners may have sought delays in marriage after ages at which reproduction was possible was that infant mortality rates were high for births to young mothers. Moreover, unions at young ages tended to be unstable. If the data on the first pair of births shown in Table 10.6 are arranged by age of the mother at first birth, then the ratio of fathers to mothers was 1.145 among those who had first births below age 20 but 1.093 among those who had first births at later ages (Steckel, 1980*b*: 418).

If permission to marry was granted, the ceremony was often delayed until a break in the agricultural work routine gave some leisure time for a festive occasion. Depositions contained in Civil War pension files about slaves who grew cotton or rice show, for example, that 33.5 per cent of marriages occurred at the end of the harvest (December or January) and about 15.6 per cent took place during the lay-by period of July (ibid. 411). The seasonal pattern suggests that slaves anticipated marriage as a significant event. Moreover, at least some slaves delayed sexual activity before or in anticipation of marriage because the seasonal pattern of first births was significantly different from the seasonal pattern of non-first births. In particular, 33.84 per cent of the first births occurred in July or August but 28.08 per cent of the non-first births took place during those months. The higher incidence of first births during the late summer is consistent with a delay in the onset of sexual activity and the concentration of marriages after the harvest.

Summary and Concluding Remarks

The American slave family endured hardship and stress. During the colonial period linguistic and cultural differences among slaves from diverse backgrounds in Africa were obstacles to the creation and operation of families. By the 1800s most slaves were second- or later-generation residents and cultural differences faded into the background, but other forms of tension emerged during the changing circumstances of the ante-bellum period. Slaves usually had freedom of partner selection, but difficulties in finding a suitable partner on the farm led many to seek arrangements with a slave who lived on a different farm and had a different owner. During the colonial period these arrangements posed few problems, but westward migration, which began during the early 1800s and increased thereafter, destroyed some of these unions. Separations could occur because slave codes did not recognize marriage and the family. Slaves also had no legal recourse against sexual advances by Whites.

Desires to stabilize the labour force led slave-owners to condone marriage and the family under a system of 'plantation law'. Marriage was a significant event; many slaves abstained in anticipation of marriage, and unions on ongoing plantations were often durable. However, American slavery was primarily a system for the production of field crops, and slave-owners gave high priority to discipline and work but low priority to child care. Therefore, debates over the incidence of separation and miscegenation are partly beside the point. Even when slaves were secure in families, infant and child mortality rates were extraordinarily high and parents had little time to socialize their young children.

References

Breeden, J. O. (1980), *Advice Among Masters: The Ideal in Slave Management in the Old South*, Greenwood Press, Westport, Conn.

Carstensen, F. V., and Goodman, S. E. (1977), 'Trouble on the Auction Block: Inter-regional Slave Sales and the Reliability of a Linear Equation', *Journal of Interdisciplinary History*, 8(2), 315–18.

Curtin, P. D. (1969), *The Atlantic Slave Trade: A Census*, University of Wisconsin Press, Madison, Wis.

Eveleth, P. B., and Tanner, J. M. (1976), *Worldwide Variation in Human Growth*, Cambridge University Press, Cambridge and New York.

Fogel, R. V., and Engerman, S. L. (1974), *Time on the Cross*, Little, Brown, New York.

Friedman, L. M. (1973), *A History of American Law*, Simon and Schuster, New York.

Gutman, H. G. (1976), *The Black Family in Slavery and Freedom, 1750–1925*, Pantheon, New York.

—— and Sutch, R. (1976a), 'The Slave Family: Protected Agent of Capitalist Masters or Victim of the Slave Trade?' in P. A. David, H. G. Gutman, R. Sutch, P. Temin, and G. Wright (eds.), *Reckoning with Slavery*, Oxford University Press, New York, 94–133.

—— —— (1976b), 'Victorians All? The Sexual Mores and Conduct of Slaves and Their Masters', in P. A. David, H. G. Gutman, R. Sutch, P. Temin, and G. Wright (eds.), *Reckoning with Slavery*, Oxford University Press, New York, 134–62.

Haines, M. R., and Avery, R. C. (1980), 'The American Life Table of 1830–1860: An Evaluation', *Journal of Interdisciplinary History*, 11 (1), 73–95.

McClelland, P. D., and Zeckhauser, R. (1982), *Demographic Dimensions of the New Republic: American Interregional Migration, Vital Statistics, and Manumissions, 1800–1860*, Cambridge University Press, Cambridge and New York.

Metzer, J. (1990), 'Efficient Operation and Economies of Scale in the Antebellum Southern Plantation' (mimeo.), in R. W. Fogel and S. L. Engerman (eds.), *Without Consent or Contract: Technical Papers*, W. W. Norton, New York.

Phillips, U. B. (1918), *American Negro Slavery; A Survey of the Supply, Employment and Control of Negro Labor as Determined by the Plantation Regime*, D. Appleton, London and New York.

Stampp, K. M. (1956), *The Peculiar Institution: Slavery in the Ante-bellum South*, Alfred A. Knopf, New York.

Steckel, R. H. (1979), 'Slave Height Profiles from Coastwise Manifests', *Explorations in Economic History*, 16 (4), 363–80.

—— (1980a), 'Miscegenation and the American Slave Schedules', *Journal of Interdisciplinary History*, 11 (2), 251–63.

—— (1980b), 'Slave Marriage and the Family', *Journal of Family History*, 5 (4), 406–21.

—— (1983), 'The Economic Foundations of East–West Migration During the 19th Century', *Explorations in Economic History*, 20 (1), 14–36.

—— (1985), *The Economics of U.S. Slave and Southern White Fertility*, Garland, New York.

—— (1986a), 'A Dreadful Childhood: The Excess Mortality of American Slaves', *Social Science History*, 10 (4), 427–65.

—— (1986b), 'Birth Weights and Infant Mortality Among American Slaves', *Explorations in Economic History*, 23 (2), 173–98.

Steckel, R. H. (1986*c*), 'A Peculiar Population: The Nutrition, Health, and Mortality of American Slaves from Childhood to Maturity', *Journal of Interdisciplinary History*, 46 (3), 721–41.

—— (1987), 'Growth Depression and Recovery: The Remarkable Case of American Slaves', *Annals of Human Biology*, 14 (2), 111–32.

Steckel, R. H., and Jensen, R. A. (1986), 'New Evidence on the Causes of Slave and Crew Mortality in the Atlantic Slave Trade', *Journal of Economic History*, 46 (1), 57–77.

Sutch, R. (1975), 'The Breeding of Slaves for Sale and the Westward Expansion of Slavery, 1850–1860', in S. L. Engerman and E. D. Genovese (eds.), *Race and Slavery in the Western Hemisphere: Quantitative Studies*, Princeton University Press, Princeton, NJ, 173–210.

Tanner, J. M. (1978), *Fetus into Man*, Open Books, London.

—— (1981), *A History of the Study of Human Growth*, Cambridge University Press, Cambridge.

Tanner, J. M., Whitehouse, R. H., and Takaishi, M. (1966), 'Standards from Birth to Maturity for Height, Weight, Height Velocity, and Weight Velocity: British Children, Part II', *Archives of Disease in Childhood*, 41 (220), 613–35.

Trussell, J., and Steckel, R. H. (1978), 'The Age of Slaves at Menarche and Their First Birth', *Journal of Interdisciplinary History*, 8 (3), 477–505.

Tushnet, M. V. (1981), *The American Law of Slavery, 1810–1860: Considerations of Humanity and Interest*, Princeton University Press, Princeton, NJ.

Wesley, C. H. (1942), 'Manifests of Slave Shipments along the Waterways, 1808–1864', *Journal of Negro History*, 27 (2), 155–74.

Part IV

Directions

11 The Centrality of Time in the Study of the Family

NORMAN B. RYDER

For an individual, the significance of the passage of time—the phenomenon of individual ageing—is in part the survival problem posed by the fact that the individual life begins with a lengthy period of immaturity. For a population, the significance of the passage of time is the problem of replacement. If the population is to persist, despite the mortality of its individual members, new personnel must be continually created and prepared to fill the roles of those who die. The family is above all the institution to which is assigned the responsibility for attempting to solve the problems of the passage of time both for the individual and for the population.

Given this viewpoint, it is not surprising that I view the central demographic questions about the family to be those concerned with delineation of the time pattern of family relationships. My own predilections compel me at least to begin with some notes on measurement possibilities. Much of the strength of demography as a social science is derived from the extent to which its theory is based on sound measurement, and its measurement on sound theory.

As a concrete social structure, the family is eligible for spatio-temporal analysis. A commonplace definition places the family at the conjuncture of the residence dimension, hence space, and the descent dimension, hence time. This simplistic dichotomy provides an opening wedge for development of an account of the implications of the passage of time for the family as a temporal pattern, and for the society and the world in which it is embedded. At the broadest level, the orientation is both the need for a theory of family change to explain demographic change and the need for a theory of social change to explain change in the family.

The central question addressed in the basic population model is change of the aggregate number of constituent elements through time. The model is both micro-dynamic and macro-dynamic. The passage of time is identified for the individual constituents as well as for the population as a whole. The central variable in the model is age, which is an index of the passage of personal time and also a link between the history of the individual and the history of the population.

Demographers specialize in the measurement of macro-biometric properties of population structures and of the temporal processes that shape and reshape those structures. The central place of time in the demographic scheme of things is most evident in the conceptualization of structure as the consequence of evolving process. The underlying dimension of the population structure is time. As a methodologist, the demographer emphasizes the study of changes of state through time, especially those changes of state capable of being characterized as well-defined shifts from one categorical location to another. Formal demography is the deductive study of the necessary relationships between those quantities serving to describe the state of a population and those serving to describe changes in that state, over time, in abstraction from their association with other phenomena.

As the population has a concrete definition, the principal definitional axes are space and time. The population serves as an organizing concept for both demography and human ecology, but there is a division of labour between them. The latter is specialized in variations in space; the former is specialized in variations in time. The basic ecological unit is the community, minimally defined by spatial co-occupancy; the basic demographic unit is the cohort, minimally defined by temporal co-occupancy. Such distinctions help to indicate some respects in which the demographer may be helpful in studying the family, and those equally important respects in which other talents are required. In any event, the concept of a population forces the sociologist to give time a prominent place in theory and research.

Proceeding from the conventional definition of demography as the study of the determinants and consequences of population change, it is clear that the study of the family is distinctively involved in both determinants and consequences. Its place in determinant analysis is an inherent outcome of the circumstance that every socio-cultural design predicates fertility as the prerogative and obligation of married couples, no matter how much exception there may be to that rule in practice. Its place in consequential analysis depends on an idiosyncratic property of the family as a group: the same processes that change the size and shape of the population are also essential in the determination of the size and shape of the family.

Furthermore, within the family, the changes of state that demarcate its history are typically responsive to specialized demographic capabilities. Demographic expertise extends to the study of what have been called quasi-populations, in the sense of characteristics that may be viewed as 'residences' for an individual over an extended period of time, with well-marked events of entry into and exit from the particular quasi-population. Such a characteristic, for example, is the married state, since marriage signals the beginning of temporal commitment to a set of social arrangements. Family relations are those exhibiting a kind of solidarity that involves a limited number of persons in total and enduring diffuse relations, in contradistinction to the partial, specialized, and limited character of contractual agreements.

One important stimulus to the development of family demography has been a reaction against the over-individualized character of conventional demography.

A predominant theme is the extent to which the behaviour of any individual is dependent upon the familial role relationships of that individual. Processes conventionally conceptualized as events occurring to individuals are in fact generally properties of the families of which the individuals are members. This viewpoint leads naturally to the idea of treating the family in the aggregate as a kind of individual, with a distinctive life history. This view is probably most cogent when the cultural design calls for an independent neo-local conjugal family, which has a clear-cut beginning at marriage, a period of maturity as its size reaches a maximum, and a senescent phase in which the family roster dwindles down to the last survivor. And yet, where the cultural design calls for a family form extended through the consanguineal axis, the appropriate analogy is rather a population, not an individual, for the family is potentially immortal: generation succeeds generation, but the 'house' endures.

The prototypical formulation of family demography is the family life cycle. The intent underlying this conceptualization is description of the time dimension of family life by dating those events most critical to its structure, critical in the sense that they signal a change in the roster of co-resident family members. Because of the inherent complexity of the assignment, this laudable ambition appears likely to be thwarted as long as we aim at comprehensive closure.

The family life cycle is generally represented as a sequence of events: marriage, birth of first child, birth of last child, first passage of child, last passage of child, first parental death. The events are dated by specification of the age of a reference person, typically the wife/mother. The first technical problem with the formulation is that the sequence of dates progressively loses coherence: not all of those families experiencing an earlier event go on to experience the next event. Thus, the sets for which two successive average dates are calculated differ in composition; the cogency of the calculation of the length of interval between them is blurred. It is strong testimony to the power of the insights generated by the family life cycle concept that they have had so strong an impact on our thinking despite their obvious technical deficiencies.

The most evident direction of resolution of the problem of an incoherent sequence of family dates is to lower our methodological sights and aim more modestly at describing each successive step in its own terms, with separate dating of the beginning of closed and open intervals. This is the course now being followed in the study of the birth history, one element in the family record. As the probability of an $(n + 1)$th birth is contingent upon the age at which the nth birth occurs, it follows that the length of time between the nth and the $(n + 1)$th birth is not equal to the difference between mean age at $(n + 1)$th birth and mean age at nth birth. Comparable considerations are involved in the measurement of divorce and remarriage, and of other components of the family life course.

A related problem concerns the loss of information implicit in confining the parameterization of distributions to some measure of central tendency. Among the many differentiating features of populations with higher levels of fertility and mortality, relative to those with lower levels of fertility and mortality, a most significant one is that their family histories have much greater variance in every dimension. It would seem to follow that less developed societies are obliged to pay disproportionate attention to normative prescriptions for the appropriate response to deviations attributable to demographic exigency.

The main strength of stochastic simulations of family histories is the full scope they give to distributional variation. Such exercises, however, are prohibitively expensive with populations of sufficient size to ensure adequate reliability for the range of interesting output parameters. Affordable models are characteristically impotent in delineating many situations of analytic importance despite empirical infrequency. In my opinion, the formulators of stochastic models have erred to date in so tolerating complexity that the principles of the underlying causal system are obscured. There is a need for models that permit scope for variance to manifest its importance yet eschew complete distributional inputs.

The family life cycle in its conventional form can also be faulted for its almost exclusive attention to the history of a family from the viewpoint of one particular generation and gender. There are as many different family histories as there are egos in whose terms that history may be described. For many important sociological purposes, one would be well-advised to choose a child as the reference person. The proposal immediately identifies a defect of the conventional formulation as the family history of an individual: basic to the sociology of the family is the circumstance that the typical individual's life involves both the family of orientation in which one is a child, and the family of procreation in which one is a parent. Focus on the family of procreation, implicit in the conventional portrayal of the family life cycle, has tended to conceal a crucial facet of family demography. The family of orientation of the average individual is larger than the family of procreation of the average individual, because those from larger sibship sizes are over-represented among the parents of the succeeding generation. The extent of the discrepancy is a function of the coefficient of variation of the parity distribution, an index that shows marked variations over space and time. Parenthetically, little is known about the relationship for an individual between size of family of orientation and size of family of procreation, relative to its evident importance for the study of change in the family.

The gender of the reference person is also critical to the analytic implications of family life cycle parameters, and in two separate respects. In the first place, suppose that one is dealing with a stable population in the formal demographic sense. Although it is indubitably the case that the intrinsic rate of natural increase for males must be the same as that for females, it is also generally the case that the components of that rate—the numerator (the natural logarithm of the net reproduction rate) and the denominator (the length of generation)—are substantially different for males and for females. These distinctive replacement designs, of major relevance for gender-specific questions about the quantum and tempo of intergenerational relationships, are lost from view in a monosexual treatment.

The second way in which considerations of the gender of the reference person are essential to interpretation of the family life cycle is the substantial likelihood of major differences in patterns of marriage formation and dissolution between males and females as a consequence of the operation of the marriage market. Marriage is a joint event. The probability of occurrence of any particular union depends not only on the characteristics of the two individuals immediately involved (and perhaps of their respective kin groups) but also on the shape of the total marriage market by age, gender, marital status, and the like, as interpreted through the norms of marital preference. Marriage transactions take place in a barter market. Each eligible person enters the market with a commodity to exchange for another commodity. The bargains that are struck presumably depend on some kind of ranking of the representatives of each gender by those of the other, with progressive sorting, and compromises contingent on bargaining-position.

The marriage market is a methodological thorn in the flesh of those who attempt to study family demography. Given any plausible representation of the interacting matrices of preference and availability, there are many more inputs to be inferred than there are outputs from which to make those inferences. The problem has proven quite intractable to technical ingenuity. It symbolizes the limits to which questions about social relationships can be pursued with a methodology designed to study the occurrences of events to individuals. This is much more than merely a cute conundrum to amuse those who enjoy playing statistical games. If the preference system in the marriage market, with respect to the age of a prospective spouse, implies an age difference between husbands and wives, as it especially does in most developing societies, then the numbers of marriages are strongly dependent on the growth rate of the population or, more precisely, on the changing size of birth cohorts over time. The growth rate is the most important determinant of the relative numbers of persons, male and female, of different ages. Moreover, the system is reflexive: a major determinant of that growth rate is the extent of marriage. The problem of the marriage market, in short, is centrally implicated in the most important single demographic parameter: the growth rate of the population.

The complexities involved in determining the dimensions of the life course for the family as a whole suggest the strategy of developing data sets and models designed to answer well some of the simpler questions that are pieces of the puzzle. Two examples may be given. First, although we have ample documentation of the conjugal histories of individuals, there is little evidence of consanguineal histories. From a familial standpoint, the individual life course may be represented as passage from membership in the junior generation of one's family of orientation into membership in the senior generation of one's family of procreation. That passage may involve no change of residence; on the other hand, there may be a hiatus of shorter or longer duration in which the individual is a sole adult. The end of life offers various possibilities with respect to co-residence with kin.

It should not be difficult to obtain, for the successive ages in an individual's life, a record of survival (yes or no) and co-residence (yes or no) for each parent and each child of an individual. The analytic utility of such a record would be substantially increased by determining also the ages of surviving parents and children, and the ages at death of the non-survivors. Also tempting with respect to the needs of family analysis would be a classification of the individual as having a dependent or providing a relationship with the parent or child in question, although it is evident that categorical responses often will be unavailable. Few records of this kind exist; that is a further complication in the lives of modellers. The justification for such inquiries is the perceived significance of intergenerational relationships, if only with respect to the numerical magnitudes of the generations immediately senior and junior to ego throughout his or her life.

The insight that distinguishes family demography from conventional individual-oriented demography is that the behaviour of an individual is dependent on familial relationships. As an alternative to focusing either on the individual or on the family as an aggregate (a most complex aggregate), a second example of a simplifying strategy would be to attempt a description of the history of a particular primary relationship. Primary relationships come in two forms: the conjugal/residential form, i.e. husband and wife; and the consanguineal/descent form, i.e. parent and child. (Although the relationship between siblings is often classified as primary, my own disposition is to treat it as secondary, in the sense that its most important characteristics derive from the circumstance that siblings share parents.) Again there is an imbalance in available data: the conjugal relationship is well-studied; the consanguineal relationship is *terra incognita*.

Consanguineal relationships are initiated by the birth of the younger member of the pair and terminated by the death of the earlier one to die. Demographic richness may be introduced through the dimensions of gender and co-residence, as well as by the commonplace formation of quasi-consanguineal relations. An evident purpose for measuring these elements of a consanguineal history is to make a beginning on the development of intergenerational demography, minimally concerned with the survival and reproduction of ego in temporal (overlapping) conjuncture with the survival and reproduction of ego's parents and children.

In such studies, a critical calculation emerges as worthy of much more attention than it has received to date. As one moves from individual to family demography, one's sights shift from individual survival to joint survival. There are various interesting and important properties of joint survival. The number of coexisting generations varies directly with length of life and inversely with length of generation. Length of joint survival varies inversely with the difference in age. As individual survival lengthens, joint survival lengthens disproportionately. Moreover, in the study of the calculus of joint survival, it is apparent that two members of the same family are not randomly drawn from the general population. Spouses select one another, they pass their genes on to their children, members of the co-resident family share (and constitute) the common environment, and the death of any one affects (positively or negatively) the viability of each of the survivors.

One somewhat uncharitable reflection about the methodological activity that was the first preoccupation of the Committee on Family Demography (described in Chapter 1, above) is that there is a substantial risk of futility in discussing measures and models in the absence of an agenda of substantive questions. At times it almost seemed as if the outputs came first, and then questions were sought for which those outputs might be answers. Most of the modelling was worth while, but that was largely a function of the fact that the constructor had implicit notions about what would be important in the study of family life and family change. In the same vein, my preceding remarks clearly reflect my prejudice that the intergenerational structure of the family is a more important line of inquiry than the conjugal ties that have to date dominated family inquiry.

Family activities may be distinguished with respect to those two dimensions, the conjuncture of which is often taken to characterize the family: residence and descent. The residence dimension is relevant primarily to meeting the family's daily need of food and protection. The implications of this are postponed for the present.

Two species characteristics establish the *raison d'être* of the family. First, from the standpoint of the individual organism, the circumstance that our species is distinctive in the length of time required to develop from birth to physical maturity implies that one or more mature individuals must be committed for a lengthy uninterrupted period to the provision of protection and energy, for sustenance and growth. This solves the problem of the passage of time for the individual. No society could be viable without regularized arrangements whereby productive adults are committed to the care of young dependants. In one sense, the family is a system for the transfer of resources over time, in this particular instance from generation to generation. Second, individual mortality implies the societal necessity of replacement, solving the problem of the passage of time in this case for the population. But the problem of replacement is socio-cultural as well as biological: it applies to all activities of society as an organization. One must inculcate in the new generation those capacities required for effective role performance as an adult. This task of socialization is generally regarded as requiring a long period of care by a limited number of individuals with whom relations of deep intimacy are developed—in short, familial relations.

I have described the family as a system for intergenerational transfer. A transfer is the provision of some goods or services by one person to another without explicit agreement for reciprocal provision at any time in the future. Yet it would be incorrect to regard the child simply as blessed by the altruism of its parents. In the process of socialization, the child is imbued with commitment to an intergenerational covenant, specifying diffuse rights and responsibilities over time. In some cultural designs, the child may be committed to contribute to the parental economy when he or she becomes productive; in other designs the commitment may be to the children he or she subsequently has. A prominent theme of current fertility theory is the importance for explanations of fertility of the temporal direction of intergenerational commitment.

As a system for resource transfer through time, the nuclear family design is insufficient in the earliest phase of family life because its needs tend to exceed its resources. The solution to what is essentially an age distribution problem is ordinarily found in inter-family transactions—contributions from related families at somewhat later stages of development, such as those headed by older brothers, or by the father's younger brothers. Most traditional societies are organized on the descent principle. Descent associates an individual with a set of relatives over his or her lifetime, for the purposes of contingent transfer, *inter alia*. Consanguineal kin groups are entered by birth to a member and exited only by death. (They are intrinsically suited to demographic analysis.)

Broadly speaking, the kinship system is characterized by its preoccupation with problems of the passage of time and by the closely associated function of sharing of risk. The descent group has greater viability than any one of its constituent nuclear families as a resource when members are unable to meet immediate responsibilities—because of chance vicissitudes as well as systemic properties of the age distribution. The descent group is not only a savings bank and insurance system, it is also the controller of property, i.e. of assets that persist over time. The resources are cultural as well as material. The activities of the kinship group are focused on what is viewed as requisite to long-term survival, and especially the preservation of the cultural design by transmission of traditions from older to younger generations. The kinship system is the ancestor of the ethnic group and the nation (as distinct from the state). Its strength is contingent upon the mode of production, in particular the ownership of land, the prototype of capital as an enduring asset.

The family is not only a unit in a descent system but also a household. This unit of co-operative living meets the day-to-day survival requirements of its members, the regular provision of energy, and protection from the elements and from competing species (and kin groups). The household is a set of persons who make joint use of capital equipment and produce joint outputs to meet these routine daily needs, exploiting the differences in their available personnel roster such as those based on age and gender. The household is an adaptation to the environment. It has many characteristics of a firm. (The original signification of the word 'economy' was household management.)

The persistence of the household depends on an appropriate balance between production and consumption. Beyond the evident circumstance that particular households may experience good or bad times, there is one prevalent feature of the household, unlike that of the firm: its membership is conditional on fertility and mortality. In consequence, households often find themselves too small, especially in a context of large demographic variance, typically associated with high levels of fertility and mortality. A household may be too small in the sense of having too few producers to meet its consumption needs. Although temporary periods of insufficient resources may be resolved by a transfer of resources between the households of kith and kin, the pervasive and enduring problems characteristic of demographic change in household size may require the movement of a productive person into the household or, more likely, the movement of a non-productive person out of the household.

The economies of scale notwithstanding, households, like firms, may also become too large, in the sense that the numbers of their producers pose problems of co-ordination and social control. In response such households may split in two. Changes in the distribution of persons by household, other than as a consequence of birth or death, may be termed fusion and fission. The most common type of fusion is marriage. Marriage is often highly responsive to economic considerations. Members of a nuclear family frequently work in teams of kinsmen. The mate-selection process is in part a means of worker recruitment. The elders devote considerable attention to the prevention of the passions of the young from overriding the work-related qualifications of mates. A second common type of fusion, particularly where mortality is high, is adoption, ordinarily by kin. The most common type of fission is the institutionalization of passage, the departure of a young adult from his or her family of orientation.

Demographic analysis of residential redistribution is exceedingly difficult. Fusions in general share the matching problem spelled out above for the marriage market. These changes in household composition represent a further level of complexity superimposed upon the already burdened depiction of the family life course; they are resistant to demographic skills. Residential redistribution of personnel is implicit in the dual character of the family. Because it is a descent unit, it is exposed to the vagaries of demographic processes; because it is a residence unit, its cross-sectional composition must make economic sense day to day.

It is evident that the family as a concrete entity experiences continual change in its roster of personnel and in the characteristics of its individual members. It is likewise evident that social systems having a precarious relationship to their environment, and demographically approximating inefficient equilibrium, must be continually exposed to the challenges of chance, with highly varied outcomes. In addressing the question of social change, I think it important to specify that such kinds of variation are not included—that they belong at a lower level of generality. I prefer to reserve the term 'social change' for transformation of the social structure, in contradistinction to the patterned sets of phases in the life cycles of individuals and other relatively invariant systems of interaction, as well as response to vicissitudes. From a demographic standpoint, one may summarize life-cycle changes with various indices of cohort behaviour as a function of age. Then change at the level intended would be constituted by systematic modification of processual parameters from cohort to cohort. Thus, demographic change occurs to the extent that successive cohorts do something other than merely repeat the patterns of behaviour (over time) of their pre- decessors.

But mere demographic change does not suffice to identify the kind of change we as sociologists should keep our eyes fixed on. Demographic behaviour can profitably be considered as the outcome, in a particular situation, of a pro- grammed response, a response determined by the application of a normative formula to the details of that situation. The normative formula specifies the appropriate behaviour for a set of circumstances. The behavioural response changes whenever the circumstances change, but that fact need not imply that the programme has changed. If $f = ax + by + cz$, where x, y, and z are input variables (measures of the relevant circumstances), and a, b, and c are para- metric constants (the normative formula), then f varies with movements in the variables, even though the parameters stay fixed. A change in the programme is a change in the parameters themselves so that, with the same values for the input variables, a different behavioural response comes to be considered proper. In this sense, social change is parametric change in the normative formula, or normative change.

Many exogenous influences may produce change in the family as a social institution. Here I discuss only two, although they seem to me to be the most important two: mortality decline and growth of the (non-family) job market. In terms of the functions of the family discussed above, these changes are located at opposite boundaries of the family: the first, the boundary between the family and the population as a macro-biological context; the second, the boundary between the family and the environment, specifically the day-to-day provision of resources.

Mortality decline changes the age distribution of the family and thus the relative numbers of children and parents, or, more pertinently, of dependants and providers. I have characterized the family and its surrounding kinship system as a set of solutions for the problem of the transfer of resources through time. Any particular normative resolution of the transfer problem, which may suffice to meet the contingencies of a particular demographic regime, may be found wanting in confrontation with the outcomes of a transformed demo- graphic regime, because the magnitudes of transfer may be dramatically altered. When the burden of junior dependency is inflated, the parents face a material problem; but it is at worst temporary, for, in due course, the children mature and increase the family labour force. This provides no stimulus for the senior generation to reduce its fertility (an evident resolution of the age-distribution problem). The costs of population growth are passed on to the younger generation. The share of family capital accruing to each heir is reduced, and the time at which that share is transferred is delayed. The disadvantages of application of the prevailing normative formula in the new context are imposed on the junior generation at the time they form their families of procreation.

The family, as a solution for the problem of the passage of time in the individual's life, has a normative design, a crucial part of which has been called here the intergenerational covenant. Such normative designs constitute the fabric of the social system. Although typically followed imperfectly, and hedged about with specifications of situations in which they may be ignored with impunity, they tend to persist as general guides to behaviour as long as they give a reasonable outcome on average. A systematic decline in mortality, unless matched by a proportionate rise in productivity, makes the fulfilment of the intergenerational covenant problematic because of change in the balance of person-years of the respective parties to it, and change in the family time-table. Incomplete fulfilment of obligations tends to produce strain and conflict, and to bring the prevalent normative formula into question. Parenthetically, a principal virtue of family demography is that its major propositions are couched not in terms of individual behaviour, but rather in terms of relationships between individuals, the objects to which normative formulas apply. Models of family demography, in brief, focus attention on the shape of the institutional structure.

The foregoing describes the import of mortality decline on the micro-level, in the context of the family itself. Parallel with the pressure mortality decline places on the intergenerational covenant, there is comparable pressure at the macro-level, impinging on the kinship system. Under equilibrium conditions, the population of a descent group achieves some kind of balance between net production and net consumption; its functioning can be described in terms of responses to statistical deviations from the standpoint of its member families. A systematic mortality decline, to the contrary, changes the age distribution of the descent group and reduces the efficacy of the entire kinship support network.

A third consequence of mortality decline for family norms has already been described. Population growth, consequent upon mortality decline, implies, with respect to any customary pattern of marriage in which an older male marries a younger female, that men from earlier, smaller cohorts are matched against women from later, larger cohorts. The upshot, if such norms were to prevail, would be an unsatisfactory surplus of unmarried females. Although equilibrium in the marriage market could technically be re-established by men marrying at a younger age, for the reasons specified above the time at which a reduced patrimony is available to finance the man's marriage is likely to be later rather than earlier.

Historically concomitant with sustained mortality decline has been a progressive differentiation of the occupational collectivity from the kinship unit. The mode of production gradually changes from one centred in the family and based on its property, to one centred in the firm, and the institutionalization of individual wage labour. This may be the outstanding characteristic of modernization. The new production mode places pre-eminent emphasis on productivity, and productivity requires individual workers, hired on the basis of achievement rather than ascription. Individualism is established not only as a requirement for an efficient economy, but also as an ideology, competitive with and antithetical to the ideology of descent.

The family, as a representative of the past, struggles with the firm, as a representative of the future, for command of the individual's time and loyalty. Where the family and the kinship system have provided the solution of the problem of transferring resources through time, the onus for life-cycle equilibration now begins to pass from family to non-family institutions, at the level of the state in the development of welfare systems, and in the development of private markets for capital and insurance, permitting the individual to solve his or her own transfer problems. In the process of modernization, there is a reduction of inter-generational transfers through the family, and an increase in both individual transfers through the capital market and inter-cohort transfers through the agency of the societal collectivity. This process brings together the two categories of stimulus for family change: mortality decline poses a new age distribution problem, and institutional differentiation provides a new solution.

In considering how normative change may occur in the family as an institution, it may be helpful to distinguish two ways in which solidarity is achieved: through socialization, and through social control.

The model appropriate to an emphasis on socialization is based on the internalization within its members of the group design. Satisfaction to the individual derives from fulfilment of responsibilities to the group. In this type of model, the covenants binding the members are not subject to the test of the extent of satisfaction that may be derived by any particular individual member. The interests of each are subordinate to and, so the myth goes, best served in the long run by attention to the needs and goals of the group. If there is to be normative change, within the orientation of this model, it will take the form of decisions by the group leaders, the senior generation, as adaptation to competition from institutional alternatives to the family as an economic entity, or in imitation of different forms of family that appear in some respects to be more successful in achieving family goals.

The second model emphasizes solidarity based on social control. In this model, the test for any covenant is not the interests of the family as a whole, but rather the interests of the particular individuals bound by the covenant. The family is a set of individuals whose actions have consequences for one another. Control over sanctions, i.e. power, is differentially apportioned by generation. Rewards and punishments are used to increase the probability that the behaviour of other members is favourable to one's own interests. The individual member is viewed as potentially rebellious. Membership in the group, and thus adherence to its covenants, is conditional on the rewards the individual receives in return for membership, relative to its costs to the individual, in comparison with a like cost–benefit analysis for affiliation with alternative organizations. Modernization is a process of development of alternatives that offer agreements more advantageous to individual interests than those within the family. Particularly subversive of the family as an institutional complex is the ideology of individualism: the assertion of individual interests as the proper test for allegiance.

These observations about the interaction of the family as an economic system pursuing an institutionalized pattern of intergenerational transfer, in competition with non-familial organizations, prompt the further observation that, if the pursuit of family demography is recommended because it raises questions about social relationships not directly encountered in conventional individual-oriented demography, then it follows that the study of the family in turn can be enriched by an orientation that encompasses the complete range of institutional complexes that constitute a society. If a theory of demographic change requires a theory of family change, then a theory of family change requires a theory of social change. The failure of the World Fertility Survey to provide satisfying analytic findings, beyond the merely demographic, was attributable not so much to the poverty of items in the questionnaire as to the level at which the questions were asked. We obtained a large inventory of information about the individual woman and her household, which could be analysed only as if these constituted essentially self-contained universes, because we neglected to consider the characteristics of the socio-cultural systems within which the woman and her household were lodged.

For purposes of thinking about the social system with respect to questions of population and modernization, I have found helpful a particular version of the functional requisite schema. Although I have no substantive propositions, derivative from this sketch, to advance with respect to the topic at hand, I am emboldened to present it in brief, because it permits a suggestive enlargement of the underlying theme of the chapter: the distinction between problems of time and problems of space.

One can consider the socio-cultural system as a mode of adaptation of a population to its environment. The areas of activity governed by a socio-cultural system are represented as an ordered array of elements interposed between the population and the environment. At the boundary of the socio-cultural system and its physical environment, we have those institutional complexes oriented at root to the problems of day-to-day survival, specifically technology (the adaptation of means to particular ends) and economy (the allocation of scarce means among alternative ends). Given a multiplicity of actors, with differentiated roles, problems of internal co-ordination and order arise, and hence the polity.

At the boundary between the socio-cultural system and the biological characteristics of the species, we find those institutional complexes oriented fundamentally to problems of persistence over time, or what is commonly called pattern maintenance. The primary position at this boundary is occupied by the family. Separating from the family in the course of modernization is education. At the top (or bottom) of the chain of pattern maintenance is religion. Just as political institutions provide a material basis for integration in a spatial sense, so does the religious system provide a moral basis for integration in a temporal sense. Religions are concerned with origins and the hereafter, and with the preservation of the system in its totality (the way of life) over time. The system may be diagrammed as follows:

Pattern Maintenance	*Adaptation*
Religion	Polity
Education	Economy
Family	Technology
Population	Environment

On the right-hand (adaptation) side, we have essentially spatial categories, concretely identifiable in the household, the community, and the state. On the left-hand (pattern maintenance) side, we have essentially temporal categories, the family, the ethnic group, and the nation. Of the many ways in which society and culture may be distinguished, one possibility exploits this spatio-temporal dichotomy: culture pertains to the longitudinal dimension of human existence; society is focused on cross-sectional interaction. If so, the demographer may find a more congenial interdisciplinary linkage with the anthropologist than with the sociologist.

Even the socio-cultural system in its entirety is insufficiently comprehensive for the purposes of studying change in the family. Although some problems are responsive to treatment as if a society were a self-sufficient entity, a major part of the process of social change we are examining is the movement of the world economy towards greater interdependency and integration. Relationships among societies are conditioned by the ease of transmissibility of some parts of the culture, by the similarity of many goals among the branches of mankind, and by the ineluctable pressure towards higher levels of aggregation and differentiation.

Modernization is a world-wide aspiration, albeit here and there tending to provoke counter-revolutionary spasms. The thrust for a higher material scale of living is propelling the populations of the world towards adaptation of their systems in directions believed to help achieve it. There is evident recognition of the differentials in command over resources, and of the technological reasons for those differentials. There is also a pervasive temptation to borrow that technology, often without full recognition of the comprehensive implications of that step for other parts of the social system the borrowers may be loath to see change. The efficiency and power of the modern system draws all nations towards it magnetically, or inundates those that may be resistant. Economic development is not only actively sought but also thrust upon weaker societies, frequently through non-free labour systems—slavery, peonage, indenture, and other systems of exploitation—and movements of capital that create economic if not political colonies. Societies with highly developed and economically oriented structures of high efficiency have invaded other, less efficient, nations militarily and economically, and transformed them in so doing. The immediate relevance of this for the family is the tenable thesis that there is a close compatibility between the achievement of high productivity and one particular family design. The logic of industrialism and individualism is transforming a culturally variegated world into one of ever greater uniformity, for good or ill.

In conclusion, I have characterized the family as a residence unit and as a descent unit. From the residence standpoint, as a household concerned with economic problems of production, the family is challenged by the development of individual-oriented labour markets and capital markets. The gradual shift from a property-based system keyed to kinship towards one based on wage labour and keyed to the individual provides an avenue along which change may intrude on the family design. From a descent standpoint, the intergenerational covenant that is the backbone of the traditional family is challenged by the decline of mortality. Relationships across time, characteristic of a descent system, are on the one hand especially resistant to change and on the other hand peculiarly exposed to the risk of change. The family is constituted of a complex of intergenerational relationships, characterized as a covenant, the roles in which are played out over time. Those bound by that covenant are by definition differently located in historical time. Should change occur, the separate parties to the covenant come to view the institutional designs that frame their world with different eyes. Any time-differentiated agreement is buffeted by the winds of social change, and the family is permeated with such agreements. Whether or not there may be institutional innovation in the family itself as a stimulus for social change, it seems evident that, should social change eventuate, for whatever reason, the family is precisely the institution one should expect to become the focus for strain, conflict, and transformation.

12 Analysing Household Histories

MEI LING YOUNG

In recent years several strands of social science research on the household and family[1] have converged on what might be called the household history approach. Historians had been concerned previously with the issue of household size and composition in families of past times (e.g. Laslett and Wall, 1972; Wall, 1983; Herlihy, 1985). Social historians such as Aries (1962), Flandrin (1979), and Stone (1979), on the other hand, examined the evolution of the modern conception of family life through the mores and mentalities of the French and English families in the sixteenth to nineteenth centuries. The concern of the anthropologists in this area stems from the fact that the family is the basic social unit from which studies of kinship structure, production, and inheritance systems in traditional societies were made (e.g. Netting, Wilk, and Arnould, 1984). Like anthropologists, sociologists view the family as an integral unit in which socialization and the transmission of values and goods occur and where ideas are perpetuated through the generations (Anderson, 1980; Goode, 1982; Harris, 1983; Rosser and Harris, 1983).

Family demographers, including the historical demographers such as Wrigley (1969), Henry (1967, cited in Wargon, 1974) and more recently T. C. Smith (1977), Lee (1977), Tilly and Scott (1978), and Tilly (1985), have examined vital demographic processes such as fertility, mortality, nuptiality, migration, and even women's work within some construct of the family boundary. According to a more contemporary view (Caldwell, 1982), the study of intergenerational transfers and their implications for fertility is related to family processes. The culmination of this interdisciplinary focus on the household approach may be seen in the recent works of Hareven (1977; 1978b; 1982) and Elder (1981; 1985). (For discussion see Wargon, 1974; Vinovskis, 1977; Hareven, 1978a; Elder, 1981; Cherlin, 1983; Tilly, 1985).

The argument for treating the household as a unit of analysis has now been accepted (see, e.g. J. Smith, Wallerstein, and Evers, 1984; Friedman, 1984; Harris, 1984; Netting, Wilk, and Arnould, 1984; Young and Salih, 1987a).[2]

---

[1] This chapter uses the terms 'household' and 'family' interchangeably. Generally a household is characterized by a task-oriented domestic group whereas a family is kin-oriented.

[2] Interest in the household approach was evidenced at the Seminar on Households and the World-Economy in 1982 (J. Smith, Wallerstein, and Evers, 1984), the Symposium on Households: Changing Forms and Functions (Netting, Wilk, and Arnould, 1984), and the two training courses and research seminars on Urbanization in Third World Countries and the Household Economy,

Taking it one step further, the household history approach, in its several variations, overcomes two conceptual inadequacies in research. First, the household is the unit of analysis rather than the individual, which had been the dominant unit of analysis in social science. Secondly, household history, by its very name, incorporates explicitly the importance of time in explaining the development of household phenomena.

The household approach involves both cross-sectional and longitudinal data, census-type (stocks) and vital registers, surveys, and oral histories. The source and nature of the data determine the type of technique employed in the analysis.

The next section of this chapter reviews these alternative methods. This is followed by presentation of a technique for analysing household histories using the life-course construct developed from the Malay Household Study, and by an examination of suggested examples of life-course analysis. The chapter concludes with a statement on the state of techniques for analysing household histories, particularly the difficult issue of macro- and micro-linkages, and its future in life-course analysis in less developed countries.

Methods of Analysing Household Histories

It is possible to distinguish conceptually between the study of households in the past, conducted by historians such as Laslett and the Cambridge Group, and that of contemporary households, conducted as household histories. The former is concerned 'with great changes over the past centuries' (Cherlin, 1983: 61), whereas the latter focuses on micro-level household structures, events, and transitions. There are, however, basic similarities between the two. Both are interested in societal change, examining this issue by analysing households or families, and both incorporate some historical perspective. The interdisciplinary concept of households forces both to use approaches and methods from a variety of social sciences, particularly history, sociology, and demography. The differences between the historical study of families and the study of household histories lie in the scale (in terms of numbers of households and historical span) and the aggregative character of the data and therefore the analysis, which are linked to the availability, type, and quality of data on the household.

In the past, historians of families made use of censuses and vital registers (especially parish records) of births, deaths, marriages, and even, where available, migration. Examples of the use of censuses and vital registers are Laslett and Wall (1972), Lee (1977), Levine (1977), and Wall (1983). T. C. Smith (1977) derived births, deaths, marriage patterns, and migration from population registers of Nakahara, supplementing his demographic information with tax and land records. The research by Hareven and Langenbach (1978) on

held in 1983 and 1985 and sponsored by the International Geographical Union Working Group on Urbanization in Developing Countries.

Amoskeag and of Hareven (1982) on New England textile cities employed company records, vital records linked to census data, and oral histories, which give their studies a richness often lacking in statistical analyses. The technique of linking different sets of data for reconstitution has also been used by Mitterauer and Sieder (1979) and Sieder and Mitterauer (1983) in their historical studies of households in Austria. Although this group is constrained by the nature of their data, generally those who work on household histories (e.g. Carter, 1984; Young and Salih, 1987*b*) have more flexibility because they use field techniques such as surveys and retrospective data such as life histories and oral histories. Their major drawback, however, is recall problems of the respondents. At a larger scale, but far rarer, is the use of panel studies. Examples are Elder's (1974) work, which used Stolz and Jones's study of adolescents in Oakland, California, in the 1930s and followed them up in the 1960s to study the impact of the Great Depression, and Elder's (1985) research based on the Michigan Panel Study of Income Dynamics. A common problem of such data sets is the high cost of collecting them. Even after the first survey is completed, the researcher who wants to follow up with another may have superfluous data from the first (as they may have been collected for different purposes) and a small, unrepresentative, group of respondents.

The study of household size and structure in past times is related to the debate about whether industrialization in Europe influenced extended households to become nuclear (Lasch, 1975). Laslett (1972*b*; 1983) concluded that the mean household size had not varied much between the sixteenth and the late nineteenth centuries in England and that the extended family was not the norm before industrialization. Similar findings have been reported for Western Europe, Japan, and North America (Laslett and Wall, 1972). Many criticisms have been levelled at Laslett's (1972*a*) conclusions, the main ones being that the evidence for England and Wales was based on cross-sectional data (from 100 parishes) that captured households at different stages of the life cycle, the operational definition of a household was too narrow and different from that used by the census takers (whose listings were not true population censuses but were prepared for tax assessments and military recruitment), they failed to take into account cultural variations between countries, and a major reason for small families in those days was that mortality was so high that three-generation families were uncommon (Berkner, 1975). From the perspective of methodology, the important point to emphasize here is that the data, being cross-sectional and devoid of information on age, were not able to reflect the different phases of the development cycle of families.

To try to overcome the inherent problems of cross-sectional data, which merely takes a 'slice' of time in the form of a snapshot, there were attempts to capture the family as process. A few methods emerged from these efforts.

A technique often employed by demographers is the cohort method, which can use census-type data by casting them into longitudinal sequence. Methodologically, the cohort technique is able to isolate specific age groups, follow them through time in an aggregative manner, and measure their changes rather than deal with a mass of undifferentiated population data gathered at one time. By selecting a group of people of the same age—say, those of age 10 at the 1870 census—and following them up—say, at age 20 in the 1880 census—it is possible to analyse historical changes in the family. According to Ryder (1965), discontinuities in a pattern—that is, how successive cohorts in each stratum differ in composition and behaviour from previous ones—signify social change. An example of how such a technique is used effectively is found in Uhlenberg's (1978) study of White American women from 1870 to 1930, comparing the timing of major events such as marriage, childbearing, widowhood, and death.

Another way of studying change over time in families is to trace differences between generations. Hill and Foote (1970) analysed changes in long-term financial planning and consumption patterns of families among three generations. Greven (1970) examined the patterns of inheritance and transmission of property across generations among the first settlers of Andover, Massachusetts. This approach has its conceptual and methodological problems, however. Conceptually, the term 'generation' may be used loosely at least three ways: to signify ascendant–descendant relationships (grandparent–parent–child), as a life stage (childhood, youth, adulthood), and as a cohort (people of the same age sharing similar historical and cultural experiences) (Troll and Bengtson, 1979). As demonstrated with many examples by Kertzer (1983), it is crucial that the concept of generation be properly defined. Methodologically, one of the major problems of using the generational approach is that one generation may contain members from different age cohorts who have had very different historical experiences (Vinovskis, 1977: 266–9).

The study of mean household size and household composition failed to take into account the developmental phases of the household. Generational analysis, while valuable for analysing transmission of values, goods, and services between parents and children, does not identify processes within the family. In contrast to these approaches, that of the family life cycle is an attempt to capture the different stages that families pass through and the major events that delineate those stages. Developing from the early works of Hill (1964), Glick and Parke (1965), Duvall (1967), and Rogers (1962), who refined Duvall's eight stages to a cumbersome 24, and also from the application of the family life cycle to India and the United States (Collver, 1963) and Japan and China (Morioka, 1967), this approach has the advantage of viewing the family as passing through stages. Useful typologies can be developed from the family life cycle, identifying important areas for analysis. Related to this concept is the emphasis on the effects of family composition and size on the household as a unit of production, accumulation, consumption, and transmission.

Although the family life cycle construct has sensitized researchers to the complexities of family research, it has a series of disadvantages. It assumes a developmental perspective on the family, giving it flexibility through role changes (Hill, 1964) and examining the family as a collective unit (Hareven,

1978a), but it remains a series of typologies based on stages of parenthood (Elder, cited in Hareven, 1978a: 99). During empirical analysis it is methodologically difficult to disentangle three effects—those of age, period, and cohort—on the life cycle even though the conceptual distinction is simpler (Oppenheimer, 1982). When applied to families in history, it is inappropriate because the stages are based on the contemporary family. Most family-cycle models rely mainly on the changes introduced by the addition and departure of children from the family. In the past these movements stretched over a longer time span, which meant that these events overlapped, blurring the sequential typology of stages. Similarly, the family life cycle approach defines stages by focusing on family members. In the past the family and non-family members in a household were less distinct, incorporating boarders, lodgers, and servants (Vinovskis, 1977: 273–4). In demographic terms, the impact of higher levels of mortality resulted in a less orderly sequence of stages, the higher birth rates meant that children were spread along a broader age range within the family, and often the family did not experience an 'empty nest' stage (Hareven, 1978a: 99–100). Finally, the family life cycle construct fails to deal with the timing and sequencing of events in the lives of family members.

It is precisely to overcome these inadequacies that the concept of the life course was formulated. This concept accepted the family as process (Hareven, 1974), that individuals in a family move through transitions rather than stages (Hareven, 1978a) and, most importantly, that the life course encompasses both the individual and collective family development, making it a truly family approach. The main proponent of the life-course approach, Elder (1977: 279), introduces it as 'processes of family adaptation and change over time' involving 'the timing, arrangement, and duration of events' in the 'ever-changing pattern of interdependence and synchronisation between the life histories of family members and the cycle of generational exchange and succession'. Of importance too is the idea that it concerns interactions between historical change and the changing household unit, and it accepts the notion that earlier transitions have a cumulative impact on subsequent ones. Thus, the concepts later propounded by Hareven (1977, 1978b, 1982) about family time (the synchronization of individual with family transitions), historical time (chronological time as it relates to important periods, e.g. the Great Depression or the Second World War), and industrial time (the industrial trade cycles) are a logical extension of the life-course construct.

Although the life-course construct is now widely accepted as an organizing framework for analysing household history, both by historians studying families in past time and by other social scientists dealing with contemporary households, the major problem is finding operational methods of analysis to implement its basic postulates. Both cohort analysis and dynamic event analysis (the choice being dependent on whether the data available for analysis are cross-sectional, as in census data, or longitudinal, as in panel studies or with retrospective data) have been used to analyse family histories, with the life-course construct used as the theoretical basis. Whereas cohort analysis, as explained earlier, relies on age-graded classifications of subject groups for comparison (Vinovskis, 1977: 276–82), event analysis focuses on the timing, sequencing, and duration of events. Life events have been classified as age-graded, non-normative graded, or history-graded (Schaie, cited in Simons and Thomas, 1983: 117). There have been some promising attempts at devising methods for event analysis (examples are Hogan's 1984 attempt to combine the two techniques in the analysis of life events and Modell, Furstenberg, and Hershberg's 1976 effort). However, no satisfactory model yet exists that can fully exploit and enhance the analytical power of the life-course construct. The Markov model has been suggested as one such technique (Tuma, Hannan, and Groeneveld, 1979). Other approaches include those suggested by Carter (1984) and the Mitterauer–Sieder method, discussed below.

Both the family life cycle approach and the event-analysis method are amenable to Markov chain techniques in the analysis of household transitions. Whereas the family life cycle format uses cross-sectional data, the event-analysis technique, as exemplified by Tuma, Hannan, and Groeneveld (1979), generalizes the transition states to critical events in the household history and thus can capture longitudinal processes. In a similar manner, when the data permit, Markov chain analysis may also be applied to the life-course approach. This requires the reduction of the family life course to some summary state of events or transitions and thus the summary or integration of individual transitions within the event-graded family life course. Therefore, although the application of the Markov chain technique to the dynamic analysis of events enables the analyst to exploit fully the rich detail of event-analysis data, as mentioned by Tuma, Hannan, and Groeneveld (1979), this latter problem is still intractable.

Carter (1984) considered the problems of modelling household histories as Markov processes. Most of the studies he reviewed had focused on household-type sequences. He suggested that such work suffered from the same ambiguities as do household types themselves. For instance, the concentration on positional definition of household members in terms of their kinship relationship to the head of household ignored such factors as seniority queues and the economic relationships between potentially independent household components. More importantly, even when a more adequate sequence of household types can be derived, as for example from the summary indexation of household events already mentioned, it is not possible to define these transition states as though they were independent of previous household types or states, a mathematical requirement of Markov chain analysis. It is in the nature of household histories that preceding states or transitions will affect current and future events. The duration of an event for a given household or the length of stay in a given state will also influence transition probabilities. Historical events such as age at marriage and mean ages at maternity and paternity will affect family formation, for instance at much later stages. Thus arises the need to focus on the events in the household history and the decisions that lead to these events. Therefore, the Markov chain approach is not necessarily a promising technique for analysing household histories.

In general, Carter (1984) believes that available methods of synchronic, cross-sectional analysis do not provide an adequate substitute for the longitudinal approach. No matter how the classification of household types is arrived at, it fails to take account of changes in household composition that may influence the subsequent actions of household members. Carter (1984: 59) suggests that the minimal elements of a household history consist of the kinship relations between any given member of the household and the head of household, the position of that member in the household personnel system, rules of seniority in the household, tracking of the movements of members in and out of the household unit, and the manner in which events affect the viability of the household unit and the opportunities of its members to pursue their own goals. Household histories thus are histories of changing household structure according to movements of personnel and resources through the household. The tracking of these developments in the household economy over time requires the calculation and tracing of relevant indicators of household change. Carter has suggested several ratios as indicative of these dynamic changes in the household: the household size, the amount or value of resources, the producer/consumer ratio, and the ratio of resources to personnel, to name a few.

Carter's approach is essentially anthropological, relying on household genealogical and compositional data and the various ratios at several time points in the household history. The results are essentially ethnographic and descriptive, and although the potential is there, the scope for quantitative analysis is hampered by less than dense data over the period of observation in his household case studies.

A similar but more graphic approach, relying heavily on family compositional data from serial records, was undertaken by Mitterauer and Sieder (1979; see also Sieder and Mitterauer, 1983; compare this with the Casalecchio Project undertaken by Kertzer and Schiaffino, 1983). The Sieder and Mitterauer project was the reconstruction of the family life course for various families in the past using census listings supplemented by vital records. The reconstruction enabled them to determine·phases in the development of the families in their study. Asserting that such serial lists are superior to cross-sectional census data, they suggest several methods of analysing these historical household data. Some of the quantitative methods relate to the analysis of changes in household composition, making it possible to establish cross-connections between population structure and development of family cycles; to analysis concerning duration, such as the length of co-residence of children with their parents; and to frequencies of certain developmental processes, for example the succession to household headship (Mitterauer and Sieder, 1979: 260–1).

A second group of methods relies upon the qualitative interpretation of specific events or sequences of events, which are not, in Mitterauer and Sieder's view, amenable to computer-generated quantitative analysis. Such analysis pertains not only to the development of individual households but also to several interacting households or to individual careers traced through different households. Such cross-connections among households would be revealed by cross-sectional data, whereas the analysis of serial lists would present most clearly 'the connections between individual biography and the development of familial groups' (Mitterauer and Sieder 1979: 281).

The problem with the Mitterauer–Sieder approach, as well as with the Carter approach, is the cumbersome detail of household micro-level data, which do not lend themselves easily to aggregative analysis. Kertzer (1985: 103–4) has criticized the Mitterauer–Sieder approach on two counts: first, that it was too difficult to generalize from the mass of pictorial representations of individual household histories, and secondly, that it failed to account for timing and sequencing of family events. Although the life-course diagrams suggested in the next section do incorporate timing and sequencing of household members' transitions, a similar problem of assimilating many complicated diagrams faces us. Summarizing these diagrams without losing the richness and complexities of the family processes represents the major challenge to methodology in the analysis of household histories.

A Framework for the Analysis of Household Histories

The Life-Course Framework

From the review of various approaches and methods in the analysis of household histories in the preceding section, the life-course framework appears to have several features useful in analysing household histories. As Hareven (1978*a*: 103) suggests,

it offers a comprehensive integrative approach, which steers one to interpret individual and family transitions as part of a continuous interactive process . . . it helps one view an individual transition as part of a cluster of other concurrent transitions affecting each other . . . and it treats a cohort not only as belonging to its specific time period, but also as located in earlier times, its experience shaped therefore by different historical forces.

Life-course analysis thus focuses on transitions in individual and family behaviour involving two levels, one being the relationship between an individual life history and the collective history of one's family unit, and the other being the relationship between individual and family change and changes in the larger society (Hareven, 1978*a*: 98).

The problem for analysts is to translate this household history framework into a practical methodology for extracting meanings and patterns from the adequacy of method and the adequacy of data. The ultimate object is both description and interpretation. The method proposed and applied within this framework involves three levels of analysis: first, at the level of representation and depiction; secondly, at the level of summary statistics in order to derive patterns of household transitions; and thirdly, at the level of linkage between household transitions and broader historical change.

The Life-Course Diagram

The approach discussed here arose out of a study of the Malay household economy in transition during a period of rapid industrialization and labour-force formation (the Malay Household Study). The research emphasized the role of the newly emergent young women workers recruited into the export-oriented factories established in the early 1970s. In particular, it examined the reasons for their migration, the effects of their participation in the industrial labour-force on their households, the generational differences between mothers and wage-working daughters, and the larger socio-political and economic processes as they affected the trajectory of village and family life in rapid transformation. Such issues are related to the question of structural change within the rural Malay family, which is undergoing tremendous change as a consequence of numerous interlinking factors such as rising educational levels, increasing Malay urbanization, and the dramatic and unprecedented rise of Malay women in the industrial labour-force.

Two important issues directly affect the Malay household. One is the question of off-farm employment in rural households, and the other is the question of proletarianization. It was felt that the household approach, rather than the individual approach, is a more effective method to capture these processes. Thus, a dynamic picture emerges of the effect of the family life cycle on the individual, as she performs different roles and assumes different responsibilities in the course of passing through these transitions. Changing configurations of the family composition make her own position change, relative to that of the rest of the family members.

The techniques used for capturing this information were those of the life-history matrix (to ensure completeness of factual data) and oral histories (to retain the richness of feelings, perceptions, and attitudes). Owing to the depth of the interviews and detailed questions, the study was limited to fifty households, most of which had at least one working daughter. The study areas were rural and peri-urban parts of Penang from which Malay factory girls had been drawn.

Using individual life-history data obtained through retrospective surveys of all members of contemporary households, it is possible to depict the history of any household by means of a life-course diagram. An example is Figure 12.1, which is organized to represent the individual, family, and external transitions (or historical time, in Hareven's terminology) with household members' individual career lines being arranged in the order of birth beginning with the household head. Events or transition points (birth, entry into and termination of schooling, entry into the labour-force, job changes, migration, marriage, birth of children, etc.) in the individual's life history are given standard symbols,

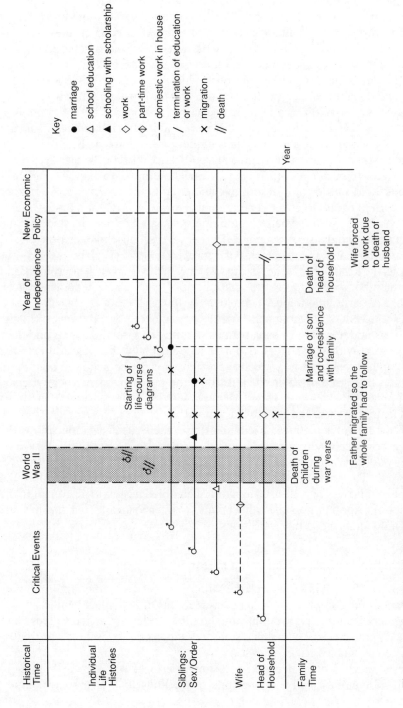

Fig. 12.1 Hypothetical Structure of the Life-Course Diagram

enabling the analyst to examine timing and duration of individual events and relate them to other members of the household. Family transitions are depicted in the lower portion of the life-course diagram, with vertical lines marking critical family events such as the death of the household head and the addition of new producers or employed household members. These events may then be related to individual members' responses and life changes. Historical time is represented in the upper portion of the diagram, where critical events or reference points that may affect the household history can be indicated, or a whole transition period, such as the war years or some other significant historical event, may be shown. Details of these transitions can be added to the diagram, depending upon the degree of significance and clarity intended.

Such a diagram can be constructed for each household, to map schematically the household's history for descriptive and comparative purposes. Extensions of the basic diagram to cover generational transitions (say, for a three-generation household history, where the data permit) can be done by 'stacking' the relevant household history diagrams. Two or several household histories can be compared by mapping the life lines of critical members of each household—for example, the heads of households, the working members of each household, and other members relevant to the analysis of a particular phenomenon (e.g. marriage patterns, migration, or employment history).

These life-course diagrams are useful in facilitating descriptions of family transitions and in narrative explanations of critical household events and their effects on individual members. Synoptic judgements of the effects of external events on household history are also possible. It is the depiction of household processes that are 'buried' in the individual life histories, seen synchronically, and supplemented by household narrative history, that constitutes the most useful feature of these life-course diagrams.

This method of depicting household histories theoretically is applicable to the analysis both of contemporary households, using retrospective life-history data, and of past households, using serial lists, linked data, or, if one is fortunate, panel data. The latter application is of course too demanding of data; thus, the life-course diagram may be used as a test of completeness to identify gaps in the description. Another possible application is to interpolate missing data in some of the individual and family transitions.

Quantitative Analysis of Household Histories

Kertzer (1985: 103) has criticized the Mitterauer–Sieder method for burdening the reader with complex pictorial representations of individual families, which limit generalizations. To avoid having the same criticism applied to these life-course diagrams, it is essential that summary statistics of household histories be generated to enable further analysis.

These statistics are calculated to examine critical variables in household histories. Being descriptive of the state of the household at particular times, analysis of the time series involving these statistics provides important insights into the development of the household. Examples of such critical variables are those calculated by Carter (1984) on household size, amount or value of resources and the technological requirements of their management, the producer/consumer ratio, and the ratio of resources to personnel. Depending upon the aims of the study, summary statistics can be calculated for various illustrations. Thus, to follow the concept of income pooling (Wallerstein, 1984; Friedman, 1984), calculations can be made of the proportion of wage income to total 'pooled' household income, the proportion of domestic labour activities, the proportion of transfer payments (gifts, subsidies, other income received without exchange of labour or commodities), etc. In the current research on how Malay households have changed as a consequence of industrialization, summary statistics will be calculated for the extent of wages from off-farm employment to total household income, the proportion contributed by working daughters, changes in income levels as members of the household move in and out of the labour-market, etc. Similarly, age-specific indicators of household transition such as out-migration and labour-force participation can be calculated for the family as it develops through its various phases.

These statistics are analysed by means of standard techniques to examine broader patterns and relationships. Specifically, demographic constraints can be isolated from effects caused by the national and international economy, such as recession in the semi-conductor industry. The range of analysis is constrained only by the availability and quality of the data. These statistics are also used in secondary analysis employing cohort methods, as discussed in the previous section, as well as methods of time-series analysis including auto-regressive models used in longitudinal analyses of household history.

Another means of analysis is to devise indicators that allow the researcher to incorporate extra-household variables into the analysis. Such variables would include economic conditions in the local economy—for example, world rubber prices as they affect the household economy. The choice of variables will depend upon the aims of the study. In a structural analysis of migration derived from life histories, for example, an index of critical moves was developed, based upon whichever variables were considered important in the process of structural change associated with the individual labour migration decision (Young, 1982a; forthcoming). These indicators may be related to household variables and other historical data. These methods allow us to consider the linkage of household and other structural variables, in this case the phenomenon of migration.

Whereas quantitative methods of analysing aggregate patterns of household transition can depict its links to the macro-framework of change, the integration with household processes in a historical sense is not so obvious unless we undertake some of the techniques of analysis, such as cohort analysis, or co-variance analysis, among the more significant individual and household historical indicators with events in the larger society.

The first method involves a panel study of every member of the family, in which at every critical point of the individual transition the family life situation is examined to determine the influence of such factors as family size, household income, average education of household members, and the occupation of the head of household. When analysed across groups of individuals, these data enable the analyst to examine household labour strategies and their relationships with local and national economic structural changes.

A second alternative, less stringent in its data requirements, considers such data only for particular conjunctures in the family demographic history, such as the death of the head of household. A slightly better method is to compare a particular conjuncture with a previous conjuncture. These conjunctures can then be related to particular structural shifts in the local or regional economy.

A more direct method is to superimpose the individual critical profiles of transition (either migration or other life transitions) on to the life-history diagram of the household, as can be done similarly with the Carter ratios. These mappings of critical household transitions on to the life-course diagram, as illustrated in Figure 12.2, allow interpretation of the household history in terms of these indicators of critical household events. Correlations among these critical household events across a sample of households, using standard multivariate statistical techniques, will provide the analyst with insights into the patterns and linkages between household processes and the larger processes in industrial and historical time.

These methods may be illustrated by case studies of the effects of industrialization on labour formation and the Malay household economy in Penang (Young and Salih, 1987*b*).

Analysing the Life Course as Household History

Life-Course Analysis of Two Malay Households

The two cases of household history illustrated in Figures 12.3 and 12.4 summarize the life histories of household members, including those who have migrated but contribute to the household income, or are subsidized by the household and therefore participate in the income pooling. They examine with more accuracy the transitions of individuals within the life course and are able to describe the integration of the concepts of individual, family, and industrial time within a household situated in 'historical' time (see Hareven, 1977; 1978*b*; 1982). Thus, we can see in a clearer time perspective how personal tragedies, such as the death of the main income earner, force the household to adapt and cope in various ways, such as by migrating and increasing the number of jobs for the other household members. Likewise, we are able to see, albeit rather starkly, the different configurations of labour input within the domestic domain and the productive work of family members through time. Such issues as sibling order,

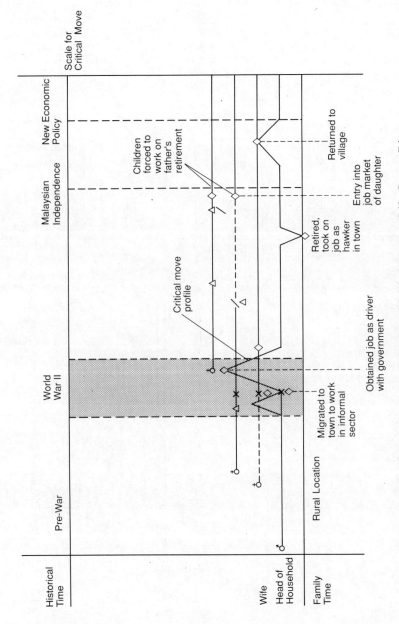

Fig. 12.2 Superimposition of Summary Statistical Index of Critical Move on Life-Course Diagram

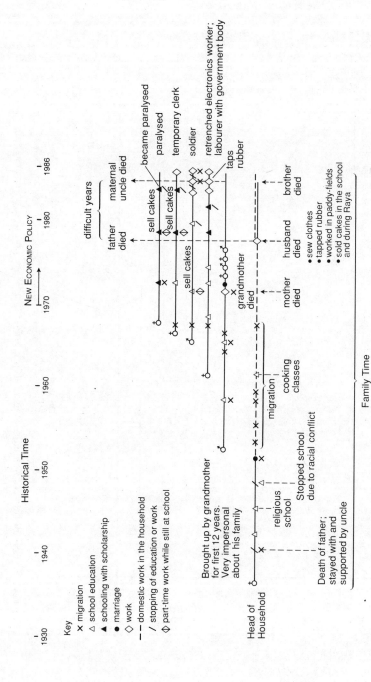

Fig. 12.3 Life-Course Diagram of Household History: Case Study 1

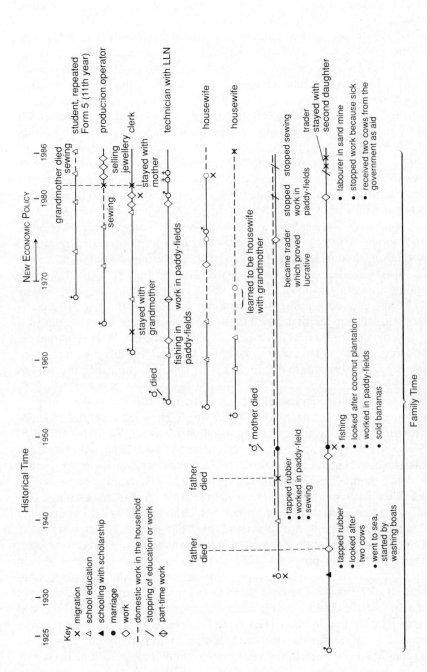

Fig. 12.4 Life-Course Diagram of Household History: Case Study 2

sex order, changing labour inputs, and income pooling within the household economy and household strategies are examined.

Figure 12.3 consists of a female-headed household with five children, in which the eldest son is already married with five children. It is a poor village household and has only the basics, although it possesses a bicycle and recently acquired a black and white television set. The life history of the head of household herself was affected by the death of her own father, which resulted in her moving in with her uncle. After her marriage, while all her children were still at school and her youngest daughter was only nine years old, the most traumatic event affected her family: the death of her husband. This rather carefree, full-time housewife of a policeman, who had enjoyed her husband's regular income and barracks privileges, and had even had time for cooking classes, was suddenly left with five school-going children, no income, and no housing. She brought her family back to her village of origin, where her brother provided her with a small house. She was forced now to survive by taking multiple jobs such as sewing, tapping rubber, working in the padi fields where she earned about 265 Malaysian ringgit (equivalent to $100) per month during planting and harvesting seasons, and selling cakes in the school and during *Hari Raya* (celebration at the end of the fasting month). She also did all types of *kerja kampung* (village work).[3] She received only $190 per month in pension payments from her husband's death for the first nine months, the period that was economically most difficult, before the final settlement at $250 per month. This meant that she had to struggle to keep her children at school. Fortunately, all of them received scholarships and were able to remain in school, supplementing their incomes by selling cakes for their mother.

It was during this economically depressed period that the eldest daughter, while still in the sixth form, left to work in a factory. She became a major contributor to the family income, donating all of her wages ($230) to the family, but was laid off when her factory retrenched in mid-1986. Afterward, to augment the family income, she tapped rubber while applying for other types of work. A few months later the fourth child, a daughter, secured a temporary job as a clerk for $200 per month and gave her mother most of her earnings. Her contribution has given the family some relief, although they worry about what will happen when her job ends. When the eldest daughter started to work in the local electronics factory, the household income situation improved somewhat, but then she was laid off again. This hardship was followed by the sudden paralysis of the youngest child, who had just reached the fifth form. Her medication is expensive. The boys in the family do not contribute to the family income. In fact, the eldest is hardly perceived as part of the family, having been brought up by his grandmother. (He was left with his grandmother because, as a policeman, his father was transferred regularly and his parents did not want the boy's schooling to be interrupted.) After his grandmother's death he lived only

---

[3] Village work encompasses a wide variety of odd jobs, from making thatched *nipah* fronds for *attap* roofs and *mengkuang* mats, to physical labour.

one year with his parents and siblings before marrying. When he married, his mother had to give him $300 to set up house (this was before his father's death). As for the other son, an unmarried soldier, he can hardly make ends meet on his meagre income, and his mother has to give him $20–$30 whenever she can. Thus, the family's economic situation is precarious, depending upon the mother and the two girls who are able to work.

The second houschold (Figure 12.4) consists of a couple and their six children, the eldest of whom (two girls) are already married. In contrast to the first household, in this one at least three children have worked in the electronics factory and two are still actively contributing to the household income. With the capable entrepreneurship of their mother as a trader, this household is well above the average economic status in the village. The house is completely renovated and full of consumer durables—furniture, refrigerator, cabinets, colour television, and carpets.

As in the first family, not only household adaptive strategies such as income pooling, but also sibling and sex order play a role in this household. The head of the household is not the husband, but the wife. Pak Cik (the husband) is quite meek, sickly, and peripheral to the family. His relationship with his wife started to deteriorate with his failing health and ended with his leaving their house to live with his second daughter in 1984 or 1985. Because of Pak Cik's inability to support a family owing to his ineptitude, Mak Cik (the wife) began to work in the padi fields and to sew clothes immediately after their marriage. She said that her life had been much easier prior to her marriage. After marriage it became very difficult, especially when the children arrived. Her first child died during those initial years of economic hardship.

The first two girls were removed from school early to help with housework and look after their younger siblings. The economic situation eased somewhat when the second daughter began working as a production worker in National Semiconductor Company at the age of 16. She was to be a major income contributor for 11 years, helping to pay for her siblings' education (none had a scholarship) and household expenses. All the other children contributed to the family income by working in the padi fields, sewing, and later, when the mother became a trader (selling crockery sets, carpets, bedspreads, pots, and eventually, jewellery), assisting her in selling those items in their work place. Even after the marriage of the electronics worker and the arrival of her son, she continued working. Her marriage ended in divorce the next year, and she and her son moved back to her mother's household. She continued working until her second marriage six years later, when her youngest sister entered the electronics factory and took over as the second major contributor to the household (after the mother). The sons do not appear to contribute, except to help the mother sell her goods.

The younger children comment on how easy their lives have been compared with those of their two elder sisters. For example, the eldest daughter is so poor that her mother has often given her money to help her family. She was married off, in a marriage arranged by her grandfather, after the second daughter had started taking over the housework. The second daughter, the one who has contributed the most to this household, has a strong say in household decisions. Although the youngest sister is now the main contributor, she defers to her eldest sister and mother.

From similar life-course diagrams constructed for the other households in our sample, it is evident that the withdrawal of these female workers from the domestic economy represented a major transition for these households. This is particularly true when we compare this current generation with the females of their parents' and grandparents' generation. Their mothers generally had little education and were removed from school so that they could look after their siblings and do housework. In turn, this enabled their own mothers to work in the fields, or to help work in padi and rubber as unpaid family workers. The essential difference between that generation and these young girls is that the latter generation substituted wage work for family labour to sustain the household economy.

This intergenerational difference reflects the changing circumstances and opportunities. Whereas their mothers had little or no education, most of it in religious schools, the younger generation was able to take advantage of widespread education in rural areas made available by the policies of the independent state in the 1960s. In the 1970s, these opportunities had been reinforced by the universal education system, more scholarships for the *bumiputras* (Malays, or literally, sons of the soil), and the New Economic Policy, which made employment restructuring—that is, the incorporation of Malays into the modern wage sector—its major plank. As a consequence of the employment-creation policy and the increasing numbers of youths entering the labour-market, transnational corporations were encouraged to set up factories in newly created Free Trade Zones (FTZs). As one of the electronics workers put it, it was easy to get a job then; if she left a job on Friday, she could find another in a different semi-conductor factory the following Monday. She herself changed jobs twice before settling into her present one. The factories even accepted girls with as little as six years of education.

Another influence on the life course of these households is that of sibling order, not only in the generation from which these workers were drawn from but also in their parents' generation. Sibling order affects the opportunties open to children. The older siblings are almost always the ones who did not have a chance to attend, or to continue, school, being forced to assist their parents in the field or with housework. Thus, it is common to see a wide educational and occupational disparity between the older children and the younger ones: in the same family an older sibling may be a padi farmer with three years of schooling, whereas a younger sibling may be a university student.

An added dimension is sex order. In one family, the older siblings, although boys, had to do housework because the oldest daughter was 16 years younger. By the time she was in the sixth form (pre-university), however, she was withdrawn from school to look after her siblings. In another case the daughter was forced to leave school, although she was the fifth child and in spite of the fact that she was a good student and enjoyed school. In this sense she was the proverbial sacrificial lamb. It was her withdrawal from school, and later entrance into the wage sector as an electronics worker, that enabled her older siblings to continue their education to the fifth form. The eldest successfully completed his university education. The future of her younger siblings at school is assured because the daughter is now contributing to the family income.

The extent of a family's dependence on its working daughters varies with the stage of its life cycle. In a family where both the parents are still able to work and the eldest child has a factory job, the family is better off than one in which the parents are too old to work, even though they may have a large number of children. Similarly, a family in which elder children contribute to the household income and a few younger children are at school is still better off than one in which none of the children is working yet because all are still at school. The most vulnerable household is one in which the parents are too old or weak to hold down a permanent job and totally dependent upon a working daughter. Such households are an object lesson about the importance of children as invest-ments for old age. In a society where state support for the aged does not exist, children become their parents' only hope.

The sibling and sex order of the children also affect the stage of the family life cycle. A family may be affected dramatically by a personal tragedy, such as the death or serious illness of the father or the major bread winner. Usually when this happens the burden falls heavily on the mother, who is forced to explore all sorts of ways to make ends meet. Such strategies can be seen in cases in which, as the husband's health failed, the mother was forced to work outside the home for the first time. As his health worsened she had to change from a part-time worker to a full-time worker on the estate. In such circumstances, it is inevitable that the children also suffer. If there is no assistance from the Social Welfare Depart-ment and their schooling is not subsidized by scholarships, they may be withdrawn from school and forced to help earn the family income. In one family, the daughter withdrew from school and started to work in the factories at age 16, the minimum legal age of employment. In both the case studies, siblings died young during sustained periods of economic stress.

The question arises as to what happens if the girls have to stop working. Two life-cycle events usually spell the end of working daughters' contributions to household income. The first is marriage and motherhood. The second is loss of their jobs.

There are not enough data to show that most daughters leave their jobs when they marry. Whether they do so or not appears to depend on whom they marry and whether the husband lives in Penang. For example, those who married civil servants had stopped working. Those who married men from outside Penang naturally had to leave. But young women who married fellow workers worked until the birth of their first child. They could continue to work if they had a relative, such as their mother or an aunt, who could look after the baby. Among Malays it is a prevalent household strategy for grandparents to look after their grandchildren while the parents are at work.

For families forced to send their children out to work, retrenchment is a perpetual threat. At the time of the field work for this study, the factories were retrenching workers owing to a recession. Many girls lived in fear of losing their jobs. Some felt shy about going back to their village and being perceived as having done something wrong in the factory. But the overwhelming concern was how their families were going to cope without their income.

The questions and observations presented here have been posed from the perspective of the working daughter in a household context. However, although marriage is one of the critical events in a household's history (although it may well be postponed as a result of a daughter's participation in the labour-force), in the discussion of the family life course, much depends on the situation of the household and the adaptive strategies adopted by each household to cope with each contingency (such as the second event, retrenchment, which relates to industrial time) and to adjust to the long-term macro-changes affecting the household. These strategies are constrained by the stage of the family life cycle and its life course. Thus, the options that family members choose have to be determined within these constraints.

What the life-course diagrams are able to show is the timing, sequencing, and duration of events affecting individuals within the configuration of the family structure. In a sense they depict the synchronization of individual events with family events, integrating them with historical time.

Conclusion

Both this review of methods of analysing household history and the case studies presented here indicate that we are still a long way from devising adequate techniques for dealing with historical data series. The life-course construct as a framework for analysing household histories allows considerable detail to be included in the analysis. Of course the application of the approach is constrained by the availability of longitudinal data. But even if data are available, as in retrospective life histories, their utilization depends upon the adoption of analytic methods that can fully exploit both the life-course framework and the available data.

A major problem in applying the life-course construct to household history remains the linkage between micro-level household data and macro-level processes. So far, the statistical aggregation of individual-level processes, as with the use of survey data and their interpretation, has been the standard approach. However, the interpretation of aggregate events through historico-analytical methods or deductions from theoretical abstractions, although intellectually satisfying, cannot capture the nuances and subtleties of micro-level processes. For those working from the ground up, it is also tempting just to leave matters at the level of idiography, extracting one or two connections no matter how tenuous the general application of the case studies.

Solving this problem involves two tasks. First is the organization of the data in such a way as to make them convenient for retrieval and analysis. The structuring of the data in the Universiti Sains Malaysia–University of British Colombia (USM–UBC) Project (which were derived from retrospective family histories) and, at a different level, in the Casalecchio Project (based on historical censuses and registers) and the Michigan Panel Study makes computer-generated analysis possible. For example, an algorithm may be programmed to draw automatically the life-course diagrams from the Malay household history data. The second task is to devise analytical procedures for summarizing household histories through the aggregation of individual transitions and their interactions with larger processes. Standard tools of multivariate statistical analyses may be used (such as the Markov chain model), but care must be exercised so as not to compromise the real-life situation as reflected in data that are inconsistent with the assumptions underlying the statistical model. The analyst needs much ingenuity to extract meaningful interpretations. The benefits from an investment in developing more appropriate and imaginative analytical tools for household histories can be considerable.

Use of household historical methods places even greater demands on data. The usual census methods of extracting data for household historical analysis suggested in this chapter may not be adequate to capture the basic household processes. But the household and life-course history, if based on micro-level information obtained through detailed household surveys, holds promise for improving our understanding of Third World household processes, especially if the object is not only to obtain parametric measurements of these households but also to elucidate processes at the household level and their integration with higher-level structures.

References

Anderson, M. (ed.) (1980), *Sociology of the Family*, 2nd edn., Penguin, Harmondsworth.

Aries, P. (1962), *Centuries of Childhood: A Social History of Family Life*, translated from the French by R. Baldick, Vintage Books, New York.

Berkner, L. K. (1975), 'The Use and Misuse of Census Data for the Historical Analysis of Family Structure', *Journal of Interdisciplinary History*, 5 (4), 721–38.

Caldwell, J. C. (1982), *Theory of Fertility Decline*, Academic Press, London and New York.

Carter, A. T. (1984), 'Household Histories', in R. M. Netting, R. R. Wilk, E. J. Arnould (eds.), *Households: Comparative and Historical Studies of the Domestic Group*, University of California Press, Berkeley, Calif., 44–83.

Cherlin, A. (1983), 'Changing Family and Household: Contemporary Lessons from Historical Research', *Annual Review of Sociology*, 9, 51–66.

Collver, A. (1963), 'The Family Cycle in India and the United States', *American Sociological Review*, 28 (1), 86–96.

Duvall, E. M. (1967), *Family Development*, 3rd edn., J. B. Lippincott, Philadelphia, Pa.

Elder, G. H. (1974), *Children of the Great Depression: Social Change in Life Experience*, University of Chicago Press, Chicago.

—— (1977), 'Family History and the Life Course', *Journal of Family History*, 2 (2), 279–304.

—— (1981), 'History and the Family: The Discovery of Complexity', *Journal of Marriage and the Family*, 43 (3), 389–519.

—— (1985), 'Perspectives on the Life Course', in G. H. Elder Jr. (ed.), *Life Course Dynamics: Trajectories and Transitions 1968–1980*, Cornell University Press, Ithaca, NY, 23–49.

Flandrin, J. L. (1979), *Families in Former Times: Kinship, Household and Sexuality*, translated by R. Southern, Cambridge University Press, Cambridge and New York.

Friedman, K. (1984), 'Households As Income Pooling Units', in J. Smith, I. Wallerstein, and H.-D. Evers (eds.), *Households and the World Economy*, Sage, Beverly Hills, Calif., 37–55.

Glick, P. C., and Parke, R. Jr. (1965), 'New Approaches in Studying the Life Cycle of the Family', *Demography*, 2, 187–202.

Goode, W. J. (1982), *The Family*, 2nd edn., Prentice-Hall, Englewood Cliffs, NJ.

Greven, P. J., Jr. (1970), *Four Generations: Population, Land and Family in Colonial Andover, Massachusetts*, Cornell University Press, Ithaca, NY.

Hareven, T. K. (1974), 'The Family as Process: The Historical Study of the Family Cycle', *Journal of Social History*, 7 (3), 322–329.

—— (1977), 'Family Time and Historical Time', *Daedalus*, 106 (2), 57–70.

—— (1978a), 'Cycles, Courses and Cohorts: Reflections on Theoretical and Methodological Approaches to the Historical Study of Family Development', *Journal of Social History*, 12 (1), 97–109.

—— (ed.) (1978b), *Transitions: The Family and the Life Course in Historical Perspective*, Academic Press, New York.

—— (1982), *Family Time and Industrial Time*, Cambridge University Press, Cambridge.

—— and Langenbach, R. (1978), *Amoskeag*, Pantheon Books, New York.

—— and Vinovskis, M. A. (eds.) (1978), *Family and Population in Nineteenth-Century America*, Princeton University Press, Princeton, NJ.

Harris, C. C. (1983), *The Family and Industrial Society*, Allen & Unwin, London.

Harris, O. (1984), 'Households As Natural Units', in K. Young, C. Wolkowitz, and R. McCullagh (eds.), *Of Marriage and the Market*, CSE Books, London, 49–68.

Henry, L. (1967), *Manuel de Démographie Historique*, Librarie Droz, Geneva.

Herlihy, D. (1985), *Medieval Households*, Harvard University Press, Cambridge, Mass.

Hill, R. N. (1964), 'Methodological Issues in Family Development Research', *Family Process*, 3 (1), 186–206.

—— (1970), *Family Development in Three Generations: A Longitudinal Study of Changing Family Patterns of Planning and Achievement*, Cambridge, Mass.

Hogan, D. P. (1984), 'Cohort Comparison in Timing of Life Events', *Developmental Review*, 4 (3), 289–310.

Kertzer, D. I. (1983), 'Generation As a Sociological Problem', *Annual Review of Sociology*, 9, 125–49.

—— (1985), 'Future Directions in Historical Household Studies', *Journal of Family History*, 10 (1), 98–107.

—— and Schiaffino, A. (1983), 'Industrialization and Coresidence: A Life-course Approach', in P. B. Baltes, and O. G. Brim Jr. (eds.), *Life Span Development and Behaviour*, vol. v, Academic Press, New York, 359–91.

Lasch, C. (1975), 'The Family and History', *New York Review of Books*, 22 (18), 33–8.

Laslett, P. (1972a), 'Introduction', in P. Laslett and R. Wall (eds.), *Household and Family in Past Times*, Cambridge University Press, Cambridge, 1–89.

—— (1972b), 'Mean Household Size in England Since the Sixteenth Century', in P. Laslett and R. Wall (eds.), *Household and Family in Past Times*, Cambridge University Press, Cambridge, 125–58.

—— (1983), *The World We Have Lost—Further Explored*, Methuen, London.

—— and Wall, R. (eds.) (1972), *Household and Family in Past Time*, Cambridge University Press, Cambridge.

Lee, R. D. (ed.) (1977), *Population Patterns in the Past*, Academic Press, New York.

Levine, D. (1977), *Family Formation in an Age of Nascent Capitalism*, Academic Press, New York.

Mitterauer, M., and Sieder, R. (1979), 'The Developmental Process of Domestic Groups: Problems of Reconstruction and Possibilities of Interpretation', *Journal of Family History*, 4 (3), 257–84.

Modell, J., Furstenberg, F. F., Jr., and Hershberg, T. (1976), 'Social Change and Transitions to Adulthood in Historical Perspective', *Journal of Family History*, 1 (1), 7–32.

Morioka, K. (1967), 'Life Cycle Patterns in Japan, China, and the United States', *Journal of Marriage and the Family*, 29 (3), 595–606.

Netting, R. M., Wilk, R. R., and Arnould, E. J. (eds.) (1984), *Households: Comparative and Historical Studies of the Domestic Group*, University of California Press, Berkeley, Calif.

Oppenheimer, V. K. (1982), *Work and the Family: A Study in Social Demography*, Academic Press, New York.

Rogers, R. (1962), *Improvements in the Construction and Analysis of Family Life Cycle Categories*, West Michigan University Press, Kalamazoo, Mich.

Rosser, C., and Harris, C. (1983), *The Family and Social Change*, abridged edn., Routledge and Kegan Paul, London.

Ryder, N. B. (1965), 'The Cohort as a Conception in the Study of Social Change', *American Sociological Review*, 30 (6), 843–61.

Sieder, R., and Mitterauer, M. (1983), 'The Reconstruction of the Family Life Course: Theoretical Problems and Empirical Results', in R. Wall, J. Robin, and P. Laslett (eds.), *Family Forms in Historic Europe*, Cambridge University Press, Cambridge and New York, 309–45.

Simons, C. J. R., and Thomas, J. L. (1983), 'The Life Cycle in Historical Context: The Impact of Normative History—Graded Events in the Course of Life-span Human Development', *Human Development*, 26 (2), 117–20.

Smith, J., Wallerstein, I. M., and Evers, H.-D. (eds.) (1984), *Households and the World Economy*, Sage, Beverly Hills, Calif.

Smith, T. C. (1977), *Nakahara: Family Farming and Population in a Japanese Village, 1717–1830*, Stanford University Press, Stanford, Calif.

Stone, L. (1979), *The Family, Sex and Marriage in England 1500–1800*, abridged edn., Harper Colophon Books, New York.

Tilly, L. A. (1985), 'Demographic History Faces the Family: Europe Since 1500', *Trends in History*, 3 (3/4), 45–68.

Tilly, L. A., and Scott, J. W. (1978), *Women, Work, and Family*, Holt, Rinehart and Winston, New York.

Troll, L., and Bengtson, V. (1979), 'Generations in the Family', in Wesley R. Burr, *et al.* (eds.), *Contemporary Theories about the Family: Research-based Theories*, Free Press, New York.

Tuma, N. B., Hannan, M. T., and Groeneveld, L. P. (1979), 'Dynamic Analysis of Event Histories', *American Journal of Sociology*, 84 (4), 820–54.

Uhlenberg, P. (1978), 'Changing Configurations of the Life Course', in T. K. Hareven (ed.), *Transitions: The Family and the Life Course in Historical Perspective*, Academic Press, New York, 65–97.

Vinovskis, M. (1977), 'From Household Size to the Life Course', *American Behavioral Scientist*, 21 (2), 263–87.

Wall, R. (ed.) (1983), *Family Forms in Historic Europe*, Cambridge University Press, Cambridge.

Wallerstein, I. M. (1984), 'Household Structures and Labor-force Formation in the Capitalist World-economy', in J. Smith, I. M. Wallerstein, and H.-D. Evers (eds.), *Households and the World Economy*, Sage, Beverly Hills, Calif., 17–22.

Wargon, S. T. (1974), 'The Study of Household and Family Units in Demography', *Journal of Marriage and the Family*, 34 (3), 560–67.

Wong, D. (1984), 'The Limits of Using the Household as a Unit of Analysis', in J. Smith, I. M. Wallerstein, and H.-D. Evers (eds.), *Households and the World Economy*, Sage, Beverly Hills, Calif., 56–63.

Wrigley, E. A. (1969), *Population and History*, Weidenfeld & Nicolson, London.

Young, M. L. (1982), 'Critical Moves: A Life History Approach to the Structural Analysis of Migration', Paper presented at the Conference on Urbanization and National Development, Honolulu, 25–29 January.

—— and Salih, K. (1987a), 'The Malay Family: Structural Change and Transformation—A Research Proposal' in J. Momsen and J. Townsend (eds.), *Geography of Gender in the Third World*, Hutchinson Educational, London, 348–54.

—— —— (1987), 'Industrialisation and Household Response: A Case Study of Penang', in D. W. Drakakis-Smith (ed.), *The Urban Totem: Economic Development and Urbanisation in the Periphery and Semi-periphery*, Croom Helm, London.

13 Family Change and Family Process: Implications for Research in Developing Countries

MARIA COLETA F. A. DE OLIVEIRA

Family Change as a Research Question

From whatever standpoint it may be analysed, the family has become an important theme for investigation in the social sciences. The reasons for this vary from one discipline to another. The family has often 'taken a ride' with other themes and issues that interest researchers, themes such as consumption patterns, income distribution, educational performance, women's work, and fertility patterns. Despite differences in emphasis, the result is that our knowledge of the multiple aspects of the family has greatly increased since a few decades ago.

One outcome of renewed interest in the family has been the development of a specific research area in demography, the demography of the family. The delimitation of this new field of interest acknowledges that the family is a relevant framework within which to look at reality, a dimension of social life deserving attention in its own right.

What about family change? This topic is immersed in a sort of 'theoretical crisis': we do not have a theory that can summarize the changes that have occurred over time and integrate them into a consistent set of hypotheses about the social, cultural, and economic mechanisms responsible for them.

For one thing, the development of historical research in the First World has destroyed a whole set of mistaken images of the past. Both the discovery that nuclear families were prevalent and the recognition that the coexistence of multiple generations in the past was impossible (or improbable) led to the dissolution of the myth of the large family as the support for high fertility (Laslett and Wall, 1974; Goubert, 1973; Uhlenberg, 1969; 1974). Paradigms such as the Demographic Transition Theory and other attempts to reconstitute changes in family patterns over time do not survive the evidence that emerges from the combined efforts of historians, demographers, economists, sociologists, and anthropologists concerned with the subject of the family (Goode, 1963; Patarra, 1973; Tabutin, 1985).

From the standpoint of the Third World, the situation is similar. What varies is the combination of factors that have led to the still evident theoretical crisis. In the case of Latin America, before historical research had gained much attention, dissatisfaction with hasty generalizations about family patterns and trends started to emerge. An appraisal of the empirical findings and interpretations of research on Latin American fertility and internal migration done in the 1960s led to acute criticism of their assumptions. It was demonstrated that suppositions about the past and expectations and desires about the future of Latin American societies were responsible for misleading statements on family change. The Demographic Transition Theory and the Theory of Modernization, in their various versions, were used in the search for signs of change (Garcia, *et al.*, 1974; Argüello, *et al.*, 1974; Aldunate, *et al.*, 1982; Patarra, 1973).

The intense theoretical debate all over the region has culminated in the formulation of alternative perspectives which have begun to be employed in research projects. The historical-structural approach, in many of its variants, has aroused the greatest attention among researchers. In-depth studies based on this new perspective have recently been joined by a renewed interest in aspects of the daily lives of various social groups and an intensification of historical research (Kuznesof and Oppenheimer, 1985). It is still too early to evaluate the results of these approaches and of the entire investigation into the family in Latin America.

The contemporary situation reflects the absence of an adequate paradigm, able to fit together all the pieces of the jigsaw puzzle. Although efforts have been made to develop alternative perspectives, we are still absorbed by the task of making sense out of many fragments of empirical evidence. Strictly speaking, we do not know what changes we are talking about when dealing with family issues.

The consequences of the situation described above are several. The old paradigm sometimes holds and stubbornly lives on in spite of its undeniable fragility. To this extent it is often the framework used by researchers in developing their procedures for observation and analysis even today, simply because they lack a better instrument to replace it. In other cases the search for theory is given up altogether, and researchers lose their bearings in multivariate approaches attempting to account for the myriad determinations that act upon the phenomenon investigated. A concern with international comparability has accentuated this trend. Despite the positive balance achieved, especially through growing formal sophistication, these approaches have not led us far towards better specifying our research questions, much less answering them.

A more promising type of response to the crisis of theory in the field of family change consists of a search for partial theories, formulated at intermediate levels of abstraction and generality. This effort entails focusing on specific aspects of family change or of changes in particular areas that are linked to the family. In both cases, interpretations are historically rooted. Examples of this approach include interpretative analyses of the emergence of the bourgeois concept of the family and of certain characteristics of family life associated with the development of capitalism (Ariès, 1962; Stone, 1979; Levine, 1977); studies that examine specific hypotheses about the relations between aspects of the family and the social changes occurring in particular regions, such as those dealing with the so-called 'proletarianization hypothesis' (Tilly, 1978; Tilly and Scott, 1978; Carvalho, *et al.*, 1981; Paiva, 1982; Levine, 1984; Merrick, 1985); and middle-range theoretical formulations based on in-depth research at the level of local communities, especially in Third World countries, such as those proposing the 'wealth-flow hypothesis' (Caldwell, 1976).

In my view, the investigations conducted in accordance with this third type of approach are the ones that, by contrast and by convergence, may lead to a better specification of our research issue. For them to do this, an even more intense effort to clarify the concept of family change will be necessary.

Family Change as a Concept

In demography the increasing importance of questions related to the family is linked to the need to contextualize demographic phenomena, which are generally apprehended as individual manifestations. Attempts to correct the atomism underlying a great many techniques of observation and research designs have led to a generalized inclusion of familial variables in models of analysis.

There are various ways of dealing with these variables. In some of the models, family characteristics appear as traits of individuals, affecting their choice of alternatives for action or behaviour. In others, the family comprises a reference micro-universe for analyses of individual behaviour. In these cases, the family is seen in isolation, shut in on itself, leaving aside the factors responsible for the characteristics of family lives and organization. In others, the family is a unit for analysis and can even become part of the phenomena or processes to be investigated.

Focusing on the family, either in itself or as the context for comprehending individual behaviour, brings with it new difficulties. One of these, which researchers often overlook, is the supposition that it is possible to take the behaviour of the familial group as univocal and consistent. This supposition has often led to the concealment of conflicts, tensions, and inequalities that are inherent to the family unit. The family is often selected as a unit for analysis to the detriment of the individual and even of the possibility of comprehending the dynamics of the family itself (Balán and Jelin, 1979).

Suppositions of this kind are present when indicators of family group characteristics are chosen. In this choice, practical considerations make only one or a few members of the family the source of information about the characteristics of the family as a whole. For example, the socio-economic characteristics of the family head serve as a basis for locating the social position of the family unit; or the age of the wife or nuclear couple is taken as an indicator of the stage of the life cycle which the family has reached. Arguments in favour of this type of solution range from purely operational considerations to ones that assert the individual or individuals chosen best represent the experience of the whole family. For a long time the debate on this question has occupied researchers on the family, especially those doing life-cycle analysis (Hill and Rodgers, 1964; Glick and Parke, 1965; Nag, 1975; Feldman and Feldman, 1975).

The difficulty of the concept of family, however, is not only that a family is a group. The term 'family' means many things. Strictly speaking, it is more a notion than a concept.

An example can be found in the discussion of the relations between the family and the household or domestic group, and the arguments for or against each conceptualization (Bender, 1967). This discussion has occurred with each new investigation. It is true that obtaining information about the family from the household alone often distorts the results.

The choice of one or another definition depends on the type of questions we are interested in formulating or the type of problem that concerns us. As Ryder (1985) has argued convincingly, the conjugal, consanguineous, and co-residential dimensions of the family point to various research possibilities. Similarly, splitting the family group into such dyadic relationships as husband/wife, mother/child, father/child, or brother/sister allows us to identify problems that help to delineate the object of research (Adams, 1960).

The importance this issue has assumed derives from excessive emphasis on aspects related to the *structure* and *function* of the family. Particularly among sociologists, the search for structural correlates of the various social institutions and the explanation of permanence and of change in terms of the functional requirements of society caused the debate to be limited to these aspects (Parsons and Bales, 1954).

This type of formulation led to the conceptualization of family change as alterations of its structure or the functions it performs. Most work in this tradition undertook an exhaustive search for factors that could explain the prevalence of one or the other type of family structure. This meant over-estimating the importance of urbanization and industrialization as the cause of changes in the family that sometimes preceded these processes. However, as Greenfield (1961–2) showed, explaining permanence or change in the form or function of the family in terms of these processes is highly problematic. The *coup de grace* for this endless wrangle came from newly developed historical research using the instruments provided by historical demography.

If the concept of change in terms of successive stages, identified by a series of correlated structural features, is a mistaken one, what notion or concept is likely to take its place? Recent work in the field, which is now interdisciplinary, indicates the existence of several equally apt substitutes. Before evaluating them, let us define the requirements they must meet.

First, an adequate concept should not condemn us to focus on general change regardless of the social groups we are dealing with. Social change encompasses movements in different and sometimes contradictory directions. Also, general factors and processes produce different impacts depending on the social condition of individuals and of groups (Patarra and Oliveira, 1974).

It may be that the intensification of social research, not only into the family but also into other dimensions of social life, present and past, will enable us to specify a concept of family change that pays respect to the historical experience of various cultures. Less developed countries entered the modern world through different paths, coming from different points of departure. In other words, although Third World populations end up adopting alien patterns, it is by no means irrelevant to their traditional forms and behaviour. That is the case, for instance, of traditional polygyny in some African countries or of high rates of illegitimacy in colonial Brazil.

Secondly, the complexity of the concept of family makes it necessary to specify what dimension the change detected refers to. It is even possible that radical changes in one direction do not necessarily lead to major changes in others or justify the assumption that something very serious must be happening to the family as a social institution. For example, changes in the average age at marriage in Western Europe have been linked with the changes that marked the proto-industrial stage of the emergence and consolidation of industry. Some scholars have argued that these changes altered the way in which families fitted economically and socially into the whole social structure, as domestic production gave way to wage labour (Tilly, 1978; Levine, 1977). Yet others have shown that age at marriage has been sensitive to various changes, not all of them structural or large-scale (Lehning, 1983; Spagnoli, 1983).

A third point that is essential in the search for a concept appropriate to research requirements is that researchers are often struck by permanence in familial patterns and behaviour even while looking for change in them (Oliveira and Madeira, 1985; Hareven, 1973; McLaughlin, 1973). This suggests that it may be advisable to think of change in terms of distinct conceptual and theoretical schemes that can guide examination of the relations between the family and society over time.

These observations lead me to point out that one of the fittest concepts to take the place of more general concepts is that of change as comprehended by the notions of the life course and the life cycle. By reducing the time scale involved, these notions make it possible to deal with those changes that occur during the life span of an individual or group of individuals. Such changes have been called vital transactions, or turning-points.

There are moments in the life course of individuals that are singled out for analysis by reason of their special characteristics. It is thus possible to focus on both specific moments and on the timing of these transitions, comparing them at different times and places, and for different groups, classes, etc. (Hareven, 1978; Hareven and Vinovskis, 1978; Elder, 1978; Oliveira, 1981; Ryder, 1985; Young, in this volume).

It is evident that from this standpoint we are not limited to comparing moments or stages in the life course as a basis for making inferences about change. While contrasts between such stages are still present, it is the transitions between them that are of interest.

Moreover, these transitions are conceived as resulting from interaction among various factors that are not merely individual but also related to the family unit of which the individual is part and to the society in which he or she lives. Both in turn are constantly changing realities. There is no assumption of a one-way causal relationship between them. These relations can thus be treated dialectically so that feedback effects can also be incorporated into the analysis.

The notion of change is replaced by the more malleable notion of *process*, and the family itself is seen as a process, not as a fixed and stable unit. This way of conceptualizing the family may be far from desirable for many engaged in the field. However, it is a more realistic, though more complex, way of looking at family relationships (Hareven, 1974; Oliveira, 1979).

Observation is reoriented in this conception, leaving behind the search for major trends in family patterns over time. It is not necessary, however, to abandon all concern with the long term. Yet it must be admitted that the wealth of information and insight about both the structure and the dynamics of society that can result from this kind of approach adds substance to the effort to construct long-range theories.

In recent years we have seen an intense development of research along the lines sketched above. Its multidisciplinary character allows this perspective to harbour various research designs, ranging from the quantification of the rhythms with which life transitions operate to in-depth anthropological studies about particular communities or social groups.

Data Requirements for Understanding Family Change

In the preceding sections, I have dwelt on aspects of concept and theory that are essential for specifying research requirements. These must be dealt with at some point in the investigation process. In this respect, I agree with those who complain that there has been too much concern with measuring phenomena without paying attention to their social and historical meanings.

This distortion is especially visible in demographic studies, in which the phenomena studied lend themselves to exhaustive quantitative refinement. When the perspective takes the family as process, development of various measures of time and the rhythm of change in family units over time has replaced emphasis on classical measures of fertility. Much of researchers' energy in this field has been spent on improving these standards of measurement.

Critiques of this type of orientation stress above all the need for adopting more complex and more flexible systems of observation. The contemporary debate over the contribution of micro-demographic studies points in this direction. A similarly critical standpoint was taken by Latin American researchers in the early 1970s. Many in-depth studies have been conducted with a view to complying with four requirements that are seen as fundamental: (1) avoidance of rigid models that assume one-way causality of factors and prevent an examination of more complex relationships; (2) avoidance of stereotyped and artificial approaches produced by excessive concern with standardization of research tools and procedures; (3) examination of the combined effects of various factors, located at different levels; and (4) consideration of the symbolic nature of behaviour, with meaning seen as an important factor in causality.

It is still too early to assess the results achieved by community-level studies. Despite criticism, however, there is no doubt that such research had brought to light questions that otherwise would have remained concealed. If it is true that this strategy requires time before it can prompt the formulation of propositions of a more general validity, this is a condition of the process of producing and accumulating knowledge. Knowledge evolves by successive approximations, step by step. This strategy is safer when compared with the usual procedure of taking scattered pieces of information out of their actual context and interpreting them in the light of an abstract and extraneous theory (Caldwell and Hill, 1985).

But flexibility of observation procedures is no substitute for necessary theoretical clarity. Observation systems are shaped by prior assumptions about the phenomenon or process being observed. This is precisely why there are such varied emphases among researchers engaged in work in local communities. In any case, when they select designs that permit global interpretation of the local social dynamics, these researchers are in a more favourable position to be able to perceive the interrelations among the various factors, independently of the emphases that result from their initial assumptions.

Let us go into some of the issues posed by the conceptualization proposed here. Our task is to understand how family life is embedded in social life. One challenge we face is finding adequate empirical data. We should be able to observe sizes, quantities, rhythms, tempos, ages at occurrence of a specific event, etc. But we also need to know the types of relationships that exist between people, the quality of these relationships, their sociability forms and patterns. The issues here are the availability and adequacy of available information, the time span of accessible data, and their variety and complexity.

Census data are the ones most readily at hand for researchers. Their advantages come mostly from the wide coverage of the census and from the systematic character of the observations over time. This is true at least for countries with fair statistical systems. Their major drawback is the difficulty of going deeper into the analysis of some important explanatory dimensions, due to the descriptive character of the observations offered by census data.

In Latin America, researchers face additional problems in using census information for family research. For example, although most of the data are collected on the basis of family or domestic units, they are not usually organized in that way (Torrado, 1971*a*; 1981*b*; Corona, *et al.*, 1986). To be able to test their hypotheses, researchers must have access either to census samples or to special and expensive tabulations. Another problem is that some relevant information is missing in Latin American censuses. Important dimensions such as age of spouses at marriage, length of marriage, and other events related to family formation are not included in census questionnaires. Recently, national household surveys have been carried out, some of them including longitudinal information on family-relevant dimensions, such as nuptiality variables. Eliminating this type of deficiency from censuses requires appropriate decisions by statistical bureaux. Such decisions are essential if we are to adopt the concept of family process as a central one in family research.

Systematic population censuses and household surveys are a recent improvement in many countries of the region. Because of this, researchers face a third type of problem, the short time span for which comparable evidence is available, a 40–50 year period at most. It is one of the reasons why *ad hoc* hypotheses are so often used to 'explain' changes within the family.

Changes in family structure over time are another example. On the basis of observation over short periods, some authors insist that the nuclearization of the family has been brought about by urbanization and industrialization. In the case of Brazil, for example, although historical research is still in its infancy, there is evidence that families were already nuclear and relatively small during the colonial period (Samara and Costa, 1984). Available evidence also indicates that forces pushing towards larger family units today are different from those in the past. It seems that in past times wealth was the basis for the incorporation of both relatives and non-relatives into a family's nucleus. Today, although they still represent a small portion of the total, large families seem to be concentrated in urban areas and are associated with poverty, female-headed households, and specific stages of the family cycle (Altmann, 1985; Bruschini, 1986).

The above observations lead me to stress, once more, that one of the basic requirements for understanding family change in less developed countries is the production of adequate evidence about the past. Inadequate knowledge about family life in previous generations and lack of information for longer periods of time are responsible for short-sighted evaluations of changes observed today.

Lack of comparability is the fourth problem researchers face when studying change. It exists even for studies involving data collected over short periods and in the same country. Brazil is a good example of the situation in Latin America. Although fairly good decennial censuses have been taken since 1940, family information from them is not strictly comparable. Such basic concepts as 'marriage' and 'family' change from one census to another. The criteria used to identify families in more complex types of household have not been consistent.

The problem of comparability is not confined to changing definitions and criteria. Changes over time and in space mean changes in the whole social, economic, and cultural environment in which phenomena and processes are apprehended.

One of the most prevalent statements about family change in Latin America is affected by a misunderstanding of this comparability aspect. It is that growing female participation in the labour force, which is associated with the process of industrialization, leads to changes in the family, including reductions in its size due to fertility control. Here of course there is a question of what causes what. One could argue that because fertility has been reduced, women have more time to work outside the home. That point aside, there is a further question of the appropriateness of comparing female employment at different times.

The statement implies that female economic participation is more limited in traditional economic systems than in industrialized ones. Available statistics from developing countries often confirm this assumption. However, we know that official statistics tend to conceal women's economic role in traditional economies because of their concentration in activities that are intertwined with domestic work. Where subsistence depends directly on workers and their families and where labour is organized on the basis of family units, female labour is often underestimated. Differences in systems of labour organization affect female economic activity, and its characteristics are not always well captured by conventional definitions of employment (Aguiar, 1984).

Such inappropriate comparisons are responsible for erroneous interpretations of factors associated with family change. What matters is not a supposed difference in rates of female employment but actual differences in systems of labour organization. Traditional systems mean fewer constraints on women in the organization of their daily lives. The central question is, who controls their use of time, the female workers themselves or their employers? Long workdays make it more difficult for women to combine productive and reproductive activities.

For recent periods, life histories collected from older informants are a worthwhile source of data. The life-history technique has been used successfully for surveys in Latin America, based on the experience in Monterrey with standardized observation instruments (Balán, Browning, and Jelin, 1973). The surveys recorded changes over time and in the individual lives under observation. Through such surveys, quantitative evaluations can be made of the time needed for changes to occur for a particular status or level to be reached (Berquó, 1981).

The recording of simultaneous occurrences in individual life courses and their location in time opens up multiple possibilities for interpreting life courses and permits comparison between generations and periods (Oliveira, 1982; also see the chapter by Young in this volume). It is thereby possible to use life histories to analyse the behaviour observed in the context of the historical conditions prevailing when it occurred, combining cohort analysis with the life-cycle perspective. Although the temporal coverage is limited because the information used comes from survivors' retrospective observations, the limited number of alternative data sources guarantees the importance of this procedure.

For studies of the more remote past, however, there is no escaping the use of vital statistics even though they present a variety of difficulties. In the Brazilian case, parish and official records have deficiencies whose seriousness is hard to assess, particularly the under-registration of certain events, such as marriages. Also, loss of information due to high spatial mobility of the population, poses some problems to research based on past records.

Some Latin American countries, including Brazil and Ecuador, have taken pre-census surveys of local populations which offer interesting possibilities for analysis (Marcílio, 1973; 1977; 1979; Kuznesof, 1980a; 1980b; 1985; Kuznesof and Oppenheimer, 1985a). If consecutive years have been surveyed, it is possible to attempt a longitudinal treatment of information, pursuing reconstruction of individual life courses and the history of households (Bacellar, 1986). In Brazil, a recent effort by researchers using this type of source may provide significant additions to historical information on family life.

It is necessary to make use of all possible sources both to fill in the gaps and to verify inferences made on the basis of incomplete information. Particular attention should be given to qualitative sources, which can provide insight into family relationships. Literature, press reports, and travellers' accounts have been used mainly by those adopting the 'mentalite' approach to history (Pescatello, 1973; D'Incao, 1982). Wills, testaments, and family genealogies can also be of great help to family research, for example in reconstructions of family alliances among the élite and even among smallholders in the countryside. Nevertheless, millions of ordinary people are not covered by this type of source. For them, in addition to parish and official vital records, we must rely on such sources as archives in local institutions, businesses, and associations (Bassanezi, 1973; Holloway, 1980; Marcílio, 1979).

This discussion suggests that much remains to be done before we can make more authoritative statements about the family, statements that do not merely reiterate myths and stereotypes about societies now undergoing profound change.

References

Adams, R. N. (1960), 'An Inquiry into the Nature of the Family', in G. E. Dole and R. L. Carneiro (eds), *Essays in the Science of Culture*, Crowell, New York.
Aguiar, N. (co-ord.) (1984), *Mulheres na forca de trabalho na América Latina*, Vozes, Petrópolis.
Aldunate, A., Benítez, R., Cardoso, F. H., Faria, V., González, F., Gianotti, J. A., Henriques, M. H., Lamounier, B., Lewis, H., Montali, L. T., Oliveira, M. C. de, Patarra, N. L., Ribeiro, A. C. T., Rodrigues, P. S., Weiss-Altaner, E., and Welti, C. (1982), *Reproducción de la Población y Desarrollo*, 2, Consejo Latinoamericano de Ciencias Sociales (CLACSO), São Paulo.
Altmann, A. M. G. (1985), 'A estrutura familiar na região Sudeste do Brasil', *Informe Demográfico*, 17, 1–30.

Argüello, O., Balán, J., Lopes, J. B., Faria, V., Pecht, W., and Stern, C. (1974), *Migración y Desarrollo*, 3, Consejo Latinoamericano de Ciencias Sociales (CLACSO), Buenos Aires.

Ariès, P. (1962), *Centuries of Childhood: A Social History of Family Life*, Vintage Books, New York (1st French edn., 1960).

Bacellar, C. de A. P. (1986), 'Herança em família: a partilha dos engenhos de açúcar do Oeste Paulista, 1765–1855', *Anais do V Encontro Nacional de Estudos Populacionais*, Associacão Brasileira de Estudos Populacionais, Aguas de Sao Pedro, i. 123–237.

Balán, J. and Jelin, E. (1979), 'La structura social en la biografía personal', *Estudos CEDES*, 2 (9), 1–25.

—— Browning, H. L., and Jelin, E. (1973), *Men in a Developing Society: Geographic and Social Mobility in Monterrey, Mexico*, University of Texas Press, Austin, Tex.

Bassanezi, M. S. C. B. (1973), 'Fazenda Santa Gertrudes. Uma abordagem quantitativa das relações de trabalho em uma propriedade rural Paulista, 1895–1930', Ph.D. dissertation, Faculdade de Filosofia, Ciencias e Letras de Rio Claro, Rio Claro.

Bender, D. R. (1967), 'A Refinement of the Concept of Household: Families, Co-Residence and Domestic Function', *American Anthropologist*, 69 (5), 493–504.

Berquó, E. S. (1981), 'Análise do ciclo vital visto da perspectiva do *'quantum' e do 'tempo'* da fecundidade: Estudo comparativo de contextos Brasileiros', in *Anais do Segundo Encontro Nacional de Estudos Populacionais*, Associação Brasileira de Estudos Populacionais, São Paulo, ii. 689–708.

—— Camisa, Z. C., Conning, A. M., Culagovski, M., Garcia, B., Jong, J. de, Quilodrán, J., Rabell, C. A., Rodrigues, A. M., Torrealba, U., and Villa, M. (1982), *Reproducción de la Población y Desarrolo*, 3, Consejo Latinoamericano de Ciencias Sociales (CLACSO), São Paulo.

Bruschini, M. C. A. (1986), 'Estrutura familiar e vida cotiadiana na cidade de São Paulo', Ph.D. dissertation, University of São Paulo.

Caldwell, J. C. (1976), 'A Restatement of Demographic Transition Theory', Population and Development Review, 2 (3–4), 321–66.

—— and Hill, A. G. (1985), 'Recent Developments Using Micro-approaches to Demographic Research', in *IUSSP International Population Conference, June 1985, Florence*, iv. 235–42.

Carvalho, J. A. M. de, Paiva, P. de T., and Sawyer, D. R. (1981), *The Recent Sharp Decline in Fertility in Brazil: Economic Boom, Social Inequality and Baby Bust*, The Population Council, Mexico.

Corona, R., Jelin, E., Llovet, J. J., Ramos, S., Oliveira, O. de, Garcia, B., Torrado, S., and Terres, M. (1986), *Problemas metodológicos en la investigación sociodemográfica*, Programa de Investigaciones Sociales sobre Población en América Latina (PISPAL), El Colégio de Mexico, Mexico, D. F.

D'Incao, M. A. (1982), 'Sobre a familia Brasileira no seculo XIX', Paper presented at the 44th Congress of the Americanists, October 1982, Manchester.

Elder, G. H., Jr. (1978), 'Approaches to Social Change and the Family', in J. Demos and S. S. Boocock (eds.), *Turning Points: Historical and Sociological Essays on the Family*, University of Chicago Press, Chicago, 1–38.

Feldman, H., and Feldman, M. (1975), 'The Family Life Cycle: Some Suggestions for Recycling', *Journal of Marriage and the Family*, 37 (2), 277–84.

Garcia, B., Figueroa, B., Conning, A., Patarra, N., Oliveira, M. C. F. A. de, Camargo, P., and Aldunate, A. (1974), *Reproducción de la Población y Desarrollo*, 1, Consejo Latinoamericano de Ciencias Sociales (CLACSO), Buenos Aires.

Glick, P. C., and Parke, R., Jr. (1965), 'New Approaches in Studying the Life Cycle of the Family', *Demography*, 2, 187–202.

Goode, W. J. (1963), *World Revolution and Family Patterns*, Free Press, New York.

Goubert, P. (1973), 'Historical Demography and the Reinterpretation of Early Modern French History: A Research Review', in T. K. Rabb and R. I. Rotberg (eds.), *The Family in History: Interdisciplinary Essays*, Harper and Row, New York, 16–27.

Greenfield, S. M. (1961–2), 'Industrialization and the Family in Sociological Theory', *American Journal of Sociology*, 67, 312–22.

Hareven, T. K. (1973), 'The History of the Family as an Interdisciplinary Field', in T. K. Rabb and R. I. Rotberg (eds.), *The Family in History: Interdisciplinary Essays*, Harper and Row, New York, 211–26.

—— (1974), 'The Family as Process: The Historical Study of the Family Cycle', *Journal of Social History*, 7 (Spring), 322–9.

—— (ed.) (1978), *Transitions: The Family and the Life Course in Historical Perspective*, Academic Press, New York.

—— and Vinovskis, M. A. (1978), 'Introduction', in T. K. Hareven, M. A. Vinovskis, and G. Alter (eds.), *Family and Population in Nineteenth-Century America*, Princeton University Press, Princeton, NJ, 3–21.

Hill, R., and Rodgers, R. (1964), 'The Developmental Approach', in H. T. Christensen (ed.), *Handbook of Marriage and The Family*, Rand McNally, Chicago.

Holloway, T. H. (1980), *Immigrants on the Land: Coffee and Society in São Paulo, 1886–1934*, University of North Carolina Press, Chapel Hill, NC.

Kuznesof, E. A. (1980*a*), 'Household Composition and Headship as Related to Changes in Mode of Production: São Paulo 1765 to 1836', *Comparative Studies in Society and History*, 22 (1), 78–108.

—— (1980*b*), 'The Role of Female-Headed Households in Brazilian Modernization', *Journal of Social History*, 13 (4), 589–613.

—— (1985), *Household Economy and Urban Development: São Paulo, 1765–1836*, Westview Press, Boulder, Colo.

—— and Oppenheimer, R. (1985*a*), 'The Family and Society in Nineteenth-Century Latin America: An Historiographical Introduction', in *The Latin American Family in the Nineteenth Century*, Special issue of *Journal of Family History*, 10 (3), 215–34.

—— —— (eds.) (1985*b*), *The Latin American Family in the Nineteenth Century*, Special issue of *Journal of Family History*, 10 (3).

Laslett, P., and Wall, R. (eds.) (1974), *Household and Family in Past Time: Comparative Studies in the Size and Structure of the Domestic Group over the Last Three Centuries in England, France, Serbia, Japan, and Colonial North America, with Further Materials from Western Europe*, revised edn., Cambridge University Press, Cambridge.

Lehning, J. R. (1983), 'Nuptiality and Rural Industry: Families and Labor in the French Countryside', *Journal of Family History*, 8 (4), 333–45.

Levine, D. (1977), *Family Formation in an Age of Nascent Capitalism*, Academic Press, New York.

—— (1984), *Proletarianization and Family History*, Academic Press, Orlando, Fla.

McLaughlin, V. Y. (1973), 'Patterns of Work and Family Organization: Buffalos's Italians', in T. K. Rabb and R. I. Rotberg (eds.), *The Family in History: Interdisciplinary Essays*, Harper and Row, New York, 111–26.

Implications for Research 213

Marcílio, M. L. (1973), 'Tendences et structures des ménages dans la capitainerie de São
Paulo (1765–1828) selon les listes nominatives d'habitants', in *L'Histoire quantitative
du Brésil; de 1800 à 1930*, Centre National de la Récherche Scientifique, Paris.

—— (1977), 'Croissance de la population Pauliste de 1798 à 1828', in *Annales de
démographie historique*, Mouton, Paris, 249–69.

—— (1979), 'Os registros eclesiásticos e a demografia histórica de América Latina', in
Memórias a I Semana de História, Universidade Estadual Paulista (UNESP), Franca.

Merrick, T. W. (1985), 'Production and Reproduction in Europe and Latin America: The
Proletarianization Hypothesis', Paper presented at the IUSSP International Population
Conference, Florence.

Nag, M. (1975), 'Social-Cultural Patterns, Family Cycle and Fertility', in United Nations
Department of Economic and Social Affairs, *The Population Debate: Dimensions and
Perspectives*, ii, New York, 289–312.

Oliveira, M. C. F. A. de (1979), *Classe social, família e reproducão: Reflexões Teóricas e
Referencias Empíricas*, Faculdade de Arquitetura e Urbanismo—Universidade de São
Paulo/Fundacão para Pesquisa Ambiental, São Paulo.

—— (1981), 'Algumas notas sobre o *ciclo vital* como perspectiva de análise', in *Anais do
Segundo Encontro Nacional de Estudos Populacionais*, ii, Associacão Brasileira de
Estudos Populacionais, São Paulo.

—— (1982), 'A producão da vida: A mulher nas estratégias de sobrevivencia da família
trabalhadora na agricultura', Ph.D. dissertation, University of São Paulo.

—— and Madeira, F. R. (1985), 'Población y fuerza de trabajo: el caso de la agricultura en
el oeste paulista', in N. Sanchez-Albornoz (comp.), *Población y mano de obra en
América Latina*, Alianza Editorial, Madrid.

Paiva, P. de T. A. (1982), 'O processo de proletarizacão como fator de desestabiizacão
dos níveis de fecundidade no Brasil', Paper presented at VIII Reunião do Grupo de
Trabalho sobre Processo de Reproducão da Populacão, Comissão de Populacão e
Desenvolvimento do Conselho Latino-Americano de Ciencias Sociais (CLACSO),
Cuernavaca.

Parsons, T. and Bales, M. (1954), *Family: Socialization and Interaction Process*, Free
Press, Glencoe.

Patarra, N. L. (1973), 'Transición demográfica: Resumen histórico o teoria de población?, *Demografía y Economía*, 3 (1), 86–95.

—— (comp.) (1983), *Reproducción de la Población y Desarrollo*, 4, Consejo Latinoamericano de Ciencias Sociales (CLACSO), São Paulo.

—— and Oliveira, M. C. F. A. de (1974), 'Apontamentos críticos sobre los estudios de
fecundidad', in B. Garcia, B. Figueroa, A. Conning, N. Patarra, M. C. F. A. de Oliveira,
P. Camargo, and A. Aldunate, in *Reproducción de la Población y Desarrollo*, 1,
Consejo Latinoamericano de Ciencias Sociales (CLACSO), Buenos Aires.

Pescatello, A. M. (ed.), *Female and Male in Latin America: Essays*, University of
Pittsburg Press, Pittsburgh.

Ryder, N. B. (1985), 'Recent Developments in the Formal Demography of the Family', in
IUSSP International Population Conference, June 1985, Florence, vol. iii. 207–18.

Samara, E. M., and Costa, I. N. (1984), *Demografia histórica: Bibliografia Brasileira*,
Instituto de Pesquisas Economicas-Universidade de São Paulo/Financiadora de
Estudos e Projetos, São Paulo.

Spagnoli, P. G. (1983), 'Industrialization, Proletarianization, and Marriage: A Recon-
sideration', *Journal of Family History*, 8 (3), 230–47.

Stone, L. (1979), *The Family, Sex and Marriage in England, 1500–1800*, abridged edn., Harper and Row, New York.

Tabutin, D. (1985), 'Les Limites de la théorie classique de la transition démographique pour l'Occident du XIXème siècle et le Tiers-Monde actuel', in *IUSSP International Population Conference, June 1985, Florence*, vol. iv, 357–71.

Tilly, C. (ed.) (1978), *Historical Studies of Changing Fertility*, Princeton University Press, Princeton, NJ.

Tilly, L. A., and Scott, J. W. (1978), *Women, Work and Family*, Holt Rinehart and Winston, New York.

Torrado, S. (1981*a*), 'Estratégias familiares de vida en América Latina: La familia como unidad de investigación censal', *Notas de población*, 9, 26–7.

—— (comp.) (1981*b*), *Investigación e información sociodemográficas*, 2, *Los censos de población y vivienda en la década de 1980 en América Latina*, Série Población y Desarrollo, Consejo Latinoamericano de Ciencias Sociales (CLASCO), Buenos Aires.

Uhlenberg, P. R. (1969), 'A Study of Cohort Life Cycles: Cohorts of Native Born Massachusetts Women, 1830–1920', *Population Studies*, 23 (3), 407–20.

—— (1974), 'Cohort Variation in Family Life Cycle Experiences of U.S. Females', *Journal of Marriage and the Family*, 36 (May), 284–92.

Index of Authors

Abu, K. 22, 62, 82–3
Adams, R. N. 204
Aguiar, N. 209
Albera, D. 41
Aldunate, A., *et al.* 202
Altman, A. M. G. 208
Anderson, David 24
Anderson, M. 23, 116, 176
Argüello, O., *et al.* 202
Aries, P. 72, 113, 176, 203
Arnould, E. J. 18, 176
Atran, S. 22
Ault, W. O. 39
Avery, R. C. 152

Bacellar, C. de A. P. 210
Bachmann, H. 22, 24
Backer, B. 24
Bacon, M. K. 81
Balan, J. 110, 203, 209
Bales, 15, 204
Banfield, E. C. 59
Barry, H. I. 81
Bassanezi, M. S. C. B. 210
Bastide, R. 125
Bastien, R. 137
Bean, L. L. 57
Behman, D. 24
Bender, D. R. 204
Bengtson, V. 179
Berkner, L. K. 178
Bhat, M. 37
Bloch, M. 74
Boesen, I. W. 22
Bohannan, P. 70, 79
Bongaarts, John 4, 8
Boocock, S. S. 115
Borsotti, C. 116
Boserup, E. 73
Boudon, R. 23
Bourdieu, P. 110
Bovin, M. 22
Breeden, J. O. 148, 153
Breman, J. 34–6
Bridenthal, R. 138
Brody, E. M. 18
Browning, H. L. 110, 209
Bruschini, M. C. A. 208
Burch, Thomas, K. 4, 8
Buvinic, M. 115–16, 138

Cain, M. 55
Caldwell, B. 56
Caldwell, John C. 10–11, 19, 21–2, 46–64,
    89, 176, 203, 207
Caldwell, Pat 10–11, 19, 22, 46–64
Camisa, Z. 118–19
Campbell, R. 18
Carmichael, G. 116
Carroll, J. 70
Carstensen, F. V. 148
Carter, A. T. 178, 181–3, 187
Carvalho, J. A. M. de, *et al.* 203
Chamratrithirong, A. 88
Chayanov, A. V. 48, 55
Chen, L. C. 53, 55
Cherlin, A. J. 89, 98, 176–7
Child, L. 81
Clark, E. 137
Coale, A. J. 55
Collver, A. 179
Cornell, L. L. 109
Corona, R., *et al.* 208
Costa, I. N. 208
Craton, M. 128
Curtin, P. D. 145

d'Abbs, P. 18
Dakuyo, M. 70
Davis, K. 117
Davis, N. Z. 59
Davis, R. B. 62
de Barbier, T. 121
de Oliveira, O. 121
Deere, C. D. 22
Degler, C. N. 133–4
del Nero da Costa, I. 126, 128–9, 131
Demeny, P. 55
Demos, J. 115
Digard, J. 18
D'Incao, M. A. 210
Dixon, R. B. 88, 111, 115, 117
Domingo, Lita J. 10, 12, 87–107
Donzelot, J. 113
Dorjahn, V. 80
d'Souza, S. 53, 55
Duben, A. 19
Dumont, L. 31, 33
Durkheim, Emil 46
Duvall, E. M. 179
Dyson, Tim 11, 31–43, 55

Ehrenreich, B. 25
Eickelman, C. 18, 22
Ekong, S. C. 24
Elder, G. H., Jr 176, 178, 180, 205
Elmendorf, M. 22
Elshtain, J. B. 113
Engerman, S. L. 127, 145, 147–8, 150
Epstein, T. S. 21
Ermisch, J. F. 112
Erny, P. 79, 81
Evans-Pritchard, E. E. 70, 77
Eveleth, P. B. 150–1
Evers, H.-D. 176

Farber, B. 23, 25
Feichtinger, Gustav 4
Feldman, H. and Feldman, M. 204
Figueras, F. 136
Flandrin, J. L. 176
Fogel, R. V. 145, 147–8, 150
Foote, 179
Forde, C. D. 71
Fortes, M. 22, 24, 70
Foster, B. L. 18–19
Foucault, M. 113–14
Frank, O. 70
Freeman, R. 116
Fricke, T. E. 96
Friedman, K. 176, 187
Friedman, L. M. 146
Fuchs, V. R. 116
Furstenberg, F. F., Jr 110, 112, 181

Gallimore, R. 72
Garcia, B., *et al.* 202
Garcia Florentino, M. 126, 129
Geertz, C. 24
Glick, P. C. 179, 204
Goldstone, J. A. 47, 59
Goode, William J. 6, 15–16, 21, 34, 176, 201
Goodman, S. E. 148
Goody, E. N. 71, 74
Goody, J. 19, 24, 59
Goody, J. R. 71–4, 76–7, 110
Gore, M. S. 37
Goubert, P. 201
Gould, H. A. 19
Graham, R. 130
Gray, R. 71, 73
Grebenik, E. 4, 8
Greenfield, S. M. 204
Greenhalgh, S. 93
Greenough, P. R. 55
Greven, P. J., Jr 179
Groenveld, L. P. 181
Gudeman, S. 132
Gulliver, P. H. 71, 73
Gutiérrez, H. 126, 130–1
Gutman, H. G. 125–7, 147–8, 150

Habenstein, R. W. 24
Hackenberg, R. 21
Hagen, E. E. 69–70
Haines, M. R. 152
Hajnal, J. 38, 40, 111
Hall, G. M. 126
Halpern, Joel 24
Hammel, E. A. 19–20
Hanna, M. T. 181
Hareven, T. K. 115–16, 176–8, 179–80, 183, 188, 205–6
Harris, C. C. 176
Harris, O. 176
Henry, L. 176
Herlihy, D. 176
Hershberg, T. 181
Hetler, C. B. 116, 138
Higman, B. W. 125–31, 133
Hill, 179
Hill, A. G. 56, 207
Hill, R. 204
Hill, R. N. 179
Hiroshima, K. 22–3
Hodge, R. W. 22
Hogan, D. P. 181
Höhn, Charlotte 3–8
Holloway, T. H. 210
Hopflinger, F. 140
Hufton, O. 109, 116

Inkeles, A. 25

Jalaluddin, A. K. M., *et al.* 48–9, 53–4
James, D. 24
Janssens, A. 19, 23
Jelin, Elizabeth 10–12, 109–22, 203, 209
Jensen, R. A. 145
Johnson, K. A. 21–3

Kanbargi, R. 37
Kapadia, K. M. 31, 33–4, 37
Karkal, M. 37
Karve, I. 31, 33–4, 37
Kertzer, D. I. 179, 182–3, 186
King, Elizabeth M. 10, 12, 87, 107
Klaus, P. 116
Klein, H. S. 127
Knight, F. W. 133
Knodel, J. 56
Kobayashi, K. 22
Kopytoff, I. 73, 79
Kumar, D. 34
Kundstadter, P. 19, 23
Kuznesof, E. A. 202, 210

Langenbach, R. 177
Lasch, C. 113, 115, 178
Laslett, P. 16, 19, 23, 38, 176–8, 201
Le Bras, Hervé 3–4

Le Play, 31
Leach, E. R. 139
Lee, R. D. 176–7
Lehning, J. R. 205
Lerner, D. 25
Lesthaeghe, R. 41–2
Levine, D. 177, 203, 205
Levine, P. 21
Levine, R. A. 71
Lewis, O. 31–2
Linares, O. F. 23
Lis, C. 21
Loyola, M. A. 118, 140

McClelland, P. D. 145
McDonald, Peter 11, 15–25
Macfarlane, A. 17
MacIntosh, A. R. 115
Mackensen, R. 4, 8
McLaughlin, V. Y. 205
McNicoll, G. 42
Madeira, F. R. 205
Mallon, F. E. 22
Malthus, T. R. 40
Mandelbaum, D. G. 33–7
Marcílio, M. L. 210
Martinez-Alier, V. 130, 132–6, 140
Marx, Karl 16, 46–7
Massiah, J. 138
Merrick, T. W. 116, 138, 203
Metcalf, A. C. 126, 129
Michael, R. T. 116
Miller, B. D. 55
Minces, J. 25
Mindel, C. B. 24
Mineau, G. P. 57
Mitterauer, M. 178, 181–3
Modell, J. 110, 112, 181
Mogey, J. 22–4
Moore, M. 55
Moreno-Fraginals, M. M. 125–6, 128, 131
Morgan, S. P. 22–3
Morioka, K. 179
Mörner, M. 130
Muhsam, H. V. 57
Murphy, A. D. 21

Nag, M. 204
Nassehi-Behman, V. 24
Netting, R. M. 18, 23, 41, 176
Newman Brown, W. 39

Ogawa, N. 22
Ojeda, N. 118
Okali, C. 24
Oke, E. A. 21–2
Okore, A. O. 48
Oliveira, Maria Coleta F. A. de 9, 12, 201–10
Oppenheimer, R. 202, 210

Oppenheimer, V. K. 180
Oppong, Christine 11, 18, 22, 69–83

Page, H. 57
Paiva, P. de T. A. 203
Palmer, B. D. 20–1
Pampel, F. C. 116
Parish, W. 21
Parke, R., Jr 179, 204
Parsons, T. 15–17, 46, 204
Patai, R. 22
Patarra, N. L. 201–2, 205
Patterson, H. O. 125
Peristiany, J. G. 20
Pescatello, A. M. 210
Phillips, U. B. 147
Plakans, A. 18
Pocock, D. 31, 33
Potash, B. 76–7
Prioux, France 6

Quilodrán, J. 118

Radcliffe-Brown, A. R. 71, 77, 79–80
Ramos, D. 134, 136
Ramu, G. N. 23
Rapp, R. 113, 138
Reddy, P.H. 19, 22, 48–9, 53, 55, 57
Rezig, I. 25
Ribeiro, Fragoso, J. L. 126, 129
Rodgers, R. 204
Rogers, R. 179
Ross, E. 138
Ross, H. L. 115
Rosser, C. 176
Rostow, W. W. 25
Roussel, Luis 5, 116
Rowntree, B. S. 39
Rugh, A. B. 25
Russell-Wood, A. J. R. 126–8, 132, 136
Ryder, Norman B. 10–11, 89, 161–75, 179, 204–5

Sahlins, M. D. 41
Salaff, J. W. 25
Salih, K. 176, 178, 188
Samara, E. M. 208
Sanjek, R. 72, 80
Sawhill, I. V. 115
Schiaffino, A. 182
Schmink, M. 116, 138
Schneewind, J. B. 114
Schoenmaeckers, I., *et al.* 79
Schofield, R. S. 38, 40, 59
Schwartz, S. B. 126, 128–33
Scott, J. W. 176, 203
Scott, R. J. 126, 128, 130–1
Scott, S. R. 116
Selby, H. A. 21

Sennet, R. 114
Shah, A. M. 35
Shorter, E. 51, 113
Sieder, R. 178, 181–3
Simey, T. S. 138
Simons, C. J. R. 181
Singer, M. 38
Slack, P. 39
Slenes, R. W. 126, 128–31
Smith, D. H. 25
Smith, D. P. 87
Smith, J. 176
Smith, K. S. 23
Smith, M. G. 137
Smith, P. C. 87–8, 96
Smith, R. J. 19
Smith, R. M. 39, 42
Smith, R. T. 137–8, 140
Smith, T. C. 176–7
Smock, A. C. 18, 22, 24
Snell, K. D. M. 42
Soly, H. 21
Souza e Silva, R. 118
Sow, F. 25
Spagnoli, P. G. 205
Srinivasan, K. 55
Stampp, K. M. 146
Stavenhagen, R. 118
Steckel, Richard C. 10, 144–56
Stolcke, Verena 10, 125–41
Stone, L. 49, 82, 176, 203
Storer, D. 24
Strong, D. 110, 112
Sukkary-Stolba, S. 21
Sutch, R. 147–8, 150
Syed, S. H. 96

Tabutin, D. 201
Takaishi, M. 151
Tanaka, K. 22
Tanner, J. M. 150–1
Thirsk, J. 110
Thomas, J. L. 181
Thompson, D. 39, 42
Thompson, E. P. 110
Thorne, B. 113
Tilly, C. 21
Tilly, L. A. 116, 176, 203, 205

Tisay, L. 20
Torrado, S. 208
Troll, L. 179
Trost, Jan 5
Trussell, J. 150, 155
Tuma, N. B. 181
Tushnet, M. V. 146

Uhlenberg, P. R. 179, 201

Vercruijsse, E. 62, 71
Vergin, N. 24
Viazzo, P. P. 41
Vicinus, M. 116
Villaverde, Cirilo 135
Vinovskis, M. A. 176, 179–81, 205
Visaria, P. M. 55
Von Elm, B. R. 88, 138

Wachter, Kenneth W. 4, 8, 19
Wales, T. C. 39
Wall, 23
Wall, R. 176–8, 201
Wallerstein, I. M. 176, 187
Ware, H. 22
Wargon, S. T. 176
Watkins, Susan Cotts 117
Weber, Max 16, 46
Weisner, T. S. 72
Wéry, R. 72
Wesley, C. H. 151
Whitehouse, R. H. 151
Whithear, D. 18
Whiting, B. B. 80, 82
Whiting, J. W. M. 80, 82
Whyte, M. 21
Wilk, R. R. 18, 176
Wilson, Chris 11, 31–43
Wolf, A. P. 19, 21
Wrigley, E. A. 38, 40–1, 59, 176

Yalom, M. 113
Yanagisako, S. J. 127, 132
Young, Mei Ling 10, 176–97, 205, 209
Youssef, N. H. 22, 115–16, 138

Zeckhauser, R. 145

Index of Subjects

abolition of slavery 127, 144–6
Africa:
  slave trade 125, 128, 131, 133, 144–5, 156, 205
  traditional family systems in rural settings 11, 69–83
  viability and vulnerability of family systems 48, 50, 55–6, 62–4
age:
  deference 48–51
  distribution 145, 149, 170, 172
  first birth 155–6
  life cycle 203
  marriage 11, 32, 34, 36–8, 40, 51, 53, 57–8, 80, 87–8, 93–8, 103, 106–7, 111–12, 114, 116, 119–20, 129, 205
  stature 150–1
  and time 161, 165–6
alliance and marriage 22, 89, 91, 95–8, 106–7
ancestor worship 50, 58, 62, 69, 71, 73
Asia:
  family and marriage in 11, 87–107
  viability and vulnerability of family systems 48–9, 52–5, 57–8, 60–3
Asian Marriage Survey 87, 94–6
authority 20–2, 34, 37, 50, 70–1, 73, 76, 139–40
autonomy 12, 62, 80, 107
  celibacy, solitude, and personal 109–22
auxology 150–4

behaviour 37, 42, 70, 76, 79–80, 89–92, 110–13, 120–1, 126–7, 131, 140, 163, 166, 169–72, 203
beliefs 47, 69–70
birth 55, 111
  age at first 155–6
  history 163
bourgeois 59, 202
Brazil 118–19, 121, 205, 208, 210
  slavery period in 10, 125–41
bride wealth 62, 73–4, 77–9

capitalism 20–1, 46, 118, 203
care:
  child 18, 37, 48, 53, 55, 63, 75, 81–2, 139, 150–4, 156, 167
  elderly 18, 24, 41–2, 53, 58, 70, 75, 93–4, 102–3, 106, 195

caste 12, 22, 31, 33–6, 38
celibacy, solitude, and personal autonomy 11–12, 109–22
census data 17, 87, 147, 150, 177–8, 180, 182, 197, 207–8
co-operation 17–18
cohabitation 62, 135, 146–7
cohort analysis 165, 169–70, 178–81, 187, 209
comparability of research 186, 202, 208–9
conjugal family 6, 15–22, 24–5, 72, 74–5, 163, 165–7, 204
consanguinial relationships 163, 165–6, 168, 204
consensual union 118, 129, 135–6, 139–40
control:
  parental 92, 95, 102–3, 107
  social 41, 93, 172
convergence theory and family structure 11, 15–20, 25
  counter examples 22–3
  evidence in favour 20–1
creolization 128, 131
Cuba, slavery period in 10, 125–41
cultural change, family systems and 31–43

depatronization 36
descent 11, 20, 70–1, 73–6, 82
development-cycle 19
diet 53, 55, 153–4
disease 53–4, 69, 81, 152–3
dowry 37, 55, 57, 74, 96

education 37, 60–4, 88, 93, 96, 98, 101–4, 106, 116, 120, 173, 184
  life-course 192–5
ethnocentrism 9
Europe 51, 63, 144, 151–2, 205
  family system in 38–43
events:
  analysis 3–4, 163, 180–1, 184, 186
  natural 54–5, 69–70
exploitation 35, 40, 72–3, 93, 126–7, 134
  sexual 132–5, 150
extended family 6, 11, 18, 20–5, 36, 38–9, 41, 63, 82, 91, 127, 131, 178

familial production 21, 46–53, 59, 63
familism 25, 117–18, 121

family change 10, 11, 82, 161, 172–4, 182
   convergence or compromise in 15–25
   implication for research 201–10
   slavery period in United States 144–56
family theory 9
fertility 111, 176, 206
   control 42, 56–61, 82–3, 92, 209
   decline 36–7, 94, 120
   explanations of 162–4, 168–70
   family structure 19
   high 69, 79, 201
   rates 47, 62, 64
   sex ratio 125, 128, 130–1
   time of marriage 88–9
fission 22, 34, 169
fostering 72, 74, 76, 82
function of family 204
fusion 169

genealogy 210

hierarchy:
   family 34
   gender 138
   labour 117
   racial 126, 133–5, 139–40
household:
   extended 24
   histories, analysis of 176–97
   multi- 17
   surveys 168, 175, 208
   types 127–30, 132, 138–40
human capital 93–4, 98
hypergamy 32–3

identity 118, 125–6, 136, 140
income pooling 187, 192–3, 195
independence 34, 37
in-depth study 9, 207
India, family systems in 11, 31–8
individualism 12, 71, 89, 110
   in Western civilization 113–14
industrialization 6, 9, 11, 15–16, 21, 23, 42,
   47, 59–60, 178, 184, 187, 204–5, 208–9
inheritance 18, 33, 50, 58, 74, 78–9, 176
intergenerational:
   covenant 164, 166–8, 171–3, 175
   difference 194
   relationships 176, 178, 201
intrafamilial transactions 53–4, 59–60, 62
isolation 15–18
IUSSP programme 3–7, 8

Jamaica, slavery period in 10, 125–41
joint family 19, 33–5, 38–9

kinship relations 19, 21–3, 25, 31, 33, 35, 37–
   8, 71–3, 79–80, 82, 96, 118, 125, 138,
   168, 170–2, 175–6, 181–2

altruism and reciprocity among 75
among slaves 127–32
systems and descent groups 75–6
terminology 76–7

labour:
   bondage 35–6, 38
   child 48–9, 56, 60, 81, 94, 130, 153
   division of 18, 48–51, 53, 69, 73–4, 110,
   121
   gender role 116–17, 120
   inputs 50, 53–4, 70, 169, 188, 192–3,
   195–6
   and land in family production 72–7
   market 41, 46–7, 58, 60, 63, 170, 175
   routine and parent–child relationship 130,
   150–4, 156
   service 40–2
   women and 49, 52, 61, 72, 90, 92–5, 98–
   100, 104, 106, 184, 187, 209
land 20–1, 34, 36, 41, 50–1, 72–7
Latin America:
   demographic research in 202, 207–10
   nuptiality in 117–22
   viability and vulnerability of family systems
   63–4
legislation, slavery 146
life expectancy 55–6, 69, 114–15
life history 9–10, 163–4, 184, 186, 196–7
life-course 19, 165, 169, 180–2, 205–6, 209–
   10
   analysis of two Malay households 10, 188–
   96
   celibacy 110, 114–15
   diagram 184–6
   framework 183–4
life-cycle 4–5, 37, 39, 50, 115, 163–5, 169,
   172, 178–80, 184, 195, 204, 209

Malay household surveys 184, 187, 188–96
Markov chain techniques 181–2
marriage 9, 10, 19, 42, 52, 79–80, 169
   across plantation 147–8
   arranged 58–60, 92, 104, 107, 113, 194
   bridge wealth 73–4, 77–8, 79
   celibacy and 109–10, 112–14, 116
   decline 55
   family and, in Asia 87–107
   formalized 118, 129–32, 135–7, 139–40
   as incentive in slavery 154–6
   interracial 134
   kinship 31, 33, 38
   labour input 195–6
   market 10, 165, 171
   slave 146
   see also age; marriage
maternalism 51, 56, 61
matriarchy 34

matrifocality 125, 127–8, 131–3, 137–41, 208
matrilineage 32–3, 62, 73, 76, 81
migration 36, 121, 176, 184, 187, 188
  slavery and interregional 148, 156
miscegenation 131, 132–3, 139, 150, 156
mode of production 16, 22, 46–7, 60–1, 168, 171
modernization 6, 9, 15–16, 24, 37–8, 46, 88, 171–4
  theory 202
monetization 20, 36
morality 47–9, 52–4, 58–61, 75
mortality:
  child 60, 62, 70, 82, 131, 147, 152–3, 155–6
  decline 37, 62, 168–72, 175
  effect on family of 161, 164, 167
  gender 55–6
  high 69
  life-cycle 192, 195
  rates 47, 58
  research into 176, 178, 180
mulattos 130–2, 136, 150

neo-local family 40, 59
norms 92, 109–12, 118, 121
North America 178–9
  slavery period in United States 10, 154–6
nuclear family 15–17, 21–2, 38–40, 42–3, 52, 59, 63–4, 71–2, 74, 91, 121, 125, 127–9, 131–3, 137, 144, 154, 168–9, 178, 201, 208
nuclearization 5–6, 8–9
nuptiality 57, 87–91, 106–7, 111–12, 115, 118, 176
  in latin America 117–22

observation research 54, 206–7
oral histories 177–8, 184

panel studies 178, 180, 186, 188
patriarchy 22, 50–4, 58, 61–3, 96, 116–17
patrilineage 20, 23, 33, 56, 58, 73, 76, 96
permanence of family patterns 205
personality 70, 81
polygamy 16, 57, 62
polygyny 11, 22, 74, 78–82, 127, 205
population structure 10, 36, 39, 51, 57, 59, 61, 63, 69, 111, 126–7, 145, 161–2, 165, 167, 170–1, 173
poverty 39, 121, 138, 208
process, family change as 163, 178, 180, 184, 186, 188, 197, 206
proletarianization 16, 20–1, 23, 184, 203
purity:
  racial 134–5
  sexual 52, 56, 58–9, 62

records:
  official 197, 210
  parish 177
  serial 182–3, 186
religion 20, 23, 47, 50, 52, 58–61, 71, 109, 114–16, 128, 130–1, 136, 173–4
replacement 10, 70, 79, 130, 161, 167
reproduction 33–4, 46, 62, 69, 71–2, 74, 77, 79–80, 89, 91, 94–5, 107, 117–18, 121
research, family change 201–10
residence 11, 58, 175
  co- 17, 24, 34, 36, 71–2, 78–9, 115–16, 165–7, 204
rights:
  conjugal 71, 77–80
  sexual 52, 56, 58, 78–9
role:
  descent 82
  gender 53, 110
  segmentation 15–16
  women 40, 69, 88, 92, 96, 101, 106

security 35–7, 41
selection of partner 91, 95–100, 104–6, 111–13, 129, 144, 146, 156
separation, slavery and 144, 148, 156
sex:
  interracial 132–4
  mating patterns 109, 111, 127–35, 137, 139–40
  order 192–5
  ratio 90, 111–12, 125, 128, 130–1
sexuality 61, 113–15
sibling:
  group solidarity 71, 74–5, 79
  order 19, 188, 193–5
size:
  family 3, 162
  household 169, 176, 178–9
  large family 34, 201, 208–9
  plantation 128–9, 144, 147–8
slavery period:
  and the family in Jamaica, Cuba, and Brazil 10, 125–41
  in United States 10, 144–56
social change 17, 46, 90, 161, 169–70, 173–5, 177, 183, 205, 207
  and family reconstitution 23–5
  impact of 58–63
socialization 71–2, 89, 106, 113, 154, 156, 167, 172, 176
socio-cultural system 94–5, 112, 139, 167, 173–4
space 161–2, 173–4
stabilization of slave labour force 134, 154, 156
status:
  ascribed 70
  family 48–9

status (*cont.*):
  gender 62
  landed 96
  socio-economic 69, 73–4, 77–8, 90, 99,
    101, 104, 111–12, 118, 120, 134–40,
    203, 209
  women 34
structural-functionalism 15
structure:
  family 15–20, 22–3, 31, 34–5, 38, 41, 162,
    184, 204, 208
  household 176, 178–9, 182
substitution 49, 71, 76
survival 10, 20, 51, 55, 58, 61, 70, 75, 121,
  166, 168, 173

time:
  centrality of, in family study 10, 161–75
  historical 186, 188
  scale and research 177, 180, 205, 207–8
transition 47, 87–9, 106–7, 110, 115, 180–1,
  183–4, 186, 188, 194, 197

theory 201–2, 205–6
transmission of culture 69, 168, 176, 179

urbanization 16, 20–1, 25, 42, 47, 56, 88, 90,
  97–8, 101–2, 104, 106, 133, 184, 204,
  208

value of daughters 12, 49, 52, 89–90, 92–3,
  95–6, 98–102, 107
  viability and vulnerability of family systems
    46–64

wealth-flow 89, 96, 203
  and family structure 53–8
welfare 39–41
women:
  freedom of choice 12, 104–6
  independence 116–17
  labour 49, 52, 61, 72, 90, 92–5, 98–100,
    104, 106, 184, 187, 209
  labour routine and children 150–4
  role 57